STATUS OF WOMEN WORKING IN THE TEA PLANTATIONS

STATUS OF WOMEN WORKING IN THE TEA PLANTATIONS

(A Case Study)

ELIZABETH KANIAMPADY FMA

AKANSHA PUBLISHING HOUSE
NEW DELHI-110 059 (INDIA)

AKANSHA PUBLISHING HOUSE
R 37-B, Vani Vihar, Uttam Nagar
New Delhi-110059
Email: ektabooks@yahoo.com
Ph. : 25640621

STATUS OF WOMEN WORKING IN THE TEA PLANTATIONS

First Edition 2003
ISBN 81–87606–41-X

PRINTED IN INDIA

Published by M.P. Misra for Akansha Publishing House, New Delhi and Printed at Tarun Offset Press, Delhi.

Dedicated to
The Women Workers of
Tea Plantations in Assam

FOREWORD

I am happy to write a foreword to this research study on the theme The Status of Women Workers in the Tea Gardens of Assam. This is a well-researched and reliable work on the Adivasi women working in the Tea Gardens of Northeast India, supported by case studies under the guidance of a recognised scholar, Prof R. K. Kàr, of Dibrugarh University. Apart from this fact, there is another reason for me to welcome this new volume. Some years back I had organized a Seminar on the "Tea Garden Labourers of Northeast India: A Multidimensional Study on the Adivasis of the Tea-Gardens of Northeast India" and published it under the same title. It was the first major book on the Adivasis of Northeast India. The book helped the Adivasi population to acquire a certain amount of collective identity with an identifiable common name, culture and kindred tribal languages.

Much has been written on the tea industry in Assam and elsewhere. But most of those works deal with tea industry and only by accident on the Adivasis who are mostly engaged in the tea industry. Instead the focus of the present study is the Adivasi people. It a valuable addition to the growing literature on the Adivasi population of Northeast India, both, of those who work in the tea plantations and those who have moved out of them and settled in Assam as agriculturists, or follow other avocations.

In my opinion, a society will change rapidly when, among many other possible catalysts for change, three major factors are introduced into it. In the first place, when literacy is introduced into a non-literate society the social and cultural profile of the society will immediately begin to change. This is due to the exposure of children to literacy and primary school education. Secondly, when the youth of a society are exposed to higher education at college and university levels, they in their turn will become agents of social transformation from within. Thirdly, if and when, factors such as a new self-awareness, conscientization of their rights, participation in various social, cultural and political activities are at work in asociety, the status of women in a given society will change, and with it also the whole society.

Kaniampady's research has highlighted one of these three major areas and dynamics of social change, namely, the status of Adivasi women workers in the Tea Gardens of Assam. Of her book, The Status of Women Workers in the Tea Gardens of Assam, is the fruit of extensive and intensive fieldwork and analysis of the data gathered. Hence, it gives the reader an insight into the present status of women workers in the Tea Gardens, its problems and prospects.

Since the establishment of the Tea industry by the British planters in India more than a century and a half ago, the labour force to work in the tea plantations of Assam was mostly drawn from the Adivasi population of Chotanagpur. They belonged to the various tribes of Chotanagpur such as Oraons, Mundas, Kharias, Hos, etc. Through forced or/and voluntary migration, and by natural growth for over a century, the Adivasi population has now grown into several millions. It is estimated that there are about six to eight million Adivasis in Northeast India.

They have been kept or are forced to remain at the lowest rungs of the society in Northeast India in politics, education, economic progress and cultural life. In the past they were denied even an identifying name such as Adivasi. Vested interests quibbled over the etymology of the word, even though there are no people in India designated by their profession or work. Yet the Adivasis have been designated as "Tea Garden Labourers" or as "Plantation Labourers." In the last 20 years or so, some change has taken place in this attitude. It is time to recognise their ethnic and cultural identity. The tribal status, recognized in Chotanagpur area, needs to be recognized in Northeast India. Their upward educational, cultural, economic and political mobility must be assured. So far they have been considered and treated as instruments of tea-industry and not as capable of becoming its subjects also.

To this end, Dr. Elizabeth Kaniampady's research on The Status of Women Workers in the Tea Gardens of Assam can make a major contribution. It is a well-researched case study and the conclusions drawn are applicable to the broad spectrum of the Adivasi population in the whole of Northeast India in varying degrees. I hope social workers, political leaders, captains of tea industry, educators, religious workers, and NGOs will take note of this major contribution to the literature on the Adivasi population of Northeast India. It should be compulsory reading for all those who are interested in the welfare of the Tea Garden workers.

The study on women workers in the Tea Gardens can also serve to open our eyes to the wider picture of the Adivasi population and their problems and possibilities. The Adivasis are represented not only in the tea industry, but also in many other key industries of Assam and Northeast India, such as oil industry, petrochemicals, jute industry, silk, paper, plywood, etc. They are found in considerable numbers in all the states of Northeast India.

A recent research seminar on Primary Education of Plantation Labourers' Children in Assam: Draft Report has studied the situation of primary education among the Plantation Labourers' Children in Assam. Another seminar is being planned by a third group to examine the problems of The Adivasis, Higher Education and Social Transformation. It is in this context that I welcome this significant publication by Dr. Kaniampady on the status of women workers in Tea Gardens of the Assam, and recommend it to the public in Northeast India and beyond.

Prof. Sebastian Karotemprel, SDB.
Sacred Heart Theological College,
Shillong.

15 June 2003.

PREFACE

Studies on the position of women and the various problems they are confronting in the society have attracted considerable attention in the recent past. An increasing number of international institutions are now concerned with defending and promoting women's interests in a global perspective.

Women are supposed to be the backbone of a society. Yet, it is a well-known fact that they are faced with many problems and atrocities. They are exploited, suppressed and subjected to harsh restrictions, discriminating rules, unreasonable customs and so on and so forth. As a matter of fact, women all over the world experience one common factor: their oppression at work , in the community and in the family.

Since the UNO's declaration of International Women's Year (1975), there has been a spurt of studies by several social scientists on women from various perspectives. The researches however, by and large , concentrate on the changing life and status of the educated women belonging to the upper and middle strata of the society.

With the ongoing march of urbanisation and industrialisation; and various push and pull factors like inroad of formal education and demographic and economic constraints etc., it may be noted, that the womenfolk from backward communities including the tribal ones , like their relatively forward counterparts too, are now-a-days taking up non-traditional jobs in both organised and unorganised sectors leading to their involvement in cash economy. Majority of them however, are involved in unskilled jobs.

Tea is one of the few industries that mainly depends upon such woman labourers. Surveys show that the entire North East India has as much as 60% woman workers and in the case of Assam alone 45% of women are employed in tea plantations.

With the shift in their economic pursuits from familial to industrial/ urban setting coupled with a changed in their economic status from being dependent to a fully or partly independent one, it is quite likely that the womenfolk would be more aware of their roles, rights and privileges in the society. From Anthropological point of view, thus, it becomes very interesting to have an understanding of the status of the working backward women on the basis of some intensive empirical investigations.

The present book is the outcome of such a study carried out in some tea plantations in Upper Assam, to have an appraisal of the status of women working in the tea industry in Assam.

The findings of the study, *Status of women working in the tea plantations: A case study*, has been the outcome of constant guidance, help, support, views, shared experiences and ideas contributed by many persons. I am profoundly indebted to all these persons without whose careful and able direction, timely help, and active encouragement, this would not have been successfully completed.

First of all, I am deeply grateful and indebted to Dr. R.K. Kar, Professor in the Department of Anthropology, Dibrugarh University. It was solely because of his scholarly genius for guidance,that I could undertake and carry out this arduous and noble venture. He has extended his valuable help step by step, progressively and methodically through teaching, exhortations, observations, remarks and continuous encouragement. Without his selfless, and efficient leadership I would not have been able to carry out and complete this project successfully.

I am grateful to all the faculty members of the Anthropology Department, Dibrugarh University, for their help and support in different phases of my study. I am also thankful to all the employees and students of the same department for their co-operation and help.

Sr. Ivy D'Souza, our former Provincial gave me this opportunity to study, and encouraged me with all possible help and guidance.To her, I am now, and always will be, very much indebted.

My heartfelt gratitude goes also to Sr. Lucy Rose, the present Provincial, who, too, has been a constant source of inspiration and encouragement throughout the course of my studies.

My special thanks to Sr. Annie V., the Principal of Auxilium College, Tinsukia and all the other sisters who were very kind and understanding during the first phase of my research, that was full of teething problems. I would like to mention in particular, Sr. Bernadette Surin who kindly accompanied me and supported me throughout the entire period of my field work in Dhelakhat and Dirial tea estates.

Grateful thanks, also, go to Sr. Mariana Kujur, the Superior and all the sisters of Little Flower School, Dibrugarh, who have always been responsive to my requests and made available all I needed especially during the last phase of my study. I thank them all for their encouragement, availability and constant support.

I am very much indebted to Dr. Sebastian Karotemprel,SDB , who , willingly availed himself and extented all the possible help to publish this book.

I extend my sincere appreciation and gratitude to Mrs. Jean Street who with much interest and accuracy has gone through the entire research so as to make it more applicable and understanding to the readers .

I am grateful to Bishop Joseph Aind and Fr. Varghese Mechery for their help and support. I also thank the staff of Sacred Heart Theological College, Mawlai, Shillong for kindly making available the facilities of the college.

A particular debt of thanks goes to the management and staff of Dhelakhat and Dirial tea estates who in various ways extended their help and support throughout the course of my field work.

Here also, I would like to express my deep sense of gratitude to all the people of Dhelakhat and Dirial tea estates. I thank them for their help, support and interest, in particular, the womenfolk who willingly made themselves available; and were ready to clarify all possible doubts. I thank them for their simplicity, delicacy and openness in sharing their notable life experiences with me. In this context, I would like to put on record my special thanks for Mr. Barjo and his family who accommodated me during my field study. I thank all the young girls who accompanied me in my door-to-door visits to collect data from the field. I thank in particular Ms. Mariam, Ms. Elizabeth, Mr. George, Mr. Asman, Mr. Bijoy and all others who extended their valuable services, especially during the intensive field work.

I am very grateful to Ms. Minati Mohapatra, a staff member of Little Flower school for typing the hand written manuscript with much patience and commitment.

Lastly, I thank my parents, all other relatives, friends and well wishers who have helped me in various ways; and have contributed either directly or indirectly to help me achieve my goal.

In fine, I would like to express my sincers thanks to Mr. M.P. Misra, who on behalf of M/s Akansha Publishing House took personal interest to bringout the publication expeditiously; and with a very impressive getup.

Elizabeth Kaniampady Fma

CONTENTS

1

INTRODUCTION

The term 'status' is difficult to conceptualise and it is often elusive to the empirical grasp. Yet, the idea of status is essential to an understanding of a social system which includes role, position and stratification.

A 'role' is the expected behaviour associated with a social position. It is not possible to list all the roles in a particular society, because there are no clear principles for deciding what is a social position. In so far as the people are conscious of themselves and others occupying positions with generally known rights and duties, then their behaviour cannot be understood without reference to their expectations about how others should behave towards them. "In order to analyse actual behaviour, the concept of role is only a beginning which must be supplemented by a battery of related concepts which give it greater utility" (Banton, 1989: 716).

In defining status as "an effective claim to social esteem in terms of positive or negative privileges", Weber (1978) emphasises its relational base and the fact that a status claimant must have an audience from which to receive or to demand differential responses. Gerth and Mills (1953)* emphasises that a status situation is not fixed; it tends to be played out on the uncertain grounds of the claimant and the audience negotiation and compromise.

---

*Cited in Kuper and Kuper 1989: 714-716.

Different scholars, in the context of different societies, have viewed the concept of status from different angles.

Thus, for example, in the words of Service (1971: 40-41), "Status terms are classificatory devices, i.e., a term that refers to a category and is not identical with an individual person who occupies it, even though only one person might occupy the position at a time, another can occupy it later. As a category, it is defined in terms of certain attributes which the person occupying it will hold, or should hold, but the category is not defined in terms of all the attributes of the person".

According to the International Encyclopedia of Social Sciences (Sills 1968: 250-302), "Age, sex, birth, genealogy and other biological and constitutional characteristics are very common bases of status. Until about 1920, the term 'status' was most commonly used to refer either to the legally enforceable capacities and limitations of people or relative superiority and inferiority".

Mazumdar (1982: 17) maintains, "status in the pure sociological sense denotes only position *vis-a-vis* others in terms of rights and obligations".

Linton (1921: 113-114) differentiates status and role and says "the polar positions in such patterns of reciprocal behaviour are technically known as statuses. The term status, like the term culture, has come to be used with a double significance. A status, in abstract is a position in a particular pattern. It is thus quite correct to speak of each individual as having many statuses, since each individual participates in the expression of a number of patterns. However, unless the term is qualified in some way, the status of any individual means the sum of all the statuses which he occupies. It represents his position in relation to the total society."

A status, as distinct from the individual who may occupy it, is simply a collection of rights and duties. Since these rights and duties can find expression only through the medium of individuals, it is extremely hard for us to maintain a distinction in our thinking between status and the people who hold them and exercise the rights and duties which constitute them. A role represents the dynamic aspect of a status. The individual is socially assigned to a status and occupies it in relation to other statuses. When he/she puts the rights and duties which constitute the status into effect she is performing a role.

From an anthropological view point, "status is primarily a position in a social structure involving rights, duties and reciprocal expectations of behaviour, none of which depends upon the personal characteristics of the status occupant". Merton (1963) observes that an individual has an array of social positions, forming a composite status.

Thus, two major conceptualisations of status are in circulation: (i) 'status', as seen by Weber and his followers as a relational and inter-subjective one; and (ii) 'status', as outlined by Linton and others as a positional and highly structured one. Much of today's researches in this sphere are however, an amalgamation of the two.

Further, from the foregoing definitions, it becomes apparent that the concept 'status' is a relative term and that it differs in its meaning from individual to individual and from society to society. A probing appraisal of the concept of 'status' thus seems to make it obvious that the status of women too differs from time to time and from society to society.

Status of Women

The National Committee on the status of women maintains (ICSSR 1955: 3-4), "Status is realised through roles. This brings into focus the rights and opportunities provided to women by the state and socio-cultural institutions to perform these roles, which may not necessarily reinforce each other. Processes of change are responsible for divergence between the expected and the actual role behaviour. . . . Status will have to relate to the living realities of the social and cultural context of the individual's present situation."

Women are in fact the backbone of a society. Yet, it is a well-known fact that they are faced with many problems. They are exploited, suppressed and subjected to harsh restrictions, discriminatory rules, unreasonable customs and so on and so forth.

Thomas and Heffron (1987) observe that the women all over the world experience one common factor: their oppression at work, in the community and in the family. They also share a belief in their own inferiority and see themselves as having no real choice for a change in their lives. Thus, the women seem to have an "undiscovered past, uncertain present and unpredictable future."

Different scholars have made different observations in this regard. Thus, for example, Lal (1979: 289-297) observes, "while the status of women in a society is determined by a number of factors, it is clear that the pattern of the task differentiation in the family also provides valuable clues to the prevailing status of women in the society. Women's status will be the lowest in a society characterised by firm differentiation between men's work and women's work."

Sacchidananda, (1978: 1) maintains, "women's role and status all over the world are generally determined by social institutions and norms, religious ideologies, ecosystem and by class position."

Hammond and Jablow (1976 : 9) however, are more specific in their observation that states : "In societies throughout the world and throughout the recorded history, women's primary roles have been family oriented. The activities and relationships that are basic to their lives are within the context of the family: The study of family roles (daughter, wife, mother, sister) is thus fundamental for the understanding of women and their place in society."

A perusal of most of the account of the definitions of status of women given by various social scientists indicates that the status of women generally centres around her family roles. Further, in any discussions of women's status, the general convention has been to assess their role in relation to men.

Mazumdar (ICSSR 1982 : 17-19) however, notes two other dimensions to facilitate such assessment. They are :

(a) the extent of actual control enjoyed by women over their own lives.

(b) the extent to which they have access to decision making processes and are effective in position of power and authority.

While dwelling on the status of women in India, it may be noted that the Hindu women form around 80% of the female population in India. Their status in the Vedic period (particularly during the period of *Rigveda*) was high; the wife was given an honoured position. She was the mistress in her husband's home: the wife of the eldest brother exercised authority even over his brothers and unmarried sisters. Remarriage and divorce were permitted under certain circumstances. Manu however, disapproved of widow marriage and divorce. But during all the Vedic periods, the main purpose of marriage was to procreate children, especially sons, who were supposed to save the father from the hell known as Puth. The main duty of the wife was therefore, to bear children, to bring them up and to attend to household duties. A mother was treated with respect, whereas a childless woman was viewed with pity and very often with contempt. Child marriages were common, for according to the ancient Hindu Law children of any age could be married as it was the result of an arrangement between the parents of both the prospective bride and the groom; and the children had no volition. A girl was to be "given" in marriage by the father or in his absence by others in particular order. Performing the marriage of daughter was through a gift to the bridegroom (Kanyadana). It was supposed to be one of the most meritorious gifts, more meritorious than the gift of land, cow or gold. According to many Smriti writers like Narada, if no one was available, the girl could approach the king and with his permission, could choose a husband herself.

As far as property rights are concerned, a wife could inherit her husband's property only in the absence of a son. But, in such a situation she enjoyed only the usufructuary right over the property. She could neither sell nor otherwise dispose of the same. After her death the property would revert to the husband's other heirs. She was however, entitled to *Stridhana*, the property gifted to her by her parents and the presents received, etc., in which she had an absolute right. On her death this would devolve on her female heirs. A woman was not entitled to adopt when her husband was living. An adoption was always a man's privilege. A widow could adopt only if her husband authorised her to adopt; and in the absence of such authority with the consent of his kinsmen. A girl could not be adopted, an adoption was only a means for the sonless man to have a son who would save him from the hell of *Puth.* This was broadly the position of the Hindu woman in ancient India.

Though the position of women in India, of late, is claimed to be better than that in many other countries, the position assigned to them is not equal to that of men. This is observable in almost all the spheres of life. Even today, in many cases, women are confined to the four walls of the house and denied equal opportunities for personal growth and social development. "They [women] are treated with discrimination, which in fact gives them their low status. The constitution has given Indian women a status which is unique, but the social, economic and political constraints have made them 'second class' citizens in real life" (Bhuyan, 1993 : V).

The traditional idea of women being confined to household activities has deprived them of adequate health care and educational facilities. The female mortality rate is higher in India due to frequent pregnancies, poor diet, and lack of proper medical care. In the field of education the picture is equally discouraging. Female literacy is 18.00% in the rural areas and 47. 00% in the urban areas. The drop out rate for the girls is 55.50% at the primary stage and 77.70% at the middle school stage. A girl's education is, to some extent, constrained by household chores and other responsibilities (Bhuyan; op. cit). In the backward communities, the picture is still gloomier.

In the economic field also, the overall situation is equally discouraging. In the rural areas, the women have to shoulder two basic economic activities, namely, to look after the children that is, to play a role of a housekeeper and to take active/passive participation in the productive economic pursuits. Even the women, employed in wage earning/salaried jobs, have by and large, not been proportionately relieved of their basic duties as housekeeper and wife in a patriarchal society.

On the political front also there has been a dismal picture. Although the women constitute approximately 50.00% of the total population, their participation in politics is disappointing. The percentage of votes casted by the female voters is always lower than that of the males in all the general elections held since the days of our independence. Their records as holders of political office is equally unimpressive. Education does not seem to be the sole factor. Because, there are some areas in India, e.g., Kerala and Mizoram, where female literacy rate is reasonably high, but their participation in the political activities is relatively poor.

With regard to the tribal women, it may not be out of place here to take note of some of their special characteristics. The tribal women have the culture of living in a self-contained community with a high degree of social freedom blended with self-dignity and self-respect. They have more commitment towards their decisions made in a group situation. They are part of an essential village-based well knit democratic structure. The tribal women are task-oriented. Since subsistence agriculture is the mainstay of 90.00% of the tribal population, the majority of the women are farmers. The tribal women however, are not entitled to inherit land in perpetuity with a few rare exceptions (e.g. the Khasis & the Garos of North-East India). Further, the village government traditionally has been dominated by men; and women generally do not find any significant place in it. In other words, women's activities, by and large, remain confined within the familial or at best kinship boundaries.

Nevertheless, with the ongoing march of urbanisation and industrialisation; and because of various push and pull factors like inroad of formal education, and demographic and economic constraints, etc., the women from the backward communities including the tribal ones, like their relatively forward counterparts too, are now-a-days taking up non-traditional jobs in both organised and unorganised sectors leading to their involvement in cash economy. The majority of them, however, are involved in unskilled jobs. With a shift in their economic pursuits from familial to industrial/urban setting coupled with a change in their economic status from being dependent to a fully or partly independent one; it is quite likely that the women folk would be more aware of their roles, rights and privileges in the society. From the anthropological point of view, it thus becomes very interesting to have an understanding of the status of backward working women on the basis of some intensive empirical investigation.

The present study, therefore, proposes to undertake a probing investigation on the status of women, with particular reference to the tribal women, working in the tea plantations in Assam.

It may be relevantly noted here that in the world scenario the status of women has begun to take a new shape and a new meaning as the various scholars have been showing varied interests in the study of the position of women at various levels in various societies in different parts of the world.

Review of Literature

Since the dawn of history up to modem times, a good number of studies on the role and the status of women in social, economic, political, religious and educational spheres have been carried out by different scholars (e.g. Altekar, 1938; Bader, 1958; Baig, 1958; Cousins, 1947; Commack, 1953; Das 1961; Indra, 1955; Kapadia, 1956; Kapur, 1974; Karve 1967; Maharani and Mitra 1911; Mehra, 1982; Misra 1967; Sachidananda, 1978 and Thomas, 1939).

But there has been a spurt in the studies relating to the position of women in different parts of the world after 1975 (The International Women's Year).

Quinn (1977 : 81), in an appraisal of anthropological studies on women's status writes that the feminist movement of the 1960s has had a striking influence on female anthropologists. Apart from their personal interest in women's status, this appraisal geared them to the intellectual role of defining women's place in a revised theory of evolution of human society. Furthermore, such anthropological discussion of women's status has borrowed the conceptualisation of the problem as a basis for analysis. Many writers begin by carefully defining what they take to mean by women's status in terms of female political participation, economic control, personal autonomy, inter-personal equality, legal adulthood, ideological position or other specific indices for the purpose of testing a particular hypothesis. However, they often end up with much loose usage in their conclusions and speak broadly of women's low status and oppression by male dominance.

Joan and Jane (1974) who studied the status of women in central and north India point out that the recent studies tend to be marked by an increasingly critical appraisal of women's place both in and out of the home. The rise of the women's liberation movement with the view of women as an oppressed class has helped to foster interest in women's studies.

Mehta (1982 : 32) in her study *(Revolution and the status of women in India)* observes, "As far as traditions and cultural values are concerned no independent status for women has been recognised by traditional Indian society. And her expression about women and their roles are important in so far as they are complementary to man. A woman in traditional Hindu society had no independent existence. She had no rights as a citizen in her own independent status".

Srinivas (1977) in a survey of " The changing position of Indian women" since the end of the Second World War points out that there has been a rapidly increasing concern both with the role and position of women. This has brought about a greater equality between the sexes than before. In fact, urban working women have taken a very bold step to greater equality with men in every field. But the village and tribal women are still lagging behind".

In the early part of the 20th century, anthropologists like Westermark, Hobhouse, Bartels and Mason attempted comparative studies on the position of primitive women in societies all over the world. They had necessarily to resort to accounts given by travellers, missionaries and others which are comparable to modem studies. All these were highly prejudiced in the light of the writers'concepts prevalent in their own societies (Pritchard, 1965 : 38).

Some scholars (e.g. Majumdar and Madan, 1956: 141; Quinn, op. cit: 182) hold that primitive societies generally assign a high status to women, whereas the other viewpoint suggests that in primitive societies women are generally a depressed group, having low status,suffering subjugation and oppression.

Lowie (1929), commenting on the position of women in primitive societies, draws attention to the two generally prevailing schools of thought which are diametrically opposed to each other. Some scholars observe that a woman in preliterate society has a very low status and is treated almost as a slave, or "beast of burden condemned to perform the hardest drudgery, bought as a commodity and without redress against her master's brutalities".

On the other hand, those who study matrilineal and matriarchal societies hold the view that woman is an "undisputed mistress of the family". However, in view of the infinite variability of social relationships from society to society, Lowie considers that any general statement concerning woman's position in society may not be strictly valid. He suggests, therefore, that "it will be best to approach the subject through a number of different avenues before venturing on even a qualified dictum".

Shah (1950), in his study of women in tribal life, states that the social structure and organisation of tribal life centres around the family. As the pivot of the family is the woman, her position and the social change that take place in her status and her daily life are most important.

With regard to the studies on the status of women working in tea plantations in general and in Assam tea plantations in particular, it must be admitted that published literature in this regard is very scanty.

A tea plantation does not need many skilled workers as the bulk of the work centres around plucking of tea leaves from the garden. The pluckers constitute about nine-tenths of the total work force. The job of plucking is done mostly by the woman workers and the strength of the woman labourers in a garden is almost equal to, and even more than, that of men.

While dealing with woman workers (mostly the tribal women) in tea plantations of North Bengal and Assam, Das Gupta (1978: 192-99) observes that the womenfolk who have involved themselves in plantation work are still shackled to their traditional domestic responsibilities like cooking and managing household affairs. Lactating mothers carry their babies to the garden and keep them under the shade of a tree or in a creche while they are busy in plucking. The babies are looked after by the old women called Dhai-Ma (nurse for babies) employed for the purpose. The mothers suckle their babies at regular intervals. Besides her work in the garden, a woman worker with her husband engages herself in raising some minor crops in the plot of land attached to the quarters given by the management. On the whole, in the industrial context, they have to maintain both the poles - the household as well as the industrial work.

In this context the author comments, "Though women have their own problems of puberty, maternity, etc., they have proved their worth as a viable economic force either in the field or in the factory".

Bhadra (1997 : 229-46) carried out a study in North Bengal to understand the family authority, role and status of the Adivasi woman workers of Chandmani Tea Plantation in Darjeeling District.

She observes that women, by and large, work due to economic necessity and with the full knowledge and consent of their husbands and other members of the family. They seem to be happy with their jobs. They never feel inadequate and inept in their roles as wives and as mothers. They do not seem to experience any observable role conflict in their family as wives, mothers and as workers. They generally integrate their work and the family in an accommodative manner.

In the context of her observations, she comments, "their low levels of aspiration and education seem to help them to adjust better to the family life than the educated middle class working women who are to compete in a shrinking job market and enter into a conflict with a rigid patriarchal family system".

In a different context she (Bhadra, 1992), however, observes that the working women of plantations do not have any role in the decision- making process in the industry, especially related to trade unions even though they are its members. Trade union leadership among the woman workers has not yet emerged. They hardly participate in the union activities. Their educational attainment is very low, and this has further perpetuated their lower status.

No intensive anthropological investigation has so far been made on the status of woman workers in tea plantations in Assam. Thus, the present study, *Status of Women working in the Tea Plantations: A Case Study*, is expected to be a maiden attempt in Assam in this direction.

The Present Study

As noted earlier, in the present study it is proposed to carry out an intensive investigation to understand the status of working women in tea plantations in Assam. It has also been noted earlier that tea is one of the few industries which mainly depends upon women labour. Surveys show that the entire North East India has as much as 60% woman workers and in the case of Assam alone 45% of women are employed in tea plantations. It is largely dependent on woman labourers for plucking operations in which they have shown their highest efficiency . Besides , pruning, Khulni (cutting away of dead wood) and Thalli (weeding), etc., are also done by woman workers. During the transplantation, the seedlings are also carried by them. In a tea plantation women labour is thus very important.

To make the study a holistic and qualitative one it was decided to confine the intensive investigation to not more than two tea plantations. Further, with the same purpose in mind and keeping in mind the fact that around sixty percent of the workers belong to different tribal groups, it was decided to confine the investigation at least to one caste and two tribal groups. It was also decided to cover, preferably, at least one hundred families in each group so as to make the study a reasonably representative one. Considering the fact that religion is an important variable in deciding the status of women, it was further decided to include at least one hundred Christian families in the total sample.

Having these points in mind and also considering the facts of relatively easy accessibility and assured cooperation from the management, the present study was carried out in Dhelakhat Tea Estate, in Tinsukia District and Dirial Tea Estate, located in Dibrugarh District in Upper Assam. A detailed description of the plantations has been provided in Chapter Three (cf. *The Field*).

Considering their numerical preponderance intensive data have been collected from the Tanti, Munda and the Parjah families. Besides, another set of available Christian families have been covered in the investigation. It may relevantly be noted here that for the Pariah and the Non-Christian Munda, data have been collected from 100 families in each group. But, in case of the Tanti and the Christian Munda, the total available number of families was 70 and 80 respectively. Therefore, data have been generated from these 150 families only (and not 100 families each). Thus, the total sample size stands at 350 families (and not 400).

Objectives of the Study

The following are the objectives of the present study:

1. To study the various day-to-day activities of the women tea labourers.
2. To analyse the role of women in the socio-economic activities of their family and community.
3. To get to know the needs and problems of women in relation to education, wage earning, employment , expenses and to find out the factors that hinder their socio-economic development.
4. To analyse the position of working women with regard to family life.
5. To analyse the position of women at their place of work.
6. To understand the level of participation of the working women in politics (Trade union activities).
7. To study the general health of woman workers (as indicated by the indices like age at marriage, fertility, infant mortality, etc.).
8. To study whether plantation Labour Act is implemented with regard to the social securities and other facilities provided to both man and woman labourers.

Working Hypotheses

The study will be guided by the following hypotheses.

I Sex variation in status exists among the tea labourers: women workers enjoy relatively low status .

2. Women have less availability to educational facilities : the majority of the tea garden woman workers are reluctant to send their daughters to schools.

3. The level of education of the couple has a direct bearing on the education of women: An educated couple is more inclined to send the daughters (as well as sons) to schools.

4. Literacy has a direct bearing on age at marriage: Literate women are not interested in being married early.
5. Hard labour with sub-standard nourishment enhances morbidity: women workers are relatively more prone to various diseases.
6. Hard labour with less nutritious nourishment reduces life span: women labourers in the tea garden live a relatively shorter life compared to the norm for women nationwide .
7. Different levels of awareness in political and community activities prevail on the basis of outside exposure : women labourers with better outside exposure have a better level of awareness.
8. Different levels of awareness in political and community activities: woman labourers have a lower level of awareness.
9. Leisure and recreation facilities are inequitably distributed: women labourers get relatively much less leisure time and far fewer recreational facilities as compared to their male counterparts.
10. Religion influences women's status: Christian woman labourers enjoy a better status in all spheres as compared to their Non-Christian counterparts.

Methodology

For any scientific research there is a necessity for proper approach to the problem, an efficient tool for collecting data and systematic method of analysis if it is to derive accurate results and conclusions. For the purpose, each step in the process needs to be systematically planned and executed. The quality of the methodology will be reflected upon the quality of the research done, since a good research cannot be expected of a poorly planned methodology.

Methodology encompasses the overall planning that includes a proper knowledge of the techniques and means of data collection;

systematic and meaningful analysis and drawing of the relevant conclusions from the same. Anthropological researches, as we know, put a greater emphasis on qualitative studies for which there are a number of field techniques. We also know that participant observation, both as a strategy and as a technique plays a very important role in generating anthropological data from the field. However, quantitative data are also necessary to have an understanding of certain spheres, e.g., demography, income and the like. Schedules are to be used to collect data in these areas.

Considering the fact that both the qualitative and quantitative approaches have their limitations, it is thought to be prudent to have an appropriate blending of both the approaches in the present study.

To start with, exploratory visits were made to a number of plantations in Tinsukia and Dibrugarh Districts to have an idea about the ethnic composition and the numerical strength of the different ethnic groups composing the labour population of the different units. Alongside, due consideration was also paid to the accessibility to the plantation as well as the assured cooperation of the management. Basing on all these factors, as well as in consultation with the supervisor of the project, two plantations, namely, Dhelakhat Tea Estate in Tinsukia District and Dirial Tea Estate in Dibrugarh District (Upper Assam) have been selected for the purpose of intensive investigation. The total number of labour families residing in these plantations are around 1294, and they are distributed in more than thirty five ethnic groups (cf . *The Field*). Out of all these groups however, there are only three tribal groups, namely the Munda , the Parjah and the Santals and one caste group namely; the Tanti who have around hundred families in each group. Independent numerical strength of the rest of the ethnic units are, by and large, not significant.

While making a search for the relevant literatures, it could be gathered that out of the three numerically dominant tribal groups, the least work has so far been done on the Parjahs. Further, it could also be gathered that between the Santal and the Munda relatively more work has been carried out among the Santals.

It has therefore been decided to select the Parjah and the Munda tribal women for the purpose of the present study. With regard to the caste group, the Tanti is the only caste that has a substantial numerical strength in the two plantations. So the group has been chosen for the purpose of the present study.

As noted earlier, religion has also been considered to be an important variable influencing the status of women working in the tea plantation. In the two tea plantations, only among the Mundas there are a good number of families subscribing to Christianity. Therefore, it has also been decided to have a representation of the Christian Mundas in the sample. Thus, the sample, drawn for the present study has been designed to have representations of (1) The Tanti (11) The Munda (111) The Parjah and (IV) The Christian Munda.

With regard to the numerical strength of each element in the sample, a decision has been taken to have 50 percent representation of the population or hundred units, whichever is greater. But, as noted earlier, for the Tanti and the Christian Munda no sampling was done as the total number of families were 70 and 80 respectively.

After the selection of the sample population, a door-to-door census survey has been conducted in these two plantations with the help of a prepared schedule. This has helped the investigator to collect the basic demographic as well as other factual information related to the families of the woman workers of the tea plantations. Besides these, the survey has also provided the researcher with an opportunity to introduce herself to the people and explain clearly the purpose of the visit and the academic aim of the study, so as to seek the respondents' co-operation during the follow-up investigation. Above all, the exercise has provided the researcher with a prolonged opportunity for establishing a very good rapport with the people in general. The initial phase of the study has been done with the help of the *Line Chowkidar.* *

This has been followed by an intensive field work for the collection of in-depth qualitative data. During this period, a number of standard anthropological techniques have been used in the field, either independently or in collaboration, depending on the nature of the data in question. The important techniques used are (i) Observation (both participant ; and non-participant) (ii) interview (both individual and group; and both structured and unstructured) and (iii) collection of concrete cases.

It is obvious that the research tools and techniques used for the purpose are not uniform throughout the study. There are many aspects in a group's day-to-day life, as well as in their social and community life, where one's penetration and in-depth understanding remain inadequate with pre-determined tools like interview schedule or questionnaire, etc. Many of the interview processes among the people are symbolic, the meaning of which can be best understood by close observation and careful scrutiny.

In order to sharpen the enquiry to facilitate the collection of data and to arrive at some meaningful conclusions, a few working propositions were formulated before going to the field. The propositions have already been incorporated elsewhere in this chapter.

The field work has been carried out between 1997 and 1999. However, occasional field visits had to be made till the last stage of the work, to fill up some of the inadvertant gaps in the accumulated data. After completion of the field work, tabulation and analysis of data have been undertaken by applying standard stastitical as well as descriptive methods. Secondary data have been collected from different sources, viz., plantation offices, research journals, books and news papers etc. The mass of the data thus collected has been systematically arranged and presented in several chapters in the

---

* Line refers to a resdiential cluster of the labourers. Chowkidar is the caretaker of a line who also maintains a liaison between the Management and the line.

dissertation. In addition, relevant photographs, necessary maps, graphs and statistical tables, etc., have been incorporated in the discourse.

The entire mass of data has conveniently been presented in eight chapters:

Chapter 1 (Introduction) deals with a discussion on some basic concepts, review of available literature, the problem at hand and the methodology used in the study.

Chapter 2 (Tea Labour in Assam) provides a brief history of introduction of tea industry in Assam; and the antecedents, mode and sequence of migration of the labour force from other states.

The land and the people where the present investigation has been carried out, have briefly been introduced in the Chapter 3 (The Field).

In Chapter 4 (Social Life), a discussion has been attempted on some relevant aspects of marriage and family life focusing the role of women.

Chapter 5 (Health and Education) provides an idea about the health and educational status of woman labourers.

A broad outline of women's level of participation in the economic activities as well as the problems they encounter in the process has been discussed in Chapter 6 (Economic Life).

Chapter 7 (Community Life) discuses the role of women in community affairs as well as political in the sphere with special reference to trade union activities.

The entire work has been summarised in Chapter 8 (Summary and Conclusion). Some relevant concluding remarks have also been incorporated here and there in the chapter.

2

TEA LABOUR IN ASSAM

Tea is one of the oldest industries in India and today it enjoys the status of one of the best organised industries in the country. More than a million workers in India are directly employed in the tea plantations and manufacturing industries. Although tea has been known since 2737 B.C. and consumed as a beverage for over 1200 years, yet, its cultivation in India commenced only recently (Misra,1986). Moreover, it still holds a considerable potential for the economic development of the country as the largest organised sector providing a stable economic base.

It is difficult to trace out the exact period when tea was first used as a beverage and how it was discovered that leaves could be used to prepare a palatable drink. Many writers have accepted the fact that tea had its genesis in China untold centuries ago, but its real history is lost in the obscurity of China's venerable antiquity and for the most part is traditional (e.g. Awasthi, 1975; David and Schapira, 1975; Misra, 1986).

The beginnings of tea are shrouded in the mists of antiquity and intertwined with myth and legend. According to David & Schapira (*op. cit*), the origin of tea seems to be associated with a tale from Japanese mythology. The legend concerning the origin of tea tells of *Bodhidharma or Daruma,* an Indian saint who founded the *Chan* (Japanese, Zen) school of Buddhism. In 520 A.D. *Daruma* travelled from India, the land where Buddhism originated, to China, where he was called *Ta-Mo* or the *White Buddha* by the Chinese. When he reached Canton, carrying the sacred bowl of the patriarchs, the Emperor, Liang Wu Ti, offered him as sanctuary a cave-temple in the mountains surrounding his capital, Nanking. Here Daruma demonstrated the particular emphasis of the Zen sect by sitting in meditation for 9 years. One day he broke his vow by falling asleep during his contemplation and when he awoke he was so vexed at that sign of weakness that he cut off his eyelids on the spot . Where the bloody lids touched the earth a strange and holy plant (the first tea bush) appeared which served as a reminder of the sage's momentary weakness and a memorial to his sacrifice. From the leaves of this holy tea plant, a drink could be made which would diminish the desire for sleep.

The magic word "tea" is associated with many corridors of history, with many battles and revolutions, inventions and social customs, minor events and interesting tales. However, tea is primarily associated with the great advancement of commerce and capitalist exploitation typical of the nineteenth century foreign investment in underdeveloped economies.

Assam is the pioneer of tea production and is known as the 'Garden of the Tea World'. The growth of the tea industry has a history that dates back to the British regime. The overall idea of the history and growth of this industry can be had from the writings of Bhuiyan (1960), Chakravorty (1997), Crawford (1924), Griffiths (1967), Harler (1964), Harlalka (1975), Halayya (1972), Jha (1996), Kar (198 1), Mishra (1986) and Phukan (1984).

History and Development of Tea Industry in Assam

The habit of drinking tea among the Assamese tribes was first noticed by Colonel Latter in 1815. The tea plant was indigenous to Assam . The Singpho tribes of Assam called it *Fanap*. David Scott, the then agent to the Governor General in Assam showed interest in producing tea in 1819. In 1823, Major Robert Bruce, the then Agent of the East India Company had come to know about the existence of tea plants in Assam and made an agreement with a Singpho chief for the supply of the same. But before the plants could be delivered, Robert's brother C.A. Bruce arrived on the scene. During the Burma war in 1823, he had been appointed to command gunboats, he could manage to penetrate the forests. He collected the promised tea plants from the Singpho chief and handed them over to Scott (Chakravorty, 1997; Gait, 1926; Griffiths, 1967; Harter, 1964).

Bhuiyan (1960), however, claims that Moniram Dewan first informed C.A Bruce of the existence of the tea plant in Assam. In 1823 when they chased the Man towards Patkai, Maniram Dewan and C.A. Bruce found two tea plants with Bisagam in the Singpho kingdom. In the hills and forests of Assam (in places like the present day Sadiya, Dibrugarh, Lakhimpur, Sibsagar, Jorhat, Golaghat, Tezpur, Mongoldoi, etc.), as a matter of fact there had long been wild tea plants. Later on, C.A.Bruce (Colonel Surgent), Moniram Dewan, Bholanath Parbatia Phukan and Badingfield (Birainfil) went to Singpho land to reorganise Sadiya. There, Badingfield offered a cup of Chinese tea to Bisagam and again at the request of Maniram Dewan, the Bisagam collected some tea plants from the forests and gave those to Badingfield. It is said that in Assam the use of tea liquor as medicine in cold and fever had long been in practice. It was Maniram Dewan who tried to convince the *shaheb* that tea plantations in Assam needed proper care. Lord Bentinck, the then Governor-General of India, formed a tea committee to make a detailed investigation into the prospect of tea plantations in Assam. In December 1834, the committee announced that the tea shrub was beyond all doubt indigenous to upper Assam .... within the territories, from Sadiya and Bessa (Griffith, 1967:40). The committee then determined to follow up the Assam discovery with vigour and formed a scientific panel that was deputed to proceed to Assam. In 1836, they searched systematically for tea jungles, they analysed soils, and collected seeds. Tea was found to be far more widely scattered in Assam than had been realised, and the new discoveries were set forth in *the Asiatic Journal* 1836.

But , a few months before the tea committee's announcement, Gordon, the then Secretary of the tea committee, had been sent to China to secure tea plants and seeds as well as to bring a select body of workers, men qualified to conduct every operation related with the production of good tea. Available China seeds were divided between the Sub-Himalayan area, Upper Assam and South India . The results in (i) South India were unsuccessful (ii) the Sub-Himalayan areas were reasonably successful , but (iii) it was in Assam that the most satisfactory results were obtained.

The seeds from China were planted experimentally in the Botanical gardens in Calcutta, in Nainital and at Sadiya . In Sadiya the tea bed was selected on *Char* (silt) near the confluence of the Kundil and Brahmaputra rivers. The poor and porous soil proved quite unsuitable for the purpose, and the plant failed to thrive. Besides, the Mighty Brahmaputra flowed over the site and washed away the first Assam tea garden altogether. Later, in 1837 another experimental garden was opened, and the seeds from China were planted at Chabua (28 km from Dibrugarh) which proved to be very successful.

With regard to the indigenous variety, however, the two localities where tea had been found growing abundantly were Sadiya and Matak.

Dr. Wallich, the botanist to the East India Company proposed to establish a large number of tea plantations in forest areas. But it was considered too ambitious, and therefore, the operations were limited to two or three areas mentioned above.

C.A. Bruce was promoted as Superintendent of Tea Forests in 1836. He made an extensive adventurous excursion through the sylvan country of the Singphos, visited Koojee on the bank of Dibru river; Ningrew, on the Bura Dihing river, and some other areas, where he found the existence of tea plants. Finally, he visited Tingri area from where he collected tea seeds.

The trained Chinese personnel started manufacturing tea at Sadiya from the locally available wild tea leaves. C.A. Bruce made an arrangement for the purchase of tea leaves. This was plucked by the Singphos and other villagers and brought at irregular intervals to the factory (Roy Burman, 1968:2).

In 1839, a sample of 12 chests of green tea, sent to London could be put to auction and with this successful manufacture of tea in Assam by the Chinese technique, the experimental stage was considered to have come to an end.

By that time, there were nurseries planted with China seeds at places like Jaipur, Chabua, Chota Tingari, Hukanphukri, Jorhat, Nazira and Gavru. One nursery with indigenous plants was established at Sadiya near the official China nursery. At the same time tracts of indigenous tea had been discovered in many parts of Upper Assam and the native chiefs had been encouraged to care for them. In all, 120 tracts of indigenous tea had been discovered by that time.

In the beginning, help was taken from some Chinese workers to open gardens, to pluck the leaves and to manufacture finished tea. At that time all the stages were worked by hand and no factory had yet developed. Further, the labourers were also not brought from other places. The local Assamese people were working in the existing tea gardens.

So far, tea production in India had been carried out under government auspices. The area in which these experiments were carried out in Upper Assam was still a territory under a local ruler. In 1839, the administration of the Sibsagar and Lakhimpur areas of Assam was taken over by the British Government. Thus, the way was opened for private enterprise to continue the production of tea. Companies were formed in Calcutta and in London in 1839 which were later amalgamated under the name of "Assam Company".

In 1840 practically all the East India Company's plantations, except those at Chabua and Dinjoy and two other small gardens were handed over to the Assam Company rent-free for ten years. In addition to cultivating the plantation handed over to them, the Assam Company took leases from the Government of jungle lands containing tea bushes and set to work, to prune and recondition them. The leases were presumably taken under the Assam Waste Rule of 1838, which provided for 20 years rent-free occupation, to be followed by an increasing scale of rent for the next 25 years, at the end of which period the land would be assessed at a rate not higher than that of the neighbouring paddy land. By 1832, there were some 2500 acres of tea beds under the company.

In 1849, the East India Company sold its remaining gardens to a Chinese employed at Chabua who sold Chabua (and presumably the other small gardens started by the East India Co.) to James Warren, the founder of a distinguished family of tea proprietors.

Till 1883 tea plantation was confined to Sibsagar and Dibrugarh districts only. Private gardens also were started by 1850-51. Lieutenant Colonel F. S. Hannay opened up a garden near Dibrugarh during that period. His example was soon followed by one Wagentribler. By 1853, there were three private gardens in Sibsagar and six near Dibrugarh. By 1859, there were, in Assam 51 tea gardens owned by private individuals or private firms - 10 in Dibrugarh, 15 in Sibsagar, 3 in Darang and the remaining in Kamrup and Nagaon.

These developments naturally drew the attention of the Government of Bengal (which included Assam) to the conditions under which waste lands were to be leased for clearance and cultivation. It resulted in the formation of the *Old Assam Waste Rules,* 1854.

Upto 1858 the Assam Company's only competitors had been private individuals or firms, but in that year preliminary steps were taken for the establishment of a second tea company in India. The

Jorhat Tea Company was incorporated in 1859. In the beginning its capital was used in buying the Cinnemaara, Oating and Kaliabar gardens.

The period from 1860 to 1866 was a period of stupendous expansion of the industry (Manoharan, 1974 : 3 -4). By 1862, annual tea production in Assam had risen to 5,00,000 kg. 57 private individuals or companies and 5 public companies owned 160 gardens. The public companies were the Assam Company, the Jorhat Tea Company, the East India Tea Co., the Lower Assam Tea Company and the Central Assam Tea Company.

It may be relevantly noted here that tea plantation and manufacturing has for long been a major industry in Assam and it occupies a very important place in the economy of Assam. There are at present around 760 tea plantations in Assam covering an area of approximately 185,000 hectares of land. This constitutes more than 51 percent of the total area under tea in the whole of India.

Assam produces 410,430,000 kilograms of tea every year to bring in a revenue of not less than Rs. 500 crore per year to the country. Assam is still considered the highest producer of tea and its quality is still unmatched worldwide, anywhere. Around the world Assam is known for tea. Assam tea plantations, at present have a resident population of more than 20 lakhs and a workforce of more than nine lakhs; they are the most important people of the state's economy (Das, 1998) .

According to Awasthi (1975) Assam has now the largest acreage under tea, producing the highest quantity. Not only does Assam lead all other Indian states in tea plantations, but also she is the second largest tea producing area in the whole world, contributing about one-fifth of the world's entire production of tea.

At present, tea is grown all over Assam. In the districts of Upper Assam Valley; namely; Dibrugarh, Dhemaji, Golaghat, Jorhat,

Lakhimpur, Sibsagar and Tinsukia, one comes across miles and miles of planted tea without any break.

Recruitment of Tea Labour in Assam

In the early days, the labour scarcity was a constant hindrance to the expansion of tea plantations in Assam. At the initial stage, however, the local people like the Kacharis, the Mataks, the Kukis, the Nagas, the Singphos and the Apatanis could be employed with active assistance of the chiefs of the respective groups (cf. Chakravarty, 1997 :29; Harlalka, 1975 : 94-97; Gait, 1926: 354; and Roy Burman, 1968: 2).

But these arrangements did not prove to be very successful. In course of time the number of tea plantations was steadily increasing and this created a constant demand for a larger number of labourers. But the need could not be filled from the local labourers, as they had gradually been showing reluctance to work in tea plantations.

About the nature of local labourers, Captain Phillips, the Assistant Commissioner of North Lakhimpur wrote, "The indigenous coolies are almost invariably residents of immediate neighbourhood of the gardens. It is a very rare thing indeed for an Assamese living at a distance to leave his home for the mere inducement of getting work in a garden. Their taking such work at all is generally attributable to temporary necessity, as for instance, inability to pay their revenues, wanting to get married and not having the necessary means, being in debt to *Kyah* and wanting if possible to escape payment of his exorbitant interest, or as more commonly happens, pawning their freedom, being in want of a yoke and bullock for cultivation purpose, etc. In cases such as these they go to the tea plantations as their last resource . . . The wants of the people were few, and could be easily supplied. Due to the enervating climate people were indolent. They would work only under the pressure of urgent necessity . . . ." (Griffiths, 1967: 101).

But in spite of all the difficulties, the tea industry grew steadily. It was obviously experienced by the then planters that in spite of abundant tea plants and lands, the great drawback to the cultivation was of labourers. So they thought of importing the labour force and inducing them to settle there.

About the incompatibility and non-avaibility of local labour force various views have been expressed by various scholars (e.g. Griffith, 1967: 19, Kar 1981 : 19; and Phukan, 1984). Besides the self-sufficient nature of their economy it has been maintained by some scholars (e.g.Griffith, 1967: 19) that the Assam peasants considered it derogatory in social estimation to work for wages under an outsider. Further, the north-eastern part of the country did not experience the existence of a landless class of people and thereby a separate labour class did not emerge in this part of the country.

Kar (1979 : 14;1980:26) maintains that in the first half of the nineteenth century, in the clearing of the land, now occupied by the Assam tea plantations, the local people were reluctant to take employment, presumably because they enjoyed an almost self-sufficient economy, and as their socio-cultural background did not incline them to work as tea labourers. Besides, the British planters might also have been reluctant to employ the willing local people, because imported labour was obviously far easier to control and exploit.

By around 1855, the problem became very acute. Not only were the local people of Assam unwilling to work in the tea gardens, but also there was acute shortage of adult population in Assam to work in tea gardens. Assam at that time was still experiencing the effect of Moamaria rebellion (1770-1795), Burmese invasion (1819-1824) and raids of hill tribes. Gait (1926 : 286) observes, " During the Burmese occupation, they had made constant raids on the hapless Assamese, carrying off thousands as slaves and reducing the eastern part of the country to a state of complete depopulation. As such, there was not enough adult population even to cultivate all the available lands to supply enough food grains to the state".

Saikia (1978) furnishes three possible reasons for the dearth of local labour in Assam for the tea plantations. First, the local people owned sufficient land for cultivation and did not need to work as wage earners for their livelihood. Secondly, they were freedom lovers, and were averse to the very idea of toiling under supervision of foreigners. The social status of women was very exalted. Hence the tea companies never succeeded in engaging the Assamese women in the tea gardens. Thirdly, the natives were heavily addicted to opium which made them very weak and lethargic. Thus, immigration of labour became imperative.

In 1834, G.J. Gordon, was appointed as the Secretary of the Tea Committee, who imported Chinese tea experts and labourers. But they were very expensive and later on turned out to be very arrogant and disobedient to the tea planters. Besides, they demanded very high wages (*ibid*).

Under these circumstances, the labourers had to be recruited from various cultural, linguistic and ethnic heritages from many other provinces; mainly from Bengal, Bihar, Orissa, Madhya Pradesh, Andhra Pradesh and Tamil Nadu (Kar, 1981 : 136).

Different groups were recruited from different places, e.g, the Munda and the Gond from Bihar and Orissa; Savara from Bengal, Bihar and Orissa; Goala from Bengal, Bihar, Orissa and Madhya Pradesh; Tanti from Bengal and Bihar; Lohar from Bihar, Orissa, Madhya Pradesh and Uttar Pradesh; Khond from Andhra Pradesh; Boya from Tamil Nadu; and Parjah from Tamil Nadu and Madhya Pradesh. Various push and pull factors like desperate poverty, indebtedness and land alienation on the country side, and false promises of "Less work and high wages" probably made available this huge supply of labour force.

It was in 1841 that the Assam Company brought the first batch of labour from Chotnagpur area but all the members died en-route. In 1859, the planters organized themselves and started recruitment of labour from different parts of India. In 1859, only about 2000 persons were recruited, but it increased to about 1. 10 lakh in 1909. It is difficult to have an exact idea about the actual number of labourers recruited from various parts of India to the tea gardens in Assam from 1859 to 1960 due to the chaotic nature of the recruitment and high mortality in transit and also in the gardens (Phukan, 1984:255).

Different Systems of Labour Recruitment

Various systems were followed while recruiting the labourers, from different parts of the country. Jha (1996) maintains that migration was a particular type of colonial government sponsored system. Its guiding principle was indenture - one of the devices through which the government transported labour from one area to the other. Under this system, the contract was provided for five years' engagement for a fixed monthly wage, food and clothing. A return passage was also promised. On the whole, the main features of the system were five years of state regulated labour, denial of the right to change the employer or employment, gross disproportion of men to women emigrants, payment of emigration charges by the employer, the denial of increased wages inspite of increased prices and profit, the entitlement of the labour to fixed wages, free housing and medicine, etc.

In order to get the labourers, mainly two systems of recruitment were followed namely, the *Contractor system* and the *Sardari system*. These two systems were operated from 1859 to 1915 and from 1870 to 1959 respectively, and provided an uninterrupted supply of cheap labour. (Jain, 1983:264)

The Contractor System

Initially, recruitment of labour was carried out through the contractors on the basis of short term contracts. The labourers were asked to serve in a garden for a fixed period of time after which they could return to their own native places. Since there was no restriction upon the contractors, the system became known as the 'free contractor system'. Recruitment to the tea plantations in Assam from 1841 was entirely in the hands of these contractors known as Calcutta contractors or *Arkati.* In order to get the labourers easily, the contractors made false promises of high pay and light work and dispatched them to the tea districts without taking any sanitary precautions for their welfare on the journey. The only way to reach the tea gardens in Assam valley was by steamer, and the journey lasted for many days and ended at a place from where the recruit had to proceed on foot. As a matter of fact, during the course of this journey, many recruits died on the way.

An enquiry committee was formed in 1861, by the Government of Bengal to investigate the unsatisfactory system of labour recruitment. As a result, the first Inland Emigration Act, Bengal Act III of 1863 was passed to control emigration to Assam. This Act provided that all recruiters should be licensed and that every intending emigrant should be produced before the magistrate of his own district so as to be examined as to his willingness and physical fitness to emigrate.

In practice, however, the licenses were produced by a handful of contractors who continued to operate under the old system by hiring many unlicensed subcontractors. The villagers were told of the easy work and availability of unlimited land for cultivation. Such alluring stories prompted them to decide for migration.

Further, the Act did not protect the labourers, after their arrival on the garden nor did it give the employer any remedy other than recourse to the Act XIII of 1859 or section 492 of I.P.C or the ordinary civil law against a *coolie* who, having been recruited at a considerable expense, refused to work or left the garden. Short work was punished with flogging and absconders, when recovered, were also flogged. The Bengal Act III of 1863 then did not bring about any significant change in the nature of recruitment except that time expired labour could legally be engaged under contract by planters who also continued to take advantage of the 1859 Act of workmen's Breach of Contract Law with regard to the re-employed labourers.

Bengal Act of 1863 was amended to Bengal Act VI in 1865, specifying minimum wages, limited hours of work, (9 hours per day and 6 days per week) and laid down that the contracts with migrant labour must not exceed three years. Besides, every estate was asked to maintain a hospital, and a Protector and an Inspector of labour were appointed and empowered to visit gardens to supervise everything including the authority-labour relation.

This modification in the Act did not work satisfactorily. "In 1886 a commission of enquiry was appointed by the Government of Bengal to examine the state and prospects of tea cultivation in Assam. It found that the *coolies* were still induced to emigrate by his [contractors] representatives. Though cases of gross cruelty were becoming rare, the death rate on many gardens as a result of bad housing, overcrowding, impure water and insufficient or unsuitable food was appalling" (Kar, 1981 : 139). Here, it should be noted that "In 1866 the employers provided rice to the workers at fixed subsidized rates to enable them to survive as they could not buy rice in the open market. With such low wages the workers were unable to survive and furthermore at that time there were no markets within easy reach of garden *coolies*. This isolation from the local markets also kept the workers unaware of the fact that in Assam a free labourer in the 1860s could easily earn Rs. 7.00 per month, while as a tea garden worker he had to accept extremely low wages as well as virtual bondage to the plantation system". (Jain, 1983 :274-75).

The Commissioners then made a very important and constructive proposal. They advocated recruitment by gardens themselves. The Bengal Act 11 of 1870 recognised the *sardari* system. But, initially this system was introduced along with the contractor system and later on, the contractor system was completely replaced by the *sardari* system.

The Sardari System

The *Sardari* System of recruitment began in 1870. According to this system the plantation did not contact any contractor for recruiting labour. Instead, they sent their own trusted *coolies* to the recruiting districts for the purpose. The *sardar* was only known by that name during the time he was employed in the recruiting districts; he was in fact nothing more than a garden *coolie* and on return to his garden, reverted to his work as a *coolie*. However, he was paid a commission over the persons he recruited. In 1871-72 the *sardari* system gained momentum, when the labourers, were allowed to proceed on the steamers without any medical check up.

According to Act II of 1870, garden *sardars* were permitted to recruit labour up to twenty persons for any particular garden with the help of a license similar to that of contractors. They were also allowed to recruit more than 20 labourers subject to the same rules applicable to other agencies (Harlalka 1975 :105).

"Garden *Sardars*, including both men and women were sent out by the planters every year in the recruiting season, which generally began in November and lasted for 3 to 4 months. They, too, used to induce men and women to come to the tea gardens in Assam, showing all the advantages of work and prospects of ultimate settlement in independent holdings. Some of the prospective emigrants desired to join their relatives already in tea gardens while others were forced to do so by poverty and scarcity at home. There were still others who came as adventurers. Planters preferred labourers to come with their families as in that case they were more likely to stay permanently on gardens" (Kar, 1981 : 141-42).

Thus, recruitment increased by leaps and bounds. "By 1921-22 some 270,000 labourers were working in Assam and by 1962 some 600,000 ex-tea garden labourers, had been able to settle on government land. In spite of frank criticism of the less satisfactory features of tea garden life, in many cases they regard emigration to Assam as an avenue of escape from destitution and even servitude" (Griffith, 1967 : 283).

The recruitment of labourers from other provinces through various means thus continued from 1841 till 1953 when the question of recruitment of the labourers in Assam was raised from a wholly different angle. The Government of Assam, seriously perturbed at the growth of unemployment and at the shortage of food stuff, suggested that recruitment of labour from outside the state should be curtailed or discontinued, and that attempts should be made to induce labour from states with excess labour to shift to the estates requiring additional labour. The Indian Tea Association, while not sanguine as to the results of such a scheme, shared the government's wishes and offered to cooperate with it. But it was soon realised that there was a big gap between the demand and the supply from within the state. The Government, therefore, permitted the recruitment of some 11,000 labourers in 1955. But, since 1959 recruitment from outside Assam had been reduced drastically. From 1960 onward, recruitment from outside was stopped and the Tea District Labour Association was abolished. Labourers were then employed only from the existing unemployed ones available within the state (Bhadra, 1990: 204-5).

A good number of these migrant labourers initially suffered from mal-adjustment, some of them died, others went back home after the expiry of the contract period, and still others fled away before the expiry of that period. A major section of the groups, however, survived that stage and had gradually been making up their mind to make a permanent settlement in the new habitat, in a new economy and remote from their original home.

Ethnic Composition of the Tea Labour in Assam

The tea labourers, in Assam are composed of various tribes and castes, and belong to multi-linglustic and multi-cultural heritages which display a kaleidoscopic pattern of ethnic mosaic.

A number of studies (eg. Bhowmick, 1981; Bhuiyan, 1960; Crawford, 1924 ; 1931 ; Das Gupta and Khan, 1983; Guha, 1977; Harlalka, 1975; Kar, 1981; Phukan 1984 and Roy Burman, 1968) have been made on various aspects of plantation labourers in Assam. All of them have observed that the tea labour force in plantations and the ex-tea labourers in the bustees (villages) are composed of different ethnic groups. Bhuiyan (1960) maintains that there are different linguistic elements among the people; these are, (i) Kolarian speaking, e.g. the Munda, Ho, Santhal and the Kharia (ii) Dravidian speaking groups, eg. the Oraon, Kondh, Gond and the Malpahara and (iii) groups speaking Oriya, Bengali and Hindi.

Roy Burman (1968:8) observes that tribal communities like the Santhal, munda, Oraon, Kharia, Gond, Khond, Kisan, Nagesia, Savara, Godva, Parjah and the Pankla were recruited for the purpose. Others include the semi-tribal communities like the Lohar, Ghasi, Turi and the Bauri. Some Hindu caste groups were also recruited and they belong mostly to the groups like the Kurmi, Tanti, Pan-Tani and the Goala, etc. Besides these major tribe and caste groups, there are a good number of other ethnic groups that have contributed to the formation of the total tea labour force in Assam.

Gohain (1974:8), Harlalka (1975:159-60) and Kurmi (1981:25-26) have recorded the names of 57, 80 and 131 different ethnic groups respectively that compose the tea labour community here.

On the basis of the available literature as well as the present investigation, a total of 60 tribes and 40 castes could be identified in the tea and ex-tea labour population in Assam. The list of these groups has been provided in Tables II.1a. and II.1b.

It is relevant to note here that the Munda, Parjah and the Tanti; along with some other groups like the Oraon, Kharia and Santhal etc., were among the early recruits of the mid-nineteenth century.

It is also relevant to note that despite the heterogenous composition of the population, they always exhibit an apparent unity and integrity amongst themselves. This kind of manifestation is, of course, one of the most often noticed feature of Indian society, that is *Unity in Diversity*. As a matter of fact, this has become a part of India's self-identity which appears to be equally applicable to the tea labourers in Assam (Kar, 1975, 1997, Kar and Barua 1979).

Table II.1.a. List of Tribes working in Assam Tea Plantations

Sl No.	*Tribe*	*Synonyms*	*Sub-Tribe*
1	2	3	4
1	Asur		
2	Basor		
3	Baiga	Ojha	
4	Bania	Teli, Sahu	Kalwar, Mohar
5	Banjara		
6	Bedia		
7	Bhumoj	Tamaria	
8	Bhuyan		
9	Bhil		
10	Bando		
11	Binjia		
12	Birhor		
13	Birjia		
14	Chick Boraik	Sutradhar, Tanti	Johi, Johla
15	Chero		
16	Dhanwar	Dhanchar	
17	Gond	Car, Media, Gata	Rajgor, Mahor
18	Gorait	Panika	
19	Ghatwal		
20	Holra		
21	Kurmi		
22	Kawar		
23	Karlali	Paharia, Pahari	
24	Korwa		
25	Kol		
26	Kalahandi	Kalendi	
27	Kharia		
28	Khumhar		
29	Kherwar		
30	Khond		
31	Khondal		
32	Koya		
33	Kondpan		
34	Khor		

Contd....

Table II.1a - Contd.

1	2	3	4
35	Karmakar	Kamar	Kamar, Lohar
36	Kisan		
37	Lodhi		
38	Mahli	Majhi, Majhuar, Malakar	
39	Mahto		
40	Malpharia	Paharia	
41	Munda	Mura, Murari	Khangor
42	Manki	munda	Ho, Khangar
43	Mirdha		
44	Mali		
45	Nunia		
46	Nagasia		
47	Nagbansi		
48	Oraon	Orang	Berga
49	Parja		
50	Pradhan		
51	Beddi	Dora	
52	Rajwar		
53	Santal		
54	Sawara	Santhal	
55	Sahora		
56	Sabor		
57	Sahsris		
58	Tassa (Chassa)		
59	Toto		
60	Mudia (Modi)		

Table II.1.b. List of Castes Working in Assam Tea Plantations

Sl. No.	Caste	Synonyms
1	2	3
1	Arya Mala	Arwa Mala
2	Basphor	
3	Bawri	Bhoi
4	Bhokta	Bhokta
5	Bhuyan	
6	Bhumiji	
7	Bedia	Sunkar
8	Belder	
9	Baraik, Barhoi	Chick, Tanti
10	Baiga	
11	Bhatta	
12	Chamar	Muchi, Tanti
13	Chowdhari	
14	Dandari	Rabidas, Roidas
15	Dandasi	Dhobi, Chakali, Dhaba, Rajak
16	Dhopi	Suklabedi
17	Dueed	
18	Dhanwar	Dhanuar
19	Ghansi	Ghansia, Haddi
20	Ganda	Sutradhar, Tanti
21	Gorait	Gorait, Rasoit
22	Gonda	Bangi, Hadi, Harhi, Mehtor
23	Hari	Keyot, Malha, Majhi, Malakar
24	Keot	Jhora, Keyot, Malha, Majhi, Malakar
25	Koiri	Mirdha, Koh, Kolia
26	Khonyor	Kaangar, Munda, Kanora
27	Motwan	Kamal, Karmakar
28	Lohar	Kerua
29	Madari	Ahir, Gwala
30	Mohli	Ahir, Gwala
31	Mahara	Ahir, Gwala

Contd....

Table II.1b - contd.

1	2	3
32	Nath	Jogi
33	Pan	Swasi, Sansia, Sansi
34	Pasi	
35	Paidi	Nayak, Don, Balmiki, Pona
36	Panika	Patowa
37	Patri-Tanti	
38	Majowar	
39	Rajbansi	
40	Sansani, Tanti Nayak, Patnayak, Pantanti, Dakua, Napit	

3

THE FIELD

Assam is a constituent state of North East India, popularly known as Sat Bhoni (seven sisters). North East India comprises seven states, namely; Assam, Arunachal Pradesh, Manipur, Meghalaya, Mizoram, Nagaland and Tripura. According to the 1991 census the total population of the region is 31.4 million which is distributed over an area of 2.6 lakh sq.km. For administrative purposes, of late, Sikkim has also been included in North East India. The anthropological importance of this strategic region is well known for its rich cultural heritage and social structure. Besides the different caste groups, the hills and the plains of the region are inhabited by more than 130 major tribal groups. They have different ethnic, religious, linguistic, social and cultural identities. (Kar, 1994 : 1).

Assam is the gateway to North East India. It covers an area of 78,523 sq.km. The state of Assam is bounded on the North by Arunachal Pradesh and Bhutan; on the South by Tripura, Mizoram, Meghalaya and Manipur; on the East by Nagaland and parts of Arunachal Pradesh; and on the West by West Bengal and Bangladesh. It is connected with the rest of India by road, railway and air as well as by water through Bangladesh.

The state comprises mainly two river valleys, namely; the Brahmaputra Valley and the Barak valley. The two hill districts of Karbi Anglong and North Cachar hills, too, form a part of the state. The Barak Valley has 3 administrative districts, namely; Cachar, Karimganj and Hailakandi, whereas there are 20 districts in Brahmaputra Valley. Brahmaputra Valley has further been divided into Upper and Lower reaches valleys (known as Upper Assam and Lower Assam). Upper Assam has 7 administrative districts, namely; Dibrugarh, Dhemaji, Golaghat, jorhat, Lakhimpur, Sibsagar and Tinsukia.

According to the 1991 census*, the total population of the state is 22, 294, 562. The population of the state is very heterogenous in composition. The caste communities include the Assamese, Bengalese, Nepalese and a good number of floating populations. Some of the important tribes are the Bodos, Kacharis, Karbis, Mishings, Rabhas and the Tiwas. Besides, a large section of the population consists of the Muslims and the tea garden labourers.

It has been noted earlier that the present investigation was carried out among the two tribal groups (Munda and Parjah) and a caste group (Tanti) inhabiting Dirial tea estate in Dibrugarh district and Dhelakhat tea estate in Tinsukia district in Upper Assam.

Dibrugarh district, situated on the southern bank and upper reaches of the river Brahmaputra, lies in the North-eastern corner of Assam. It extends between 94° 44' E and 95° E longitudes and 27° 3'45 N and 8° N latitudes. It is bounded on the North by the rivers Brahmaputra and Lohit, on the East by a part of Lohit of Arunachal Pradesh, and the South Western boundary of the district runs along the eastern boundary of Sibsagar district.

Population of the district is composed of the members of various ethnic, linguistic, social and religious affiliations. Apart from the proto-Mediterranean and Australoid elements, brought in by the labourers of the tea plantations, the area is characterised by the prominence of Mongoloid and Caucasoid elements and an admixture of these two. This is, however, reflective of the population composition of the state as whole.

A large number of tea plantations are located in Dibrugarh district. Around 30 per cent of the plantations of the state are situated

* According to the provincial census Report, 2001, the total population of Assam stands at 26, 638, 407 (The Assam Tribune, 27th March, 2001)

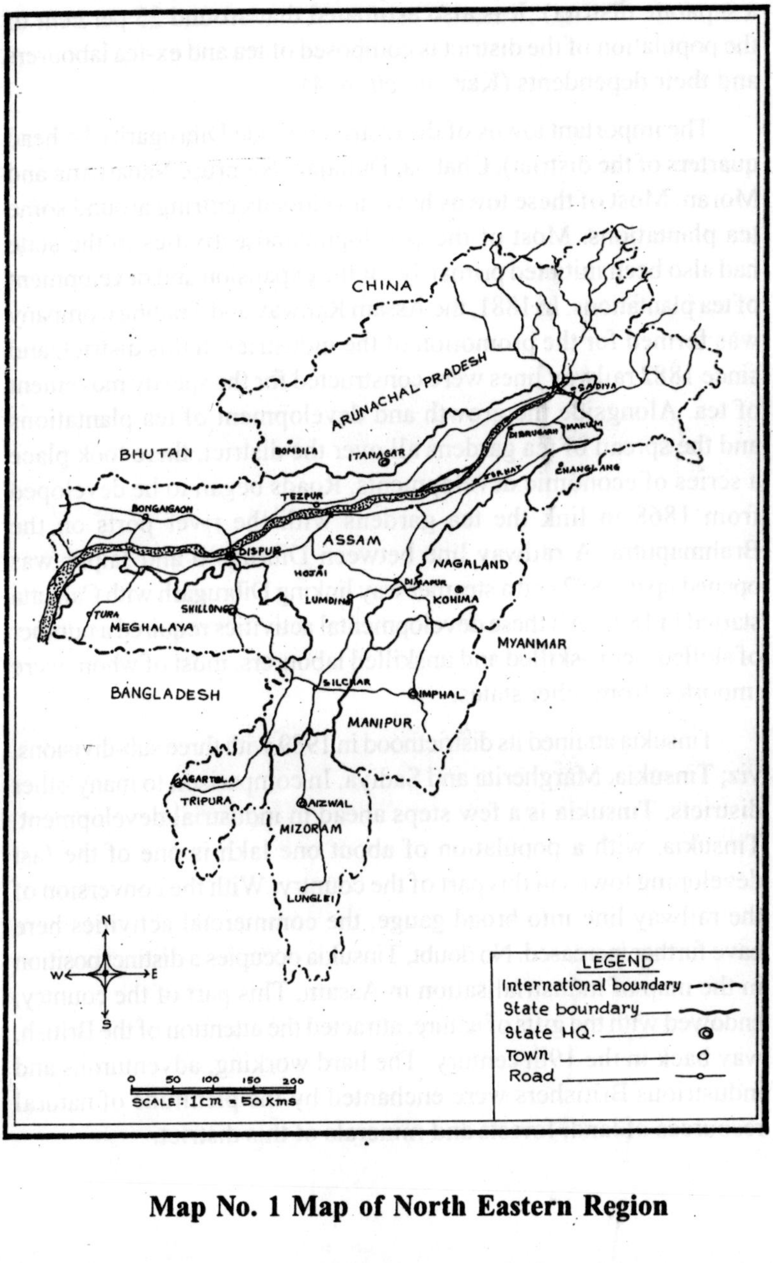

Map No. 1 Map of North Eastern Region

here (including Tinsukia district which has very recently been made a separate district). It is also estimated that around 25 per cent of the population of the district is composed of tea and ex-tea labourers and their dependents (Kar, *op. cit.* p. 4).

The important towns of the district include Dibrugarh (the head quarters of the district), Chabua, Duliajan, Namrup, Naharkatia and Moran. Most of these towns have developed centring around some tea plantations. Most of the developmental activities in the state had also been initiated primarily for the expansion and development of tea plantations. In 1881, the Assam Railway and Trading Company was formed for the promotion of the industries in this district, and since 1882 railway lines were constructed for the speedy movement of tea. Alongside the growth and development of tea plantations and the spread of tea gardens all over the district, there took place a series of economic developments. Roads began to be developed from 1868 to link the tea gardens with the river ports on the Brahmaputra. A railway line between Dibrugarh and Jaipur was opened up in 1882 and a steamer way linking Dibrugarh with Calcutta started in 1893. All these developmental activities required a number of skilled, semi-skilled and unskilled labourers, most of whom were imported from other states.

Tinsukia attained its districthood in 1989 with three sub-divisions, viz; Tinsukia, Margherita and Sadiya. In comparison to many other districts, Tinsukia is a few steps ahead in industrial development. Tinsukia, with a population of about one lakh is one of the fast developing towns in this part of the country. With the conversion of the railway line into broad gauge, the commercial activities here have further increased. No doubt, Tinsukia occupies a distinct position in the map of industrialisation in Assam. This part of the country, endowed with the gifts of nature, attracted the attention of the British, way back in the 19th century. The hard working, adventurous and industrious Britishers were enchanted by the plenitude of natural resources of land, forests and minerals of this district.

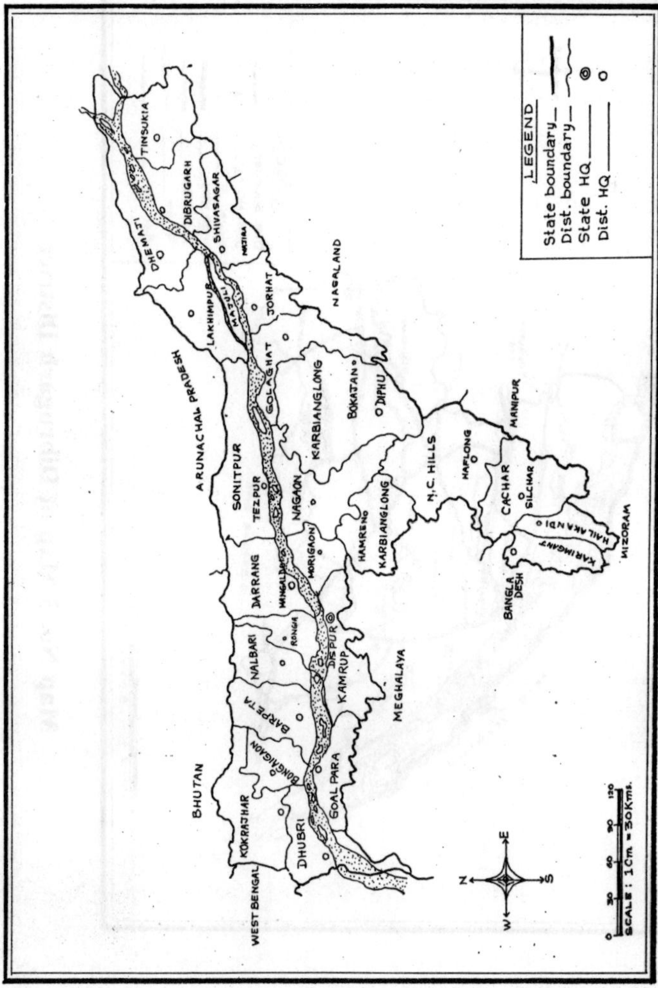

Map No. 2 Map of Assam

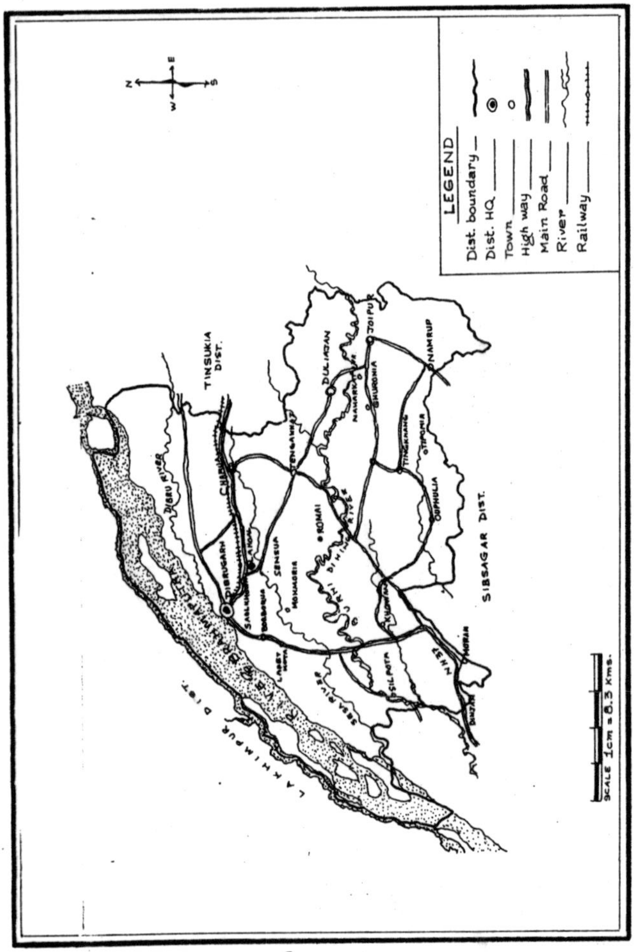

Map No. 3 Map of Dibrugarh District

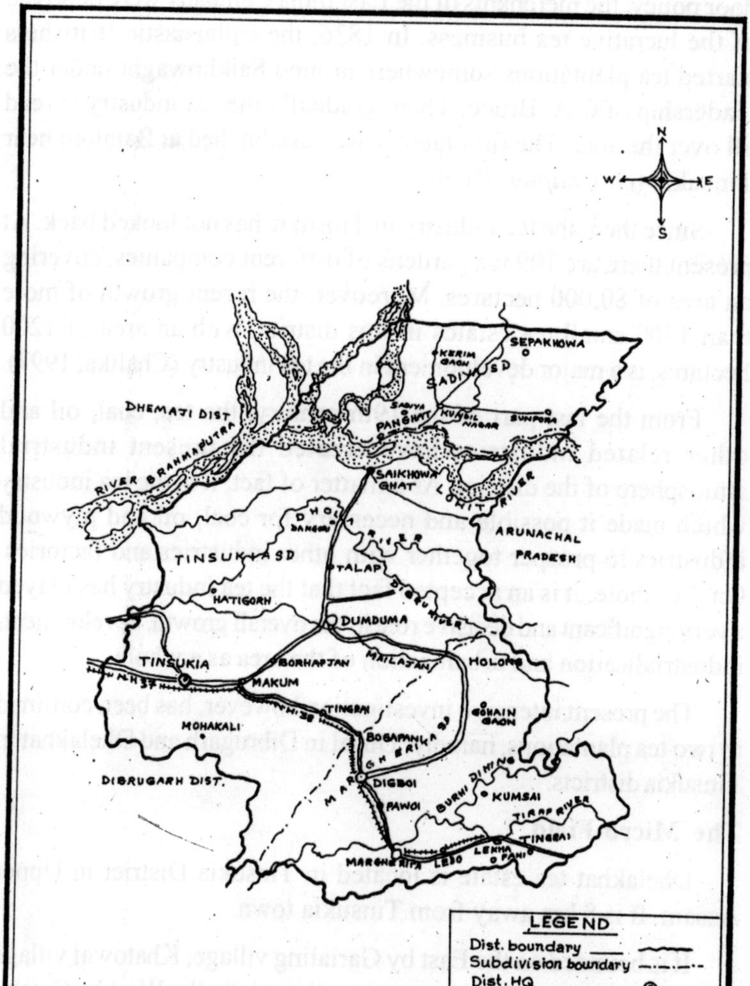

Map No. 4 Map of Tinsukia District

In the beginning of the 19th century, as China adopted a closed door policy, the merchants of the East India Company were deprived of the lucrative tea business. In 1836, the enthusiastic Britishers started tea plantations somewhere around Saikhowaght under the leadership of C.A. Bruce. Then, gradually the tea industry spread all over the area. The first factory was established at Bajaloni near Tinsukia (*cf. Chapter Two*).

Since then, the tea industry in Tinsukia has not looked back. At present there are 109 tea gardens of different companies, covering an area of 80,000 hectares. Moreover, the recent growth of more than 1300 small tea estates in this district, with an area of 1200 hectares, is a major development in the tea industry (Chalika, 1997).

From the last part of the 19th century, the tea, coal, oil and other related industries have created the present industrial atmosphere of the district. As a matter of fact, it is the tea industry which made it possible and necessary for coal, oil and plywood industries to prosper together with other industries and factories. On the whole, it is an accepted fact that the tea industry has played a very significant and decisive role in the overall growth, development, industrialisation and urbanisation of the area as a whole.

The present intensive investigation however, has been confined to two tea plantations, namely; Dirial in Dibrugarh and Dhelakhat in Tinsukia districts.

The Micro-Field

Dhelakhat tea estate is located in Tinsukia District in Upper Assam. It is 8 km away from Tinsukia town.

It is bounded on the East by Gariating village, Khatowal village and Tagukhowa village (Assamese villages); on the West by Gatang and Nimouguri tea estates; on the South by Chanmari and Gilaphukri tea estates; and on the North by Bazlan tea estate and Matun Rangagara gaon (Assamese village). The plantation covers an area of 592.12 hectares.

Dhelakhat tea estate belongs to M/S Dhelakhat Tea Company Ltd. which is a sister group of M/s Jardine Henderson Ltd. Its head office is situated in Calcutta and at present Mr. S.G. Mehta is its chairman.

Dirial tea estate, however, is located in Dibrugarh district, Upper Assam. It is situated at a distance of 35 km from Dibrugarh. Though under Dibrugarh district Dirial tea estate is nearer to Tinsukia than to Dibrugarh. Tinsukia town stands at a distance of about 13 km from the plantation.

It is bounded on the North by Hatimara tea estate; on the South by Duliajan town and Kacharipathar village (Assamese village); on the East by Bordubi town and Keyhung tea estate; and on the West by Balijan tea estate and Dringkhat village (Assamese village). It covers an area of 893.35 hectares.

Dirial tea estate is owned by M/S George Williamson (Assam) Ltd. It was started in the year 1868/70 by M/S Tingri Tea Company. In 1969, Hoogrijan tea estate also was amalgamated with Dirial. At present it has two divisions, namely; Pailabari and Old Dirial Division.

The Plantation is located on the plains area. Barring the labour settlements, staff quarters, administrative offices, educational institutions, club house, play ground, drains and burial ground etc., the entire land consists of tea beds interspersed with shade trees of various types.

Some of the bungalows of the managerial personnel are situated very close to the office.

Communication and Transport

Dhelakhat, as noted earlier, stands at a distance of about 8 km from Tinsukia town, the district headquarters of Tinsukia. There are neither proper means of communication nor regular transport facilities to the plantation. The road that links the tea estate with Tinsukia is a *kuccha* one. No public or private transport runs to or through it. The labourers and the members of the staff often have

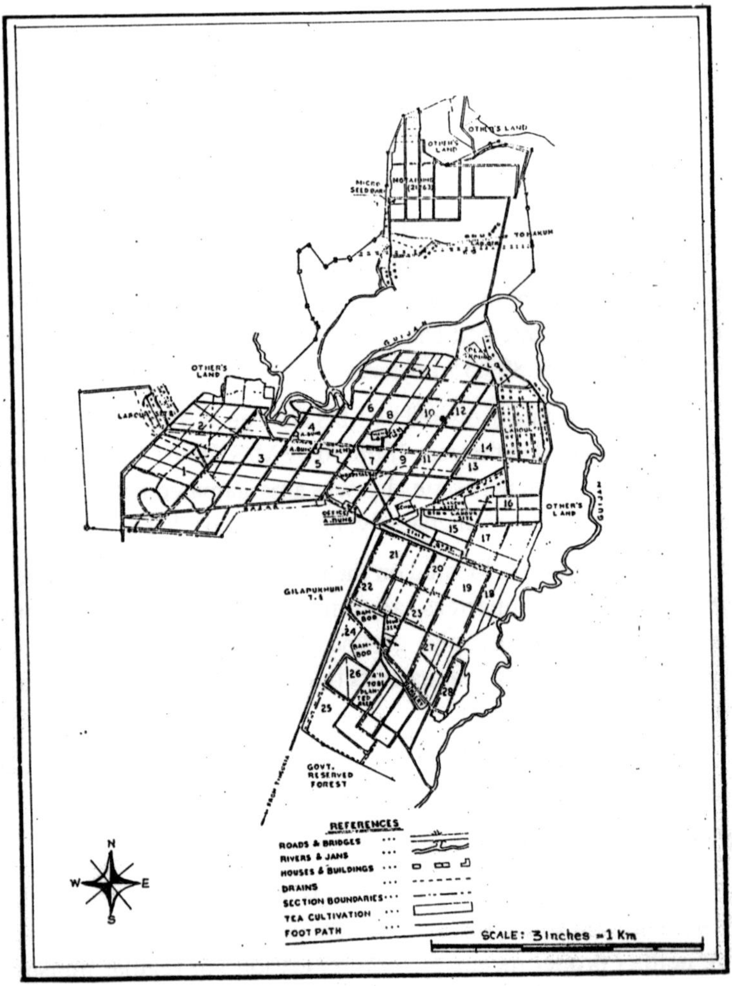

Map No. 5 Map of Dhelakhat Tea Estate

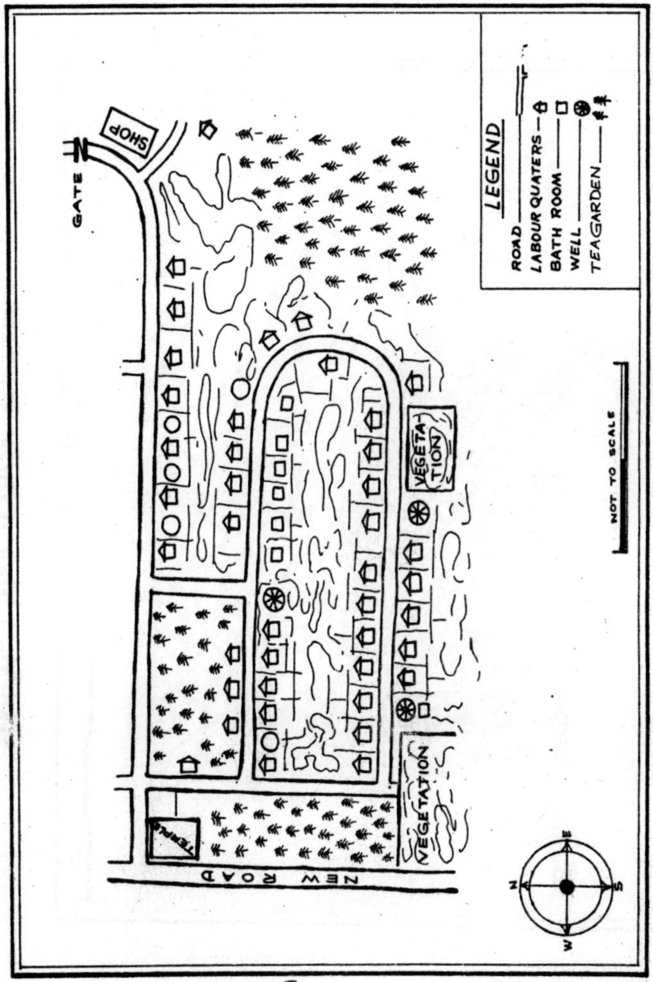

Map No. 6 Dhelakhat Tea Estate L. No.2

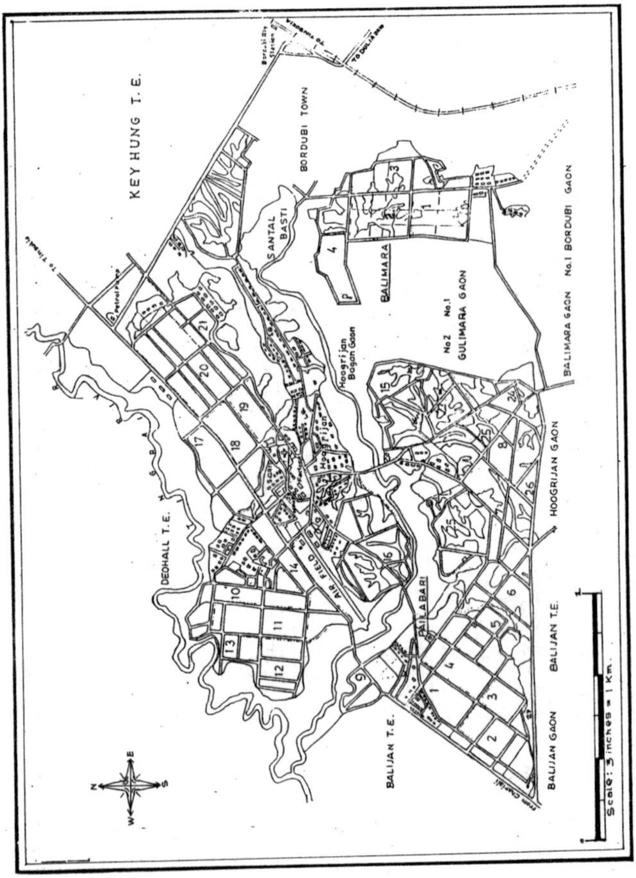

Map No. 7 Map of Dirial Tea Estate

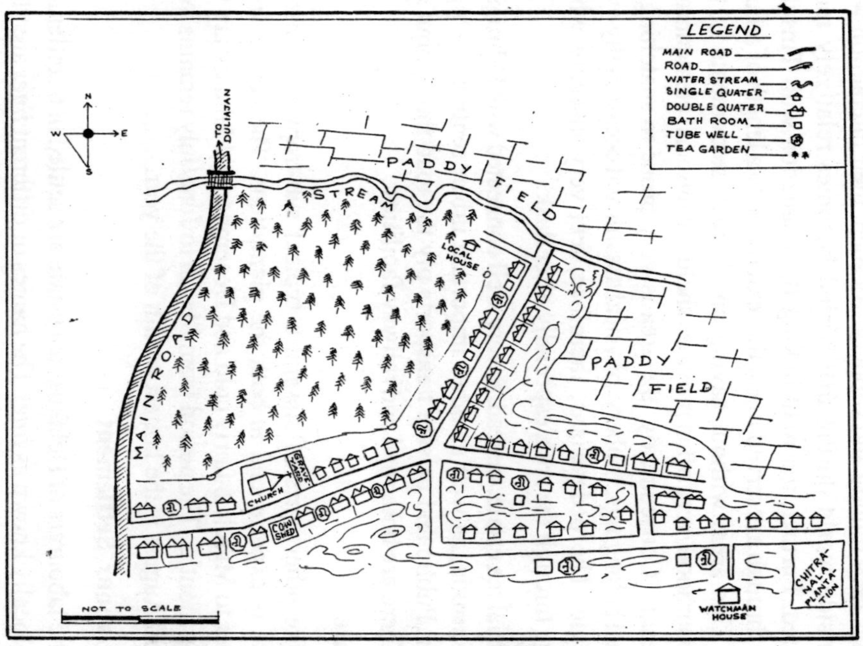

Map No. 8 Dirial Tea Estate L, Pailabari-2

to find their own means to come out of the plantation. The labourers normally use bi-cycles and the woman members usually travel on foot to go to Tinsukia. During the rainy season however, the road becomes very muddy and slippery. As such, their interaction with the outside world during that period becomes relatively more restricted. Further, the road linking the plantation with Tinsukia passes through a reserved forest that extends upto a length of around I km. This area, without having any human settlements in the neighbourhood, very often provides shelter to unsocial elements and miscreants. Consequently, the area is very prone to snatching of personal belongings, robbery, physical assault and occasionally even homicide. The pedestrians, therefore, feel very insecure while moving through the area, especially after dusk.

Dirial tea estate, instead, is very well connected with Dibrugarh and Tinsukia, as well as other important urban centres in Upper Assam. Public and private transports ply the road throughout the day. There are both road and railway facilities .

Climate

Like other parts of Assam, a typical sub-tropical monsoon climate is experienced in both the plantations. The period from October to March is fairly cold and December and January are the coldest months. The period from March to June/July remains very wet and August is the hottest month of the year.

The Labour Settlement

The labourers of Delakhat tea estate are settled in 6 settlement units, locally known as *lines*.The names of different *lines* are : No. 2 (72 families), No. 13 (50 families), No. 14 (160 families), Dhonjan (28 families), Hattipatti (36 families), and Mottapung (122 families). Thus, a total number of 468 labourers' families reside in Dhelakhat tea estate.

In Dirial tea estate, on the other hand, there are two divisions, namely, New Dirial (Pailabari) and Old Dirial. In New Dirial there are eleven labour *lines*. They are: Karat (21 families), Sambalpuria

(40 families), New (100 families), Jungle (64 families), No. 21 (39 families), Kachariya (55 families), P.B. 1 (34 families), P.B. 2 (70 families), P.B. 5 (39 families), Gutibari (58 families), and factory lines (49 families), accommodating a total number of 567 families.

In the second division (Old Dirial), there are only six *lines*. They are: Balimara (37 families), Boro (39 families), Dhora (94 families), Oria (35 families), No. 1(17 families), and No. 7 *lines* (26 families). Thus, in Old Dirial there are 248 families.

Besides, from the two nearby *Bastis* (rural settlements) the labourers from 72 families come to work in either of the two divisions,

Most of these quarters in a line are constructed on both sides of one or more bylanes, in a linear fashion. The lines are hetero-ethnic in composition. Each *line* is situated at a reasonable distance from the other.

The Creches

Article 46 of the Assam Plantation Rules of 1956, provides that in every plantation wherein 50 or more women workers are employed or were employed on any day of the preceding twelve months, the employer shall provide and maintain creches for the use of the children who are below 2 years of age, at suitable sites at the work places to the scale of one for every 25 hectares of tea or part thereof. It also provides that there should be creches for the use of children who are between the age of 2 and 6 years, to the scale of at least one for each of the main and the out gardens; and all the creches shall be according to the standard laid down in these rules.

(1) Every creche shall be conveniently accessible to the mothers of the children accommodated therein.

(2) There shall be not less than 15sq.ft., of floor area for each child to be accommodated therein.

(3) The building in which the creche is situated shall be of sound construction with a good plinth.

(4) The plan of the creche building shall be in accordance with the standard plan laid down by the Chief Inspector , provided that , where no standard plan has been laid down or where it is proposed to deviate from a standard plan, the Chief Inspector's approval shall be obtained.

(5) The creches shall be furnished with suitable furniture such as couches for reclining, benches , a hammock for each child below the age of 2 years, etc. and provided with toys and other playthings as may be specified by the Chief Inspector of the plantations with prior approval of the State Government.

(6) A suitably fenced and shady open air playground shall be provided for the older children.

(7) The employer shall appoint: (i) a woman as creche-in-charge to look after the children during the absence of their mothers, who shall possess such qualifications and training as may be approved by the State Government, and (ii) such other staff, to the scale of one for every twenty children or part thereof as may be approved by the said authority.

During the present investigation, it has been found that both the gardens do not have the creche facilities as per the provision of the Act. For instance, in Dhelakhat tea estate it has been found that there exists a creche structure which is non-functional. On enquiry it could be gathered that a few years back the creche had been functioning and was being attended by a caretaker named Miss Stella Hasa. She was a permanent employee of the garden. Gradually, however, the creche ceased functioning, probably because the garden authority failed to maintain a regular supply of milk and other facilities. Dr Dilip Borkakoty, the physician of the plantation hospital reported that they had also a mobile creche which used to bring the children from the different areas of the garden. But, that too, has not been found to be in operation during the present investigation.

Similarly, Dirial tea estate too possesses a structure which was established in 1950. It is attached to Dirial Hospital. At present, it is used for the out patients for their check up; and distribution of medicines.

Thus, both the gardens have the structure for the creche, but these do not function as per the provision of the Act.

Drainage System

Article 20 of the Assam Plantation Labour Rules 1956, along with the Plantation Labour Act 1951, provides that all drains carrying waste or sullage water shall be constructed in masonry or with other impermeable materials and shall be regularly flushed and the effluent disposed of by connecting such drains with a suitable drainage line.

Provided that, where there is no such drainage line, the effluent shall be deodorized and rendered innocuous and disposed of in a manner to the satisfaction of the health officer.

The drainage system of the gardens under investigation does not appear to be upto requirement. During the rainy season, the non-metalled by-lanes of the plantations become water logged and filled with mud. Water remains stagnant here and there. This is not only inconvenient for their movement along the lanes and by-lanes, but also instrumental in afflicting the people with a number of diseases.

IMPORTANT PUBLIC PLACES

Educational Institutions

Section 14 of the Plantation Labour Act, 1951 states that where the children between the age of six and twelve of the workers employed in any plantation exceed twenty five in number, the State Government may make rules requiring every employer to provide educational facilities for the children in such manner and of such standard as may be prescribed.

There are two primary schools within the jurisdiction of Dhelakhat tea estate. Both the schools are located in different labour *lines* (settlements). One of the schools has a reinforced concrete building with 141 students (cl. 1:82; 11:23; 111:20; IV: 16) in 1998. All of them are the children of the tea labourers. The school is run by two teachers. It functions from 9.00 a.m to 3.00 p.m.

The second school is housed in kuccha structure and does not have tables and desks, etc. The total roll strength during the present investigation in 1998 was only 48. The line committee started this school in 1993. Later on, in 1995, it was taken over by the garden authorities. There is only one teacher. The school functions in two shifts. Classes I and 11 students are taught from 8.00 a.m to 12.00 noon. The rest are taught from 1.00 p.m to 5 p.m.

In both the schools, the students do not wear any school uniform. Further, the text books have not been found to be distributed among the students free of cost.

There are a few other schools that are located very close to the garden. The ME school located in the immediate neighbourhood was established in 1965. In 1997 it has been upgraded to a high school. At present it has students upto class IX There are facilities for high school and higher education at Tinsukia, located at a distance of 8 km from the garden.

In Dirial tea estate, there is only one primary school run by the garden authorities. It was established in 1948. The school is housed in a *pucca* structure. It has 180 students enrolled at the time of investigation (class A:30; 1:72; 11:43; III:20; IV: 15). The students are taught from 9.00 am to 3.00 p.m. They have to wear school uniform, and text books are given free of cost. The teaching staff has three members who run the school.

For higher education they have to go to the neighbouring towns like Tinsukia (which is around 13 km away from the garden), Bordubi (2 km.) and Duliajan (I km).

The Club

For the purpose of recreation, clubs are provided for the labourers in the tea plantations.Dhelakhat tea estate however, there does not exist any such club. Earlier, there was a *kuccha* house for this purpose. But, at present it has been found to be non-functional and the house is being used to accommodate a labour family.

In Dirial tea estate, on the other hand, there are three clubs for the purpose of recreation of the labourers. All the permanent workers of the garden are members of the club. The garden authority provides materials for playing, different indoor and outdoor games like table tennis, carom board, cards and football. All the infrastructural facilities, including electricity are provided by the management.

The Play Ground

In Dhelakhat there is only one playground for outdoor games. That is situated adjacent to the L.P. school which is in No. 13 *line*, whereas in Dirial tea estate there are three playgrounds and an air field, a large field used for landing of helicopters, etc. It is used by the management personnel coming from England. Most of the games conducted by the tea garden for both children and adults usually take place in the air field, which is situated at the entrance of the tea garden close to the main road.

The Hospital

As per the provision of the Plantation Labour Act 1951, the garden hospital in Dhelakhat was established in 1940. The labourers working in the plantation attend the hospital for necessary medical services. There are two wards, one for the male and the other for the female patients. There are 36 beds for the Inpatients.

With regard to the composition of the staff, during the present investigation, there was one doctor, one nurse, one pharmacist, one health assistant, four female attendants and two male attendants. Because of lack of proper infrastructural facilities, most of the surgical cases cannot be attended here. Barring a few minor cases, the surgical cases are generally referred either to Tinsukia civil hospital or to Assam Medical College Hospital, Dibrugarh.

No definite information could be collected with regard to the exact year of establishment of the Dirial hospital. However, in 1989, Dirial hospital had been amalgamated with the Central Hospital in Dirial tea estate. The central hospital caters to the referred cases from 16 other tea plantations belonging to the same company. The hospital is well equipped and by and large self-sufficient. All treatment is provided free of cost.

There are in all 115 in-patient beds in the hospital that has 6 whole time and 2 visiting trained physicians, 6 nurses, I pharmacist and two assistants, one for the X-ray unit and the other for the pathological laboratory.

Shops and Market

There are 3 shops in the premises of the Dhelakhat tea estate. One of these is run by a Marwari family and it deals in stationery and grocery goods. The other two shops are owned by two Assamese families and these deal only in stationery goods.

In Dirial tea estate too, there are three shops run by some families who migrated from Bihar. These three shops, too, deal in stationery and other grocery goods. There are three other petty shops run by the labourers, but very few stationery items are available there. Besides, very often from Tinsukia, some hawkers come to the *lines* with fish and some stationery items. Since there are nearby urban centres like Bordubi and Duliajan, the labourers very often visit those centres to purchase their essentials.

Occasionally, the people of both the gardens go to Tinsukia for some major purchases. Besides, on every alternate Friday, the people get the benefit of a temporary market that sits within the premises of the gardens. Flying businessmen from Tinsukia town and its neighbourhood come to the market to sell various types of commodities. Generally, they deal in groceries, vegetables, clothes, ready-made garments, stationery and fancy articles, cosmetics and various other necessary and luxury goods. It may be noted here that the floating market day coincides with the payment day of the labourers.

Places of Worship

In Dhelakhat, there are 4 Shiv temples, 2 churches and I Nam Ghar (temple for the Assamese Vaishnavites) for the purpose of worship.

In Dirial there is only one Shiv temple for the Hindus and a church for the Christians. There is no Nam Ghar in this plantation.

Cremation/Burial Ground

For the purpose of the disposal of the dead bodies, there are two burial grounds in Dhelakhat and Dirial tea estates: one for the Hindus and the other for the Christians. The burial ground for the Christians is located in the vicinity of the lines, whereas the other one stands on the bank of the river that flows in the neighbourhood. The cremation is also done by the Hindus on the river bank.

Ethnic Composition of the Labourers

It has been noted earlier that the ethnic compositions of the labour forces in both Dhelakhat and Dirial tea estates are heterogeneous. Table III.1 shows the ethnic composition of the labourers working in these gardens. It will be seen from the table that a total of 1035 families are distributed in 36 different ethnic groups.

The Mundas however, are the numerically dominant group. There are in all 225 (21.74%) Munda families in the two plantations (Dhelakhat - 75 and Dirial 150).

The table further reveals that the Parjahs have the next numerical strength. There are 167 (16.14%) families that are, however, very unevenly distributed in the two plantations (Dhelakhat - 149 and Dirial - 18). The total number of the Majhi families is also reasonably high (121, 11.69%).

Table III. 1. Distribution of the Labourers in Different Ethnic Groups (Dhelakhat and Dirial Tea Estates)

Sl. No.	Group	No. of families
1	2	3
1	Munda	225
2	Pariah	167
3	Majhi	121
4	Tanti	80
5	Karmakar	53
6	Oriya	37
7	Goala	34
8	Bhumij	27
9	Kharia	24
10	Lohar	23
11	Gorait	23
12	Oraon	20
13	kishan	20
14	Mirdhaa	19
15	Mahato	18
16	Johla	18
17	Bhuyan	17
18	Nagasia	14
19	Paharia	11
20	Dandasi	11
21	Nepali	7
22	Bawri	8
23	Sahora	8
24	Mahara	7
25	Manki	6
26	Saharia	5
27	Ghansi	5
28	Nayak	5
29	Panika	4
30	Ghatwal	4
31	Korwa	3
32	Sahora	3
33	Khond	3
34	Sabor	2
35	Kurmi	2
36	Muslim	1
	Total	1035

Among the caste groups, the Tanti with 80 (7.91%) families has the highest nunierical strength.

The other major groups are Karmakar (53:5.13%), Oriya (37:3.58%) and Goala (34:3.29%) etc. The rest of the ethnic units are by and large not very significant in numerical strength.

Before concluding the chapter, in the following pages, an attempt is being made to include a brief ethnographic introduction of the three communities under investigation.

The Mundas

Next to the Santhal and the Oraon, the Mundas are the third largest tribe living in the state of Bihar; and are one of the numerically dominant tribes in India. With regard to their probable origin, different scholars have maintained different views. Thus for example, Crawford (1924 : 210) observes, " They entered India from the south and south-east at a period when India had land connection with Australia and was cut off from Northern Asia".

However, Roy in his book, *The Mundas and their country,* maintains that the earliest traces of the groups are found in the sunny valleys of Northern India. It is mentioned in the Hindu legend that an ancestor of Jarasandha, named Yayah made a division of his empire amongst his five sons. Northern India was allotted to one of his sons Kola, whose descendants are the kols, the generic name applied to the Mundas and other allied tribes (cited in Baruah, 2000).

Saran (1974) maintains that next to the Santal and the Oraon, the Mundas are the third largest tribe living in the state of Bihar having a total population of 6,28,931, out of which 4,65,093 (73.90%) live in the district of Ranchi in the east and south-east of Ranchi district and they are one of the earliest inhabitants of the Chotanagpur plateau.

With regard to their distribution in Bihar, Belfour (1976 : 1008) observes that the group comprises about two-thirds of the population of the five parganas of Silli, Tanar, Baranda, Rabey and Bundu; all others being recent settlers.

The mundas are divided into two principal endogamous sub-groups, namely; (i) the *Khangar or Tamaria Munda* and (ii) the Kompat Munda . The two groups have been found to maintain a hierarchy. With regard to their hierarchy, Dasgupta and Sarkar observe that the Khangar group is ritually impure. It seems, there is a legendary origin of the two groups to explain in this hierarchial inter-relation. It goes as follows :

There were two Munda brothers who started a journey on foot. The younger brother with his family was going much ahead of the elder brother with his family. The younger brother's wife was pregnant and on the way she delivered a child. The placenta was buried and the family proceeded further with the new born child. After they left the place a jackal came there and dug out the placenta. Afterwards, on reaching that particular place the elder brother noticed the unearthed placenta and mistook it as the intestine of a deer. At that time, they were very hungry and cooked the placenta and consumed it. When both the brothers met at a point the elder brother described all their experiences during the journey. He also told the incident of his eating the deer's intestine due to excessive hunger. The younger brother then realised that it was not deer's intestine, but human placenta. So the elder brother was excommunicated. Ultimately, the younger brother formed the *kompat* group which holds a relatively high status for his purity than the *Khangar* group of the elder brother which is regarded as impure due to the consumption of human placenta, and since then *roti-beti* (commensal connubial) relationship between the two groups is avoided (cited in Baruah, 2000).

The Mundas are patrilocal in residence and patrilineal in descent and inheritance. Traditionally, they follow the joint family system. When the father of the family dies, the married sons are often separated; but generally they remain in the same village.

As per custom, marriage must take place within the tribe, but outside one's own *killi* or Sept. The bride is formally adopted into her husband's *killi* and the ceremony of putting *sindur* (vermilion) by the bridegroom on the forehead of the bride is a relic of the old ceremony of the mingling of blood. It is the essential part of the actual celebration of marriage. The bride has to adopt the totem of her husband.

Among the Mundas, child marriage is unknown and bride price is paid to the parents of the bride by the bridegroom's parents in cash or in kind. An interesting item is binding of a mango tree with a thread and the social recognition of the tree as a witness to the marriage. Widow remarriage is permitted.

As for religion, the Mundas believe in a number of gods, spirits and ghosts. These gods and deities are known as *Bongas* who may be either benevolent or malevolent. They also believe in witchcraft and sorcery.

When a person dies, the body is anointed with oil and turmeric and then covered with a sheet of new cloth. While disposing of the dead body, generally the Non-Christian Mundas follow the system of cremation, whereas the Christian Mundas bury the corpse.

The Parjah

The Parjahs are a comparatively small group and are believed to be an off-shoot from the Gonds. The word "parja" is derived from the Sanskrit word *Praja*, which means a subject, in contradistinction to *Rajah* or a king.

Russell and Lal (1975 : 371-379) report that the Rajas and the Parjahs were brothers; But the Rajas took horse riding as a profession whereas the Parjahs became the carriers of burdens.

According to a legend, one of their ancestors was the elder brother of the first Raja of Bastar. While in Tamilnadu, they had to flee on account of an invasion by the Muhammedans. They were accompanied by their tutelary deity, the Goddess *Danteshwari*. In accordance with the command of the Goddess, the younger brother was considered to be the *Raja* and rode on horse back, while the elder one carried the baggage. The Goddess followed them, guiding their steps, but she strictly enjoined the *Raja,* not to look behind to see her. However, when at a certain point he could not hear her footsteps, he looked back and as such she could no longer go with him, and asked him to march as far as he could, and settle down. The two brothers settled in Bastar where the descendants of the younger brother became the ruling clan and those of the elder brother became their servants, who constitute the present day Parjah tribe (Crawford, *opcit*, 166-167; Russell & Lal, *opcit*, pp. 372). It is also interesting to note that the Parjahs still refer to the *Rani* (Queen) of Bastar as their *Bohu* or younger brother's wife (Crawford, *opcit* pp. 167).

Thus, it seems the term Parjah refers to a group with a particular occupational calling that occupies a relatively lower position in occupational hierarchy.

Russell and Lal (*opcit*) further observe that the Parjahs in Bastar are held to be a branch of the Gonds, and have a considerable admixture of the Khonds, or other tribes in different localities, as the rules of marriage are very loose in this part of the country. Thus, it affirms that the Parjahs have affinities with both the Gonds and the Khonds, as they were originally one tribe.

According to Grigson they include at least seven different tribes, some speaking Mundari, some Dravidian and some Aryan dialects. Some of them belonged to the old Jaypore state, and some primitive Parjahs lived beyond the Kolab Subari river in the old Sukma Zamindari around the mount Tulsi Dongri (cited in Mehta, 1984). In Orissa they are known as *Porjas*.

The tribe, as a whole is endogamous, but there are a number of exogamous totemic clans. Some of the clans have names such as *Bagh* (a tiger), *Kachins* (a tortoise) and *Bokda* (a goat), etc. These animals are never killed by the members of the respective clans.

Whenever any member of the family kills a totem even accidentally, the family observes mourning, pollution and purification rites.

Though marriage is prohibited between the members of the same clan, sometimes clan exogamy is negotiated with village exogamy.

Monogamy is the general rule. But polygamy in the form of polygyny is permitted. By and large, they go for negotiated marriage. While initiating the process, the proposal of the marriage is generally made by the boy's father, who offers a cup of liquor to the girl's father in the *bazar*, and subsequently explains the purpose of his mission. If the girl's father, after consulting the members of his family, disapproves of the match, he returns an equal quantity of liquor to the boy's father as a token of his decision. The girl is usually consulted. Now-a-days the girls seem to have a greater say in the matter, though ultimately the negotiations are made by the parents.

The Parjahs are patrilocal in residence and patrilineal in descent and inheritance. The marriage takes place at the house of the boy, where two marriage sheds are made. It is also interesting to note that the bride, while going to the bridegroom's house, is accompanied by her female relatives only.

The remarriage of widows is permitted. A man can divorce his wife if she is adulterous, or if she is considered to be inauspicious or under an unfavourable star; or if her children die in infancy. But the society does not approve of the woman divorcing her husband even if he is involved in adultery or they are otherwise maladjusted. A divorced woman can marry again if she becomes a widow.

The Parjahs worship the class of divinities of the hills and forests, as well as *Danteshwari*, the tutelary Goddess of Bastar. Most villages have a man who is possessed by the deity and his advice is taken in religious matters. The dead are invariably buried, the corpse being laid on the ground with head to the east and feet to the west.

The Tanti

Although the Tantis admit weaving to be their immemorial profession, many of them have recently been driven by the influx of cheap machine-made goods, and have taken to agriculture. They are patriarchal, patrilineal and patrilocal.

Their tradition maintains that they descended from Siva, the powerful Hindu god. As per the legend, Siva Das was born from the sweat that fell from Siva when he was dancing. Siva Das's wife Kushati was created by Siva from a blade of kusa grass. Kushati and Siva Das had four sons namely; Balaram, Uddhap, Purandar and Madhukar. They are believed to be the ancestors of the present day four sub-castes of the Tantis (Crawford, opcit pp. 281).

Among the Tantis, there are a large number of sub-castes, bearing various names. Each of these sub-castes is further sub-divided into various groups taking the names of different animals, plants and birds.

The ancient dwelling places of the Tantis include places like Bengal, Bihar and Orissa.

Except in Bihar, where adult marriage is still practised by the poorer members of the caste, the Tantis generally marry their daughters before they have attained puberty. The bride-price demanded for a girl usually does not exceed Rs 50 to Rs 60, but it is deemed more respectable for a man to give his daughter free of price.

Polygamy is recognized to the extent that a man may take a second wife if the first one proves to be barren. Widow remarriage and divorce are forbidden in Bengal, while in Bihar widows can marry again.

In religion, marriage and funeral customs, the Tantis resemble other similar Hindu castes. In Chota Nagpur and Orissa, however, their Hinduism is tinged by the Animism of those among whom they live. The Tantis worship *Krishna* and they celebrate *Janmashtami* or birthday of their god *Krishna.*

In West Bengal *Vaishnavism* is the characteristic subscription of the caste. Reverence is also paid to *Durga* and *Siva*, but no sacrifice involving the taking of animal life is offered to them. Images are sometimes made, but more commonly the weaver's looms or some of the tools of the craft are regarded as the dwelling places or symbols of the god.

4

SOCIAL LIFE

Social life grows out of constant patterning of social interactions and relationships that take place within some institutionalised groupings among human beings.

Man does not live alone, and at the same time he has to meet his basic needs like food and shelter, and social needs like companionship, recreation, religious activities and games, etc. He thus forms groups or associations with the help of other men, and builds up certain institutions. With the help of those groups, he satisfies his needs. To quote Firth (1961:41), "All community life involves methods of grouping and grading people for an effective carrying out of the various types of activities demanded by the common existence."

Fortes (1945, 1949) puts particular stress on the corporate groups of society. For him, the principal corporate group is the lineage, a stable structure, the warp, and the organised domestic life, the woof. He compares the two components to the blood and tissues of an animal organism.

In this context, it may be emphasized that the family is considered to be the most important element in the social life, as it forms the first sphere in which individuals combine. It is the fundamental social institution that fulfills the various needs of a human being in his life. Lowie (1950 : 215) takes it to be an association that corresponds to the institution of marriage, the socially approved form of sex relations.

From the dawn of history, it may relevantly be noted, documented evidence concerning woman shows that women's primary role has been family oriented. The study of women's role in the family as daughter, sister, wife and mother are thus fundamental for understanding women and their status in a society (Hammond and Jablow, 1976: 9).

The activities and roles played within the family by women through different stages as daughter, daughter-in-law, sister, sister-in-law, wife, mother, mother-in-law, separated, divorcee, and widow throw light on their position in the society (Raju, 1988 : 23).

As a matter of fact, social status actually concerns the total life in the society through various social institutions. But family being the basic and the smallest unit of the society, the status of any of its members, primarily centres round the family.

In the present chapter, therefore, an attempt has been made to have a reasonably detailed understanding of the family life of the people under investigation as revealed by the data generated from the field on different aspects of family. Marriage being very intimately related with family, a brief discussion has also been included on some aspects of the institution. In the process of discussion, all possible attempts have been made to put particular focus on the role of women in different spheres.

The Family as a Social Unit

The term 'family' is derived from the Roman word *Famulus,* meaning servant. It is the most universal cultural institution and is the basis of every human society from the most primitive to the present day modern one. In other words, it is the basic unit of society and the smallest of all human social life.

A family may be defined as a bio-social group, characterised by common residence, economic co-operation and reproduction. It includes members of both sexes, at least two of whom maintain socially recognised sex relations; and one or more children, their own, or adopted, of the sexually co-habiting adults. The meaning of the family and its boundaries, as a matter of fact, are culturally determined and differ widely from one society to another.

Gisbert (1984 : 83) observes, " It is not a mere association but also an institutional complex or system of institutions. The family, especially the nuclear or individual family is the most basic social group and of primary importance in the socialization of the young".

As a matter of fact, it ordinarily consists of a man and a woman, permanently united, with one or more children. About the union of a man and a woman, Herskovits (1974 : 17 1) elaborates, " The family in all societies is distinguished by a stability that arises out of the fact that it is based on marriage". Lowie (*op.cit*, p. 25) also emphasizes the marital relationship when he says that the family be considered as an association that corresponds to the institution of marriage.

Mandelbaum 1972: 42), while dwelling on Indian family, observes that in India, as elsewhere, it is a corporate group where members get together to meet their common purpose. Typically, they live the same house and eat food prepared in the same kitchen; they work together, pool their income, expenditure and property and perform religious rituals as a family. With regard to the family life in the tribal and other simpler societies, Radcliffe - Brown maintains that the relationship between the members is to be understood in a sociological as much as psychological sense; thus, the family will include not only the husband, wife and their minor children, but also parents, in-laws and wife/husband of son/daughter. The ideal household in most tribes would include two or more married couples and their children (cited in Kattakayam, 1983 : 87).

To sum up, the important features of family are : (i) It is the fundamental instrumental foundation of the larger social design. (ii) Some version of family as a type of social organization exists everywhere. (iii) Participation in family activities by all the individual members is its quality. (iv) Every member of the family is duty-bound to assume a direct role or responsibility in the family. (v) It acts as a source of force on an individual to adjust to work or with need. (VI) It is a functional unit for all such purposes as reproduction, socialization, social control, social order, economy, etc. (Vidyarthi and Rai, 1977).

Family Among the Tea Labourers

For the purpose of the present discussion, the term 'family' has operationally been synonymously used with the term. 'household'. A family, then, includes all the members dwelling under the same roof and sharing common food from the same hearth. Put in another way a household (for the people under investigation) is a small patrilocal, elementary, broken or joint family.

Though broadly classified as patrilocal, in fact they are neolocal in the sense that after marriage a couple generally settles in separate individual quarters as soon as a house becomes available. It is thus neolocal though patrivicinal. There are, however, instances where patriliny is not associated with virilocality or neolocality as in the case of *gharjuain*, when a man comes to stay in the house of his father-in-law.

With regard to the relation between the socially recognised marriage and the establishment of a family, the people show some unique features. In more than 50 percent of the cases, it has been observed that the couples having children are not yet socially married. The society, however, prescribes that they should get married any time before they give their children in marriage.

The Munda, Parjah and the Tanti are patrilineal in inheritance and patrinymic in descent. After the death of the father, the sons inherit his property in equal shares. In the event of their not having a son, the parents sometimes adopt a son who will reside with them and inherit their property in due course of time. Generally, the sonless parents adopt a boy who is usually their near kin. A family without a girl child normally does not go for adoption. During the present investigation, however, at least two families have been found to have adopted girl children as they do not have daughters.

Nuclear Family or Elementary Family : It denotes a family composed of the parents and their unmarried children. Families not having children and those having one/two dependants have also been grouped under this category.

Extended or Joint Family : This category includes those cases where extension of the elementary families has taken place by marriage either horizontally, where more than one brother live together with their respective families, or vertically, where a married son lives with his parents, or in both dimensions. When the extension takes place only in vertical direction, it will be called a lineal type, and the other will be called a fraternal type of extended family.

Broken Family : When a household either has lost or lacks one or more relationship to be qualified as an elementary family in the true sense of the term, it has been grouped under "broken family". For example ; a single parent with unmarried children is considered a broken family.

Miscellaneous type : This category includes those families which do not fit in to any of the above types of families.

Size of the Family

As mentioned in the previous chapter, a total of 350 families have been selected for the purpose of the study. The total population is 1975 (Male : 1004, female : 971). The size of the family has, for the sake of convenience, been classified according to the number of children as "single member family", "small" (2-3 members), "Medium" (4-6 members), "Big" (7- members) and "very big" families having more than 9 members.

Data on the family size has been presented in Table IV.1.

It will be seen from the table that the average size of a family among the people is 5.64. With regard to the distribution in different categories, it seems there is a preponderance (56.57) of the medium category with an average size of 5.21. This is followed by the "big" one (27.71%). "Very big" families are very rare whereas the "single member" one is totally absent in the population.

Table IV. 1. Distribution of the Studied families according to Size and Group affiliation (Dhelakhat and Dirial Tea Estates)

Sl No.	Category of family	Size	No. of House Holds					Total Population					Average
			Christian Munda	Non - Christian Munda	Parjah	Tanti	Total	Christian Munda Munda	Non- Christian	Parjah	Tanti	Total	
1	2	3	4	5	6	7	8	9	10	11	12	13	14
1	Single Member	1	-	-	-	-	-	-	-	-	-	-	-
2	Small	2-3	7 (8.75)*	11 (11.00)	20 (20.00)	12 (17.15)	50 (14.29)	19	28	60	33	140	2.8
3	Medium	4-6	43 (53.75)	61 (61.00)	47 (47.00)	47 (67.14)	198 (56.57)	226	331	238	236	1031	5.21
4	Big	7-9	29 (36.25)	24 (24.00)	33 (33.00)	11 (15.71)	97 (27.71)	230	180	256	86	752	7.75
5	Very Big	10 & above	1 (1.25)	4 (4.00)	-	-	5 (1.43)	10	42	-	-	52	10.4
	Gand Total	-	80 (100.00)	100 (100.00)	100 (100.00)	70 (100.00)	350 (100.00)	485	581	554	355	1975	5.64

*The figures within parentheses in this and the subsequent tables represent the percentage.

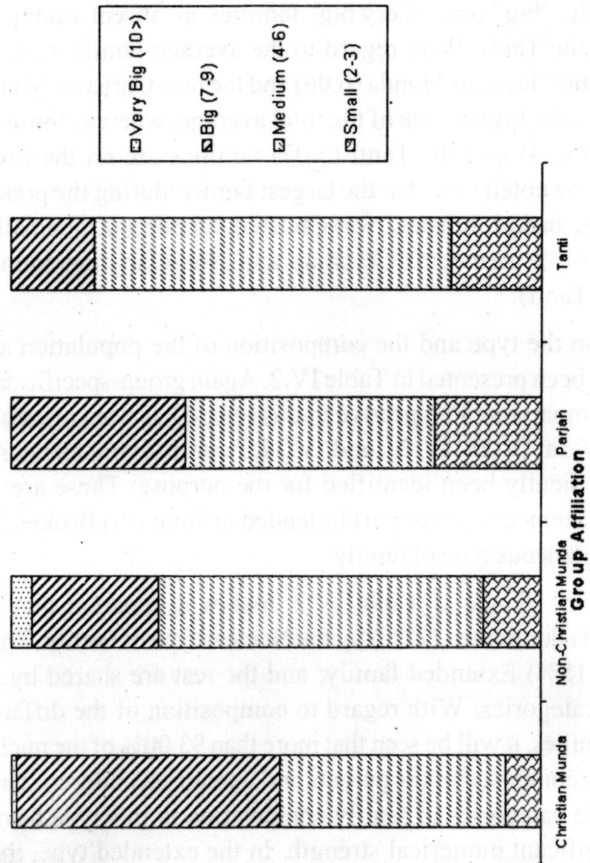

Figure No. IV.1.

A column Bar diagram showing the distribution of the studied families according to the size and group affiliation

Group-wise analysis of the data shows more or less the same trend in the distribution of the families in different categories. "Medium" families are in the highest frequencies in all the groups. However, among the Tantis , it is followed by the "small" category in place of the "big" one. "Very big" families are absent among the Parjah and the Tanti. With regard to the average family size, the figures for the Christian Munda (6.06) and the non-Christian Munda (5.81) are on the higher side of the total average, whereas those for the Parjah (5.54) and the Tanti (5.07) families are on the lower side. It may be noted here that the largest family, during the present investigation, had 11 inmates (Non-Christian Munda and the smallest one was with 2 members (Christian and Non-Christian Munda, Parjah and Tanti).

Data on the type and the composition of the population as a whole have been presented in Table IV.2. Again group-specific data, tohave a comparative Perspective in this regard has been presented in Table IV.2a, IV.2b, IV.2c, and IV.2d. Four different categories have conveniently been identified for the purpose. These are: (i) Nuclear or Elementary type. (ii) Extended or Joint (iii) Broken and Five Miscellaneous type of family.

A cursory glance at Table IV.2. makes it apparent that the population is dominated (72%) by the Nuclear type of family. There are 60 (17.15%) Extended family; and the rest are shared by the other two categories. With regard to composition of the different types of families, it will be seen that more than 93.00% of the nuclear families are composed of the parents and unmarried children. There are six more categories of family composition in this type having very insignificant numerical strength. In the extended type, there are six different categories of composition. Around 42% of them consist of parents, their married sons, unmarried children and grand children. 12 (20.00%) families have either of the parents, their married sons, unmarried children and grand children as inmates.

There are in all 20 (5.71%) Broken families, most of which (85.00%) consist of either of the parents and their unmarried children.

Table No.IV.2. Distribution of the Studied Families according to Type and Composition (Dhelakhat and Dirial Tea Estates)

Sl. No.	*Type*	*Composition*	*No. of Families*	*No.Total Population*	*Average Size*
1	2	3	4	5	6
1	Nuclear or Elementary Family	1. Husband & Wife (3.97)	10 (1.46)	20	2.00
		2. Parents with unmarried children	235 (93.25)	1304	5.55 (95.18)
		3. Husband and wife with unmarried children and wife's sister	7 (0.40)	5	5 (0.36)
		4. Husband and wife with their children and husband's unmarried brothers and sisters	3	23 (1.19)	7.67 (1.68)
		5. Husband and wife with their unmarried children and widowed daughter	7 (0.04)	5 (0.36)	5.00
		6. Husband and wife with unmarried son and wife's brother's daughter	1	4 (0.40)	4.00 (0.29)
		7. Husband and wife with their unmarried children and wife's widowed sister and her son	7	9 (0.39)	9.00 (0.66)
	Sub. Total		252 (72.00%)	1370. (69. 37%)	5.44
2	Extended or Joint Family	1. Parents with married sons, unmarried children and grand children	25 (41.67)	191 (46.36)	7.64
		2. Parents with married sons and grand children	4 (6.67)	23	5.75 (5.58)
		3. Parents with their married sons and unmarried children	4	31 (6.67)	7.75 (7.52)
		4. Either of the parents with married sons and grand children	14 (23.33)	84 (20.39)	6.00
		5. Husband and wife with their married son, unmarried children and husband's brother's son	7 (1.67)	9 (2.18)	9.00
		6. Either of the parents with married son, unmarried children and grand children	12 (20.00)	74 (17.96)	6.17
	Sub Total		60 (17.15)	412 (20.86)	6.87

1	2	3	4	5	6
3	Broken Family	1. Either of the parents with unmarried children	17 (85.00)	68 (79.06)	3.58
		2. Widow with her unmarried children, her nephew and niece	7 (5)	6 (6.98)	6.00
		3. Widow with her widower son, unmarried daughter and grand child	2 (10)	12 (13.95)	6.00
		Sub Total (5.71)	20 (4.35)	86	4.30
4	Miscellaneous Family	1. Parents with their married daughters, sons-in-law and grand children	4 (22.22)	22 (20.56)	5.50
		2. Widow with her married daughter, son-in law and grand children	7 (38.89)	35 (32.71)	5.00
		3. Widow with her daughter, sister and adopted son	7 (5.55)	4 (3.73)	4.00
		4. Widow with her married daughter, son-in law and unmarried children	3 (16.66)	20 (18.69)	6.66
		5. Widow with her married son, daughter-in law, unmarried children, unmarried brother and mother-in-law	7 (5.55)	9 (8.41)	9.00
		6. Widow with her married son, unmarried son, daughter-in-law and son's father-in-law	7 (5.55)	8 (7.48)	8.00
		7. Widow with her unmarried children and her younger sister's husband	7 (5.55)	9 (8.41)	9.00
	Sub Total		18 (5.14)	107 (5.42)	5.74
	Grand Total		350 (100.00)	1975 (100.00)	5.64

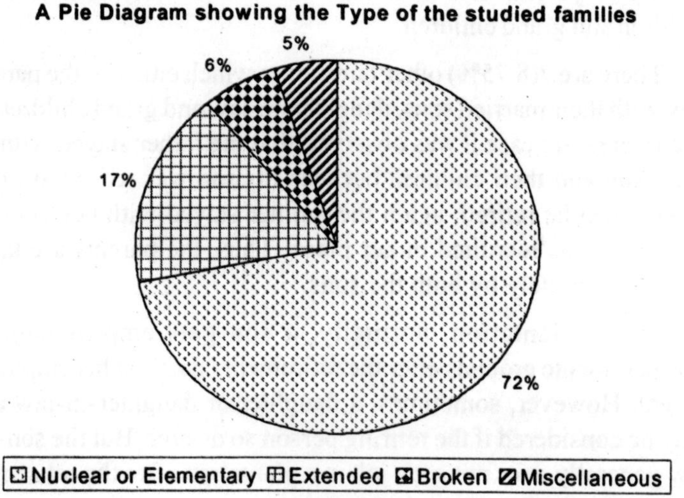

Figure No. IV.2

There are 18 (5.14%) families that could not be included in any of the three categories; and as such grouped under "Miscellaneous type". In order to have a group-wise idea of the distribution of the families according to type and composition, let us now have a quick glance at the other four tables.

In Table IV.2.A the type and composition of Christian Munda families have been presented. Out of 80 families 58(72.5%) are of nuclear type; of this 52(65.00%) are with parents and their unmarried children. As noted earlier, soon after marriage the majority of the couples prefer to establish their own family. There are at least 3 families in which the husband's unmarried brothers and sisters, and one family where the wife's unmarried sister lives in the household; and there are two couples who do not have any children. In one case, the only child died a few days after birth; and in the other case the couple had been married very recently.

The nuclear family is followed by the extended or joint families. There are 13 (16.25%) families in this category; of these 5(6.25%)

consist of parents and their married sons as well as unmarried children and grand children.

There are 7(8.75%) other families in which either of the parents stay with their married sons, daughter-in-law and grand children. In one interesting case it was observed that the father stayed with his elder son and their children because his son was recruited in his place when he retired; again the mother stayed with her younger son as he was recruited in her place. Thus, the parents are taken care of separately by both the sons.

In the plantation, normally, a son gets employment on compassionate grounds after the retirement / death of his employed parent. However, sometimes, a daughter or daughter-in-law also may be considered if the retiring person so desires. But the son- in-law generally does not get a job in a plantation after the retirement of his father-in-law or mother-in-law.

It will be seen from Table IV .2.A that all the extended families among the Christian Mundas fall under lineal type. The average size of an extended family is 6.06.

Table IV.2.B depicts the type and composition of the families of the Non-Christian Mundas. The table reveals that out of 100 families 71.00% belong to the nuclear type and its average size is 5.38. There are 3 families with couples alone and 68 consist of parents with their unmarried children. It will be interesting to note here that there is at least one family with eleven children. This may be however, because of his having two wives (a case of polygyny).

The table further reveals that there are a total of 21 (21.00%) extended families having an average size of 7.09. Here also, all the families are of lineal type.

There does not exist any broken family among them. The remaining 8 families could not be included in any defined category; and as such included under "miscellaneous" head. Among these, 6 families are headed by the widows having other inmates of different nature. Again, in 7 of the families married daughters with their

Table No.IV.2.A Type and Composition of Christian Munda Families (Dhelakhat and Dirial Tea Estates)

Sl. No.	Type	Composition	No. of Families	Total Population	Average Size
1	Nuclear or Elementary Family	1. Husband & Wife	2 (2.5)	4	2
		2. Parents with unmarried children	52 (65.00)	310	5.96
		3. Parents with their children and wife's sister	1 (1.25)	5	5
		4. Husband and wife with their children and husband's unmarried brothers and sisters	3 (3.75)	23	7.67
	Sub Total		58 (72.5)	342	5.96
2	Extended Family	1. Parents with married sons and unmarried children	5 (6.25)	45	9.00
		2. Parents with their married sons and un-children	1 (1.25)	6 (3.75)	6.00
		3. Either of the parents with married sons and grandchildren	7 (8.75)	46	6.57
	Sub-Total		13 (16.25)	97	7.46
3	Broken Family	1. Either of the parents with unmarried children	5	24	4.8
		2. Widow with her unmarried children, her niece and nephew	1 (1.25)	6	6
	Sub Total		6 (7.5)	30	5
4	Miscellaneous Family	1. Widow with her married daughter, son-in-law and grand children	1 (1.25)	4	4
		2. Widow with her daughter, sister and adopted son	1 (1.25)	4	4
		3. Widow with her married son, unmarried son, daughter-in-law, son's father-in-law	1 (1.25)	8	8
	Sub Total		3 (3.75)	16	5.33
	Grand Total		80 (100)	485	6.06

Table No.IV.2.B Type and Composition of Non-Christian Munda Families (Dhelakhat and Dirial Tea Estates)

Sl. No.	*Type*	*Composition*	*No. of Families*	*Total Population*	*Average Size*
1	2	3	4	5	6
1	Nuclear or Elementary Family	1. Husband & wife (3.00)	3	6	2
		2. Husband & wife with unmarried children	68 (68.00)	376	5.53
		Sub Total	71	382	5.38
2	Extended Family or Joint Family	1. Parents with married sons, unmarried children and grand children	15	110	7.33
		2. Parents with their married sons and grand children	1	5	5
		3. Widow with married sons and grand children	4	25	6.25
		4. Husband & wife with their married son, unmarried children and husband's brother's son	1	9	9
		Sub Total	21	149	7.09
3	Miscellaneous Family	1. Widow with her married daughter, son-in-law and unmarried children	3	20	6.66
		2. Widow with her married son, daughter-in-law, unmarried children, unmarried brother and mother-in-law	1	9	9
		3. Parents with married daughter, son-in-law and grand children	2	10	5
		4. Widow with married daughter, son-in-law and grand children	2	11	5.5
		Sub Total	8	50	6.25
		Grand Total	100	581	5.81

Table No.IV.2.C Type and Composition of the Parjah Families (Dhelakhat and Dirial Tea Estates)

Sl. No.	*Type*	*Composition*	*No. of Families*	*Total Population*	*Average Size*
1	2	3	4	5	6
1	Nuclear or Elementary Family	1. Husband & wife	2	4	2
		2. Husband & wife with unmarried children	75	415	5.53
		3. Husband & wife with their unmarried children and wife's widowed sister and her son.	1	9	9
		Sub Total	78	428	5.49
2	Extended Family	1. Parents with married and unmarried children.	3	25	8.33
		2. Widow/er with her married son, unmarried children and grand children.	9	54	6
		Sub Total	12	79	6.58
3	Broken Family	1. Widow with her widower son, unmarried daughter and grand child	2	12	6
		2. Either of the parents with unmarried children.	7	26	3.71
		Sub Total	9	38	4.22
4	Miscellaneous Family	1. Widow with her unmarried children and her younger sister's husband	1	9	9
		Sub Total	9	9	9

husbands and children are also permanent members. It is reported that the parents who do not have any son generally prefer to bring their son-in-law to live with them permanently (*Ghar Juain* System).

The type and composition of the Parjah family is shown in Table No. IV. 2.C. Here too, the number of nuclear families are relatively higher (78.00%) and are mostly composed of the parents and their unmarried children. The average size of the nuclear family is 5.49.

There are 12 families that belong to the "Extended" category. The average size of an extended family is 6.58. There are also 9 families that are grouped under "Broken" category. The average size is 4.22.

There is one family that consists of a widow, and her younger sister's husband. It has been included in "Miscellaneous" category. The average size of a Parjah family is 5.54.

Table IV.2.D. depicts the type and composition of the Tanti families. The nuclear family has the highest frequency (45 : 64.28%). Again around 89% of these families have the parents and their unmarried children as the inmates. In one family, the widowed daughter and in another, the wife's younger brother's daughter happen to be the dependents.

Case: IV. 1.

Nawaker Sona, aged 60 years; and his wife Sakuntala, aged 55 years stay in Dhelakhat tea plantation. Though Nawaker is a daily labourer outside the garden, Sakuntala is a permanent worker in the said garden. They belong to the Tanti community. They have three daughters of whom the two elder ones got married. The eldest daughter Panchami, aged 38 years old became mentally ill due to the premature and sudden death of her husband. Due to her illness she was unable to perform any normal activity. Therefore, she was brought back to her parents and they willingly take care of her.

Case IV. 2.

Kethra Bag (aged 45 years) and Jayanti (aged 40 years) have two sons. They too belong to the Tanti community. Since they do not have a daughter, they have adopted Juri, Jayanti's younger brother's daughter in their family. Juri's mother died during the delivery of this child. During the time of investigation Juri was 6 years old. The family takes care of her as their own daughter.

Table No. IV.2.D Type and Composition of the Tanti Families (Dhelakhat and Dirial Tea Estates)

Sl. No.	Type	Composition	No. of Families	Total Population	Average size
1	2	3	4	5	6
1	Nuclear or Elementary Family	1. Husband & wife	3 (4.28)	6	2
		2. Husband & wife with unmarried children	40 (57.14)	203	5.08
		3. Husband & wife with their unmarried children and widowed daughter.	1 (1.43)	5	5
		4. Parents with unmarried son and wife's brother's daughter.	1 (1.43)	4	4
		Sub Total	45 (64.28)	218	4.84
2	Extended or Joint Family	1. Parents with their married, unmarried children & grand children.	5 (7.14)	36	7.2
		2. Parents with their married son and grand children.	3 (4.28)	18	6
		3. Widow with her married son and unmarried children and grand children	3 (4.28)	20	6.66
		4. Widow/er with her/his married son and grand children	3 (4.29)	13	4.33
		Sub Total	14 (20.00%)	87	6.23
4	Miscellaneous Family	1. Parents with their married daughter, son-in-law and grand children	2 (2.86)	12	6
		2. Widow with her married daughter, son-in-law and grand children	4	20 (5.71)	5
		Sub Total	6 (8.57)	32	5.66
		Grand Total	70 (100)	355	5.07

The average size of a Tanti nuclear family is 4.84. The number of extended family is 14 (20.00%) all of which are of lineal type. The average size is 6.23. There are in all 5 broken families, whereas, 6 have been categorised as belonging to "miscellaneous" type. In all the 6 miscellaneous type families, the sons-in-law live with their parent/s. The average size for this category of family is 5.66. The overall average size of a Tanti family is 5.07. While dwelling on the Tanti families, it may be noted here that there is at least one family where the head has three wives and 10 children born of them.

The data on family size, and type and composition thus make it apparent that in the present setting, the communities by and large prefer to have a relatively small size and nuclear family. Though there are some inter-community variations in these regards, the variations do not seem to be very significant. With regard to composition, it seems, the majority of the nuclear families have the parents and the unmarried children as the inmates.

The size of a nuclear family, however, shows a wide variation. It ranges between 2 and 9 members.

On the whole, on the basis of the data at hand, it may be said that the present trend among the people is towards adhering more to a nuclear family than to an extended one.

A probe, however, reveals that the tendency results more out of economic compulsions than because of social disorganisation. Apparently, it seems to be a contradictory contention as it is believed that joint living is expected to provide economic relief rather than hardship. But, as a matter of fact, joint living saves expenses only when (a) housing is a recurring expense in the shape of high rent or so; and (b) the high price of board and lodging in general and fuel in particular makes it less expensive to cook the food of several families together. In a plantation, however, both these needs for each family, irrespective of its size, are uniformly met by the plantation management. So, in the present setting, joint family does not seem to lead to relatively more economic solvency.

Bhadra (1992) also makes a similar observation in a study among the labourers working in tea plantations in West Bengal. She observes that although there are few joint families, in plantations the nuclear families are predominant. The plantation's recruitment policy has strengthened such nuclearization. They consider a nuclear family as a basic unit to receive working facilities and other benefits. Certain facilities such as free quarters, free fire wood, cultivable land and rations at subsidised rates are given to each family. This naturally encourages the workers to form such families. In many cases these are the main factors responsible for splitting up of large joint families into constituent nuclear units.

It will be interesting to note in the present context that in many cases, though the agnates live separately, they carry on their economic activities in the agriculture fields in collaboration and participate in common ceremonies and rituals. A son generally takes interest in the important affairs of his natal family. A brother also behaves accordingly towards his other brothers living in independent nuclear families. It has also been observed that the sons and the brothers occupying separate quarters do not appear to have any sense of guilt about it; and the society in general has also accepted the trend as a convenient arrangement and not as an amoral exercise.

In some cases, of course, the separation has taken place as a result of strained relation between the in-laws , particularly between the daughter-in-law and mother-in-law. Nevertheless, in most of the cases harmonious relations are maintained with the natal families.

Case IV.3.

Tarun Parjah, aged 22 years; and Saganti Tanti, aged 20 years got married 2 years ago. After the marriage Saganti went to stay with her in-laws in her husband's natal home. She had her father-in-law, mother-in-law and 3 unmarried sisters-in-law in the family. During the course of her stay over there she experienced ill treatment from all her in-laws including her father-in-law and mother-in-law. Her parents-inlaw, very often under the influence of country liquor used to abuse and ill-treat her. As she could not endure all this illtreatment for a prolonged period, she with her husband left the house for her own parents' one; and they stayed there for some time. In course of time they got independent quarters from the plantation management. During the present investigation they were living in the quarters and did not have any kind of interaction with her in-laws.

In this context, it may also be noted that though not in favour of the joint family system by and large, they include their widow mother/widowed father in the nuclear family. And this addition does not seem to cause any observable strain on the day-to-day life of the other members of the family.

With regard to the change in the size and structure of the family, it may finally be stated that this trend has an important bearing on the woman's status in the family. In an extended family, in the midst of all the elderly kin the newly married woman's liberties are curtailed to a great extent. She is expected to remain submissive and to abide by the commands of the elders. In a nuclear family, with a co-operative husband, many of her liberties are restored, and she can, by and large, participate in many of the decision-making processes in the family.

Family Life

Philosophers and social analysts have noted that society is a structure made up of families, and that the peculiarities of a given society can be described by outlining its family relations (Kar, 1981:92). In view of the fact that family is the initial platform for socialisation and enculturation, an overall idea of the family life involving the members of the two sexes is expected to reflect on the position of a woman in the family in particular and the society in general. In the following pages, an attempt is made to have some idea about the childhood of a girl baby, marriage, widowhood, intra-family relationship, husband-wife relationship, the role of women in the process of decision making, relationship between the other members of the family and the daily life of different members.

Childhood

The attitude of the members of a family towards the sex of a baby is considered to be moulded by the overall position of the particular sex in the society. It may also be considered to be reflective of the same. Thus, it is very often found that a boy and a girl child are differently welcomed in a good number of societies. During the present study an attempt was made to know the sex preference of a prospective baby in a family. A total of 200 respondents were interviewed for the purpose. The responses have been presented in Table IV.3. It will be seen from the table that a very small number of people (14.00%) prefer to have a girl child. The respondents showing a secular attitude (44.50%) and those preferring a boy-child (41.50%) are more or less the same in number.

People who prefer to have a girl-child do it mainly because of the prospects of better domestic assistance as well as a sustained emotional attachment even after the girl is given in marriage. A boy is preferred mainly because he is considered to be an economic asset of the family as well as one who continues the father's lineage in the next generation.

The Table (No. IV.3.) also provides us with a comparative idea as to the preferences shown in this regard by the different groups under investigation. It will be very interesting to note that while only 6.00% to 10.00% of the respondents among the Munda and the Parjah prefer to have a girl child, among the Tantis it is 28.00%. It seems, at least one of the reasons for the deviation may be the demographic scenario. As reported by the people, non-availability of a suitable Tanti bride sometimes results in inter-group marriage. If there are more girls, they believe, the group endogamy can possibly be maintained more consistently.

It will also be interesting to note that a very high number(82.00%) of the Christian Mundas prefer a boy child, and 72.00% of the Non-Christian Mundas show a secular trend.

Table No. IV.3. Distribution of the Respondents according to their preference of Children (n=200) (Dhelakhat and Dirial Tea Estates)

Sl. No	Prefernces	*Christian Munda*			*Non-Christian Munda*			*Parjah*			*Tanti*			*Total*		
		Male	*Female*	*Total*	*Male*	*Female*	*Total*	*Male*	*Female*	*Total*	*Male*	*Female*	*Total*	*Male*	*Female*	*Total*
1	2	3	4	5	6	7	8	9	10	11	12	13	14	15	16	17
1	Boy Child	22 (44.00)	19 (38.00)	41 (82.00)	6 (12.00)	3 (6.00)	9 (18.00)	10 (20.00)	3 (6.00)	13 (26.00)	10 (20.00)	10 (20.00)	20 (40.00)	48 (24.00)	35 (1 7.50)	83 (41.50)
2	Girl-Child	1 (2.00)	2 (4.00)	3 (6.00)		5 (10.00)	5 (10.00)	2 (4.00)	4 (8.00)	6 (12-00)	9 (18.00)	5 (10,00)	14 (28.00)	12 (6.00)	16 (8.00)	28 (14.00)
3	Either or Both	2 (4.00)	4 (&00)	6 (12.00)	19 (38,00)	17 (34.00)	36 (72.00)	13 (26.00)	18 (36.00)	31 (62.00)	6 (12.00)	10 (20.00)	16 (32.00)	40 (20.00)	49 (24.50)	89 (44.50)
4	Total	25 (50.00)	25 (50.00)	50 (100.00)	25 (50.00)	25 (50.00)	50 (100.00)	25 (50.00)	25 (50.00)	50 (100.00)	25 (50.00)	25 (50.00)	50 (100.00)	100 (50.00)	100 (50.00)	200 (100.00)

With regard to the "least preference" however, there is unanimity, and it goes to a "girl child". The next preference again shows inter-group variation. For the Non-Christian Mundas and the Parjahs, it is "either or both", whereas, for the other two groups it goes to a "boy child".

It may be noted in this context that even the respondents who have preferred a girl-child, do want to have at least a son in the family. This is mainly because of the desire for the perpetuation of the lineage in a patrilineal society.

As a corollary of this weakness/bias toward the particular sex of the child, it has been observed that during pregnancy both the parents get worried about the sex of the prospective child. An attempt was made to have a quantitative idea of the frequency of this worry among the people. The data in this regard has been recorded in Table No. IV.4. It will be seen from the table that a majority of the parents(51.500%) become worried about the sex of the prospective child. A total of 41.50% of them have been found to try to accept the outcome sportingly. However, at least 7.00% of them are ambivalent in their replies.

With regard to inter-group variation, it seems, the Non-Christian Mundas and the Tantis are relatively more in number (62.00% and 68.00% respectively) to be preoccupied with the sex of the child. Though here, it seems to be contradictory to what has been observed previously, yet the explanation given by the respondents is that they all want to have at least one boy-child. Until this desire is satisfied, they continue to worry to a great extent. The worries become less as the number of male children increases.

When we look for a comparative state of affairs in this regard on the basis of sex, it will be seen that the women are by and large more in number in almost all the groups to be worried about this matter. Most of them become worried, not on their own account, but they think that their husbands, other relatives and even the society may be disappointed with the birth of a girl child.

Table No. IV4. Distribution of the Respondents according to their Worry About the Sex of the Child (n=200) (Dhelakhat and Dirial Tea Estates)

Sl. No	Responses	Christian Munda			Non-Christian Munda			Parjah			Tanti			Total		
		Male	Female	Total	Male	Female	Total	Male	Female	Total	Male	Female	Total	Male	Female	Total
1	2	3	4	5	6	7	8	9	10	11	12	13	14	15	16	17
1	Yes	2 (4.00)	16 (32.00)	18 (36.00)	8 (16.00)	23 (46.00)	31 (62.00)	13 (26.00)	7 (14.00)	20 (40.00)	10 (20,00)	24 (48.00)	34 (68.00)	33 (16.50)	70 (35.00)	103 (51.50)
2	No	22 (44.00)	4 (8.00)	26 (52.00)	11 (22..00)	2 (4.00)	13 (26.00)	12 (24.00)	16 (32.00)	28 (56.00)	15 (30.00)	1 (2.00)	16 (32,00)	60 (30.00)	23 (11.50)	83 (41.50)
3	Not Always	1 (2.00)	5 (10.00)	6 (12.00)	6 (12.00)	—	6 (12.00)	—	2 (4.00)	2 (4.00)	—	—	—	7 (3.50)	7 (3.50)	14 (7.00)
4	Total	25 (50.00)	25 (50.00)	50 (100.00)	25 (50.00)	25 (50.00)	50 (100.00)	25 (50.00)	25 (50.00)	50 (100.00)	25 (50.00)	25 (50.00)	50 (100.00)	1oo (50.00)	100 (50.00)	200 (100.00)

It may be relevant here to note that the attitude of the parents and the other members of a family towards a baby at birth, does influence the type of rearing the new-born undergoes. All these in turn, influence intra-familial relationship as well as the development of the total personality of the new-born.

In view of the fact that the "attitude" and the "practice" may not always go hand-inhand, an attempt was made to ascertain the acceptability of a girl child in the family that craved for a boy. It seems, in most of the cases that the members do reconcile themselves to the birth and accept the baby as a family member. The responses in this regard have been presented in Table no. IV.5. It is apparent from the table that 78.00% of them do not show any hesitation to welcome a girl-child as such, whereas 11.50% show some reservations. Again, there are at least 10.50% of the respondents who show a fluctuating stand in this regard. Their stand as a matter of fact, is reported to depend on the order of the birth of the child.

The table further reveals that there does not exist any significant inter-group variation in this regard. The variation with regard to the sex of the respondents is however, conspicuous. The male respondents (42.50%) seem to be relatively more lenient in accepting a girl child than their female counterparts (35.50%).

In order to have a deeper understanding as to the position of a female child in the family, a further attempt was made to know if a female child was considered a burden or not. The opinion of the respondents has been presented in Table IV.6. It will be seen from the table that a majority of the people (79.50%) do not consider the female child a burden. In conformity with the earlier observations, the table conspicuously reveals that there has not been a single Tanti respondent replying in the affirmative. Among the other three groups however, the Christian Mundas are more in number (36.00%) to consider the female child a burden; the Parjah and the Non Christian Munda share more or less the same attitude in this regard.

Table No. IV.5 Distribution of the Respondents with regard to their acceptability of a girl child (n=200) (Dhelakhat and Dirial Tea Estates)

Sl. No	Responses	Christian Munda			Non-Christian Munda			Parjah			Tanti			Total		
		Male	Female	Total	Male	Female	Total	Male	Female	Total	Male	Female	Total	Male	Female	Total
1	2	3	4	5	6	7	8	9	10	11	12	13	14	15	16	17
1	Yes	23 (46.00)	17 (34.00)	40 (80.00)	16 (32.00)	12 (24.00)	28 (56.00)	22 (44.00)	19 (38.00)	41 (82.00)	24 (48.00)	23 (46.00)	47 (94.00)	85 (42.50)	71 (35.5 0)	156 (78.00)
2	No	2 (4.00)	4 (8.00)	6 (12.00)	6 (12.00)	4 (8.00)	10 (20.00)	3 (6.00)	2 (4.00)	5 (10.00)	1 (2.00)	1 (2.00)	2 (4.00)	12 (6.00)	11 (5.50)	23 (11.50)
3	Not Always	--	4 (8.00)	4 (8.00)	3 (6.00)	9 (18.00)	12 (24.00)	--	4 (8.00)	4 (8.00)	--	1 (2.00)	1 (2.00)	3 (1.50)	18 (9.00)	21 (10.50)
4	Total	25 (50.00)	25 (50.00)	50 (100.00)	25 (50.00)	25 (50.00)	50 (100,00)	25 (50.00)	25 (50.00)	50 (100.00)	25 (50.00)	25 (50-00)	50 (100.00)	100 (50.00)	100 (50.00)	200 (100.00)

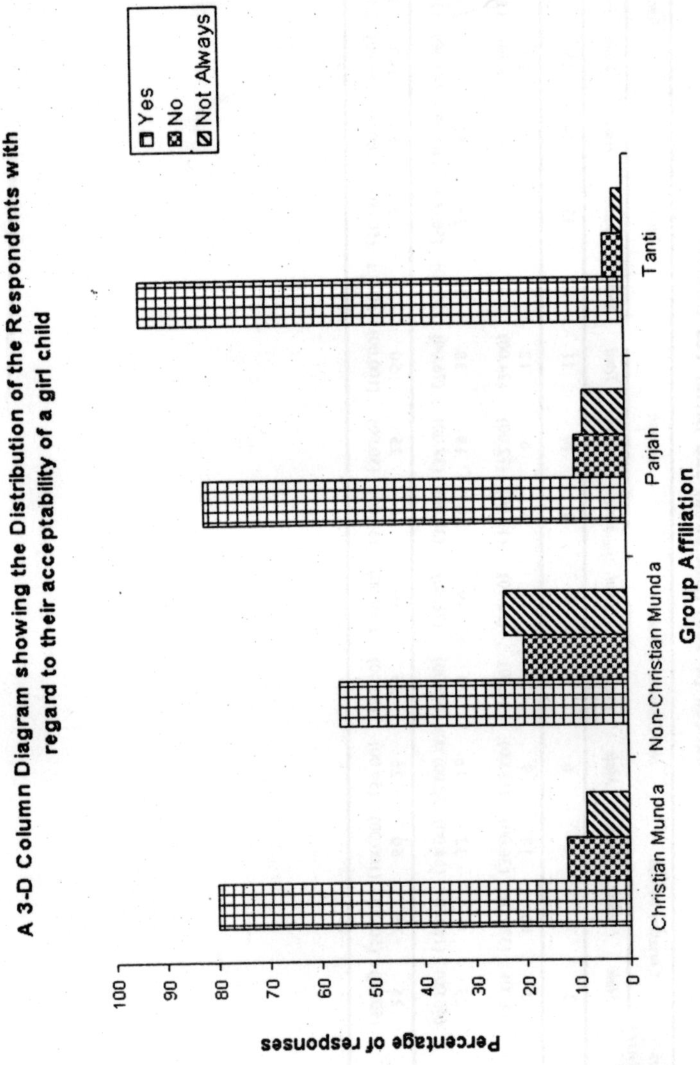

Figure No. IV.3.

Table No. IV.6 Distribution of the Respondents with regard to their Opinion as to whether or not the female child is a burden (n=200) (Dhelakhat and Dirial Tea Estates)

Sl. No	Res-ponses	Christian Munda			Non-Christian Munda			Parjah			Tanti			Total		
		Male	Female	Total	Male	Female	Total	Male	Female	Total	Male	Female	Total	Male	Female	Total
1	2	3	4	5	6	7	8	9	10	11	12	13	14	15	16	17
1	Yes	2 (4.00)	16 (32.00)	18 (36.00)	9 (18.00)	2 (4.00)	11 (22.00)	6 (12.00)	6 (12.00)	12 (24.00)	-			17 (8,50)	24 (12.00)	41 (20.00)
2	No	23 (46.00)	9 (18.00)	32 (64.00)	16 (32.00) 00)	23 (46.00)	39 (78.00)	19 (38.00)	19 (38.00)	38 (76.00)	25 (50.00)	25 (50.00)	50 (100.00)	83 (41.50)	76 (38.00)	159 (79.50)
	Total	25 (50.00)	25 (50.00)	50 (100.00)	25 (50.00)	25 (50.00)	50 (100.00)	25 (50.00)	25 (50.00)	50 (100.00)	25 (50.00)	25 (5C.00)	50 (100.00)	100 (50.00)	100 (50.00)	200 (100.00)

With regard to inter-sex variability, the table makes it apparent that there exists a significant variation in this regard only among the Mundas (both the Christians and the Non-Christians). Among the Christians it is the womenfolk, whereas, in the other group it is the menfolk who are more in number to answer in the affirmative. It may be noted here in this context that many of the respondents answering in the negative have maintained that the female child is an asset to the family. Many of the Tanti respondents opine that without a girl child it is rather difficult to run a family. They maintain that a girl child is very helpful to her mother, especially to a working mother. She looks after her younger siblings, takes care of the house and does all types of household chores when the mother is away at work. They further maintain that without a female child, the working mother's work-load will be doubled as the boys are hardly any help in the household chores.

However, 41(20.00%) of them agreed that the female children are a burden to their parents. According to them, to bring up a girl child is rather difficult, particularly, it is difficult to take care of a grown up girl. Besides, they consider girls as somebody else's property as they are to be given in marriage in some other family. All of them however, do agree to a great extent that the girls give a lot of help in domestic work. On the whole, it may be said that unlike in many other communities, among the plantation labourers, the people accept the birth of a female child, relatively more liberally.

In order to have a further and corroborative understanding as to the extent of their acceptance and welcome of a girl child, and if there is any discrimination in their treatment towards the children of the two sexes, the people were interviewed in this regard. The responses have been systematised and presented in Table No. IV.7. The table reveals that the majority (52.50%) of the respondents provide a preferential treatment to the boys. The boys are by and large, given more opportunity and care than the girls. The discriminating treatment is reflected in almost all spheres, eg., education, food distribution and health care, etc. However, there are at least 94(47.00%) respondents who provide equal treatment to both the son and the daughter.

With regard to inter-group variation in this regard, the table shows that the discriminatory treatment favouring a boy-child is maximum (80.00%) among the Christian Mundas. The next frequency (62.00%) is shown by the Non-Christian Mundas. Instead, among the Parjahs 82.00% of the respondents extend equal treatment to the children of both the sexes. Again, among the Tantis the frequency of the respondents providing secular (48.00%) and discriminatory treatment (52.00%), favouring a boy, are by and large equal.

Case IV.4.

Krishna (aged 40 years) and Santhi (aged 33 years) belong to Dhelakhat Tea plantation. Krishna is a temporary worker while Santhi is a permanent labourer. They belong to the Parjah community. Both of them are illiterate. They have 7 children; 3 boys and 4 girls. The eldest daughter Sumi, too, works in the tea plantation as a child labour. Though all the elder children are daughters, none of them have been sent to school to study. Instead, the boys have been admitted for the purpose. When asked to share their reasons for the apparent discrimination, they said that education for a girl was useless for the family. The reason, they maintained was that the girl would finally go to some other family after marriage.

Case IV.5.

Ramlal (aged 45 years) and Gurubari (aged 40 years) are inhabitants of Dirial Tea Estate. They belong to the Munda community. Both of them are employed in the tea plantation as permanent workers. They have 4 children; two boys and two girls. Both the sons are school goers, but the daughters are at home, engaged in the household chores and looking after their brothers. The reason for not sending the girls to school was that they should learn to work at home so that they would be able to look after their future family properly.

Table No. IV.7. Distribution of the Respondents according to their treatment to Children (n=200)
(Dhelakhat and Dirial Tea Estates)

Sl. No	Nature of treatment	Christian Munda			Non-Christian Munda			Parjah			Tanti			Total		
		Male	Female	Total	Male	Female	Total	Male	Female	Total	Male	Female	Total	Male	Female	Total
1	2	3	4	5	6	7	8	9	10	11	12	13	14	15	16	17
1	Equal	5 (10.00)	5 (10.00)	10 (20.00)	15 (30.00)	4 (8,00)	19 (38.00)	21 (42.00)	20 (40.00)	41 (82.00)	14 (28.00)	to (20.00)	24 (48.00)	55 (27.50)	39 (19.50)	94 (47.0 0)
2	Not Equal	--	--	--	--	--	--	--	--	--	--	--	--	--	--	--
3	Boys are given more opportu-nity and care	20 (40.00)	20 (40.00)	40 (80.00)	10 (20.00)	21 (42.00)	31 (62.00)	4 (8.00)	4 (8.00)	8 (16.00)	11 (22.00)	15 (30.00)	26 (52.00)	45 (22.50)	60 (30.00)	105 (52.50)
4	Girls are given more opportunity& care	--	--	--	--	--	--	--	1 (4.00)	1 (4.00)	--	--	--	--	1 (0.50)	1 (0.50)
5	Total	25 (50.00)	25 (50.00)	50 (100.00)	25 (50.00)	25 (50.00)	50 (100.00)	25 (50.00)	25 (50.00)	50 (100.00)	25 (50.00)	25 (50.00)	50 (100.00	100 (50.00)	100 (5 0.00)	200 (100.00)

Case IV.6.

Saidev (50 years) and Asa (40 years) belong to the Tanti community. Both of them are employed in the Dhelakhat tea plantation as permanent labourers. They have 5 children; 4 boys and I girl. Though the youngest, Rupa, their only daughter has not been sent to school while all their sons are attending the nearby school. Rupa is only 10 years old. But she is asked to look after the family and do the household chores while the parents are at work.

Case IV.7.

Markus is 46 years of age and Augustina is 39 years old. They belong to the Munda tribe. They have 7 children, 4 boys and 3 girls. All the sons are sent to school to study. Gita, their daughter was also sent to study. But when their youngest son was born, Gita, who was studying in class II was asked to discontinue her study as there was no one at home to take care of the youngest baby. Though very young Gita was asked to look after the family affairs in the absence of her parents.

The intensive investigation thus makes it apparent that there does exist a difference, though in varying degrees in the different groups, in the treatment extended towards male and female children.

Marriage

Marriage may be defined as a union between a man and a woman such that the children born to the woman are recognized as legitimate offsprings of both parents (*Notes and queries in anthropology* 1971:7 1). Most men and women marry at least once in their life time. Emphasizing its importance in human society, Herskovits (*op. cit* p. 17 1) observes, "... the family in all societies is distinguished by a stability that arises out of the fact that it is based on marriage". As a *rite de passage*, marriage involves a change in status from single to married person, and often a change from youth to adulthood. Further, it means that an individual acquires a whole new set of relatives and must work out new forms of interaction.

With regard to a woman, in particular, marriage may be considered as a very important phase in one's life. Marital union does influence her entire life in respect of role, position and other associated facts. After marriage, a woman assumes new roles and her individual life changes as per the roles and duties assigned to her according to the prevailing custom. Before marriage she is a daughter and a sister in her natal home; but after marriage she becomes a wife and an in-law in her husband's family. This change in status generally involves a radical change also in other spheres of her life. Therefore, some knowledge of marriage customs is necessary to understand the social life of the people more fully.

The following few pages have been devoted to discussing some aspects of marriage among the people as revealed in the present investigation. As has been permitted by the nature and mass of data, analysis has been made with regard to forms of marriage, marital status, age at marriage and inter-ethnic marriage, etc.

Marriage among the members of all the three groups under investigation appears to be a social contract and is generally reversible. Traditionally, they practise group-endogamy and clan-exogamy. Though polygyny is permitted, specially in cases of barrenness of the first wife, monogamy is the general practice. However, at least 4 cases of polygamy have been reported from the population. There are three polygynous families among the Non-Christian Munda and one among the Tanti.

Case IV.8.

Sibei, a temporary worker in Dirial tea plantation is 45 years old. He belongs to the Munda community. He is an illiterate man. At the age of 29 years he married Suknumoni who was 24 years old at the time of marriage. She too is an illiterate woman and works in the same garden temporarily. After having the first son, he took another woman as his second wife and brought her to his home. Her name is Sumita (aged 30 years) who belongs to the same community. She too is an illiterate woman. She works in the same plantation as a permanent labourer. He has five children from the first wife. They are four sons and one daughter. From the second wife he got two daughters and one son. He continues to have sexual relations with both his wives. During the time of the investigation both the wives and their children were with him. When asked about the reason for bringing the second wife, he replied that he loved her even before his first marriage. Therefore, he included her in his family. After the initial teething trouble was over, the two wives somehow adjusted between themselves and were leading a harmonious life.

Case IV.9.

Gonath, aged 41 years, is working permanently in Dirial tea estate. He is an illiterate person. He belongs to the Munda community. He got married at the age of 37 years with Bina who was 21 years old at the time of marriage. She too belongs to the same community. She is also an illiterate woman,working in the same plantation. She is a permanent worker. He got two sons from Bina. The eldest son is 3 years old and the second son is only three months old. Very recently (1999) he took another woman (named Panchami) as his wife and brought her to his home. She is 28 years old and belongs to the Munda, community. She too is illiterate and is working temporarily in the same garden. According to him, the reason for having two wives is that he is able to maintain both of them; and that the first wife has no objection to his taking a second woman. At the time of investigation both of them were staying together in the same house. Though initially there were disagreements and quarrels, gradually they came to a mutual understanding to adjust as co-wives.

Case IV. 10.

Maharati Sona is 40 years old and is a temporary worker in Dhelakhat tea plantation. He belongs to the Tanti community and is illiterate. He first married Namsita whose age was 26 years. She too belongs to the Tanti community. Now she is 38 years old. Namsita is an illiterate woman permanently working in the same garden.

She has two sons and two daughters. Before his first marriage with Namsita, he had courted with Kirmo who belongs to the Parjah community. She was ten years older than Maharati. Kirmo too is illiterate and works temporarily in the same garden. Maharati had pre-marital sex with Kirmo who gave birth to a daughter. Since they belong to different ethnic communities, Kirmo's parents did not allow her to get married to Maharati. So, she remained unmarried. After two years of his first marriage, without the consent of his first wife Maharati brought Kirmo and her daughter into his family and kept her as his second wife. Though, in the beginning the two wives disagreed and quarrelled with each other, later on, they gradually came to a mutual understanding. At the time of investigation they were found living together harmoniously. Kirmo had two more daughters by the time of investigation. After around one year, once again he fell in love with Saradha a co-worker, who belongs to the Rajput community. She is also illiterate . She was a 29 year old spinster, when he took her as his wife. Now she is 35 years old and has one son and four daughters. The first two wives did not agree to bring Saradha home. So he has kept his third wife and her children separately, visiting them frequently.

In this context, it may be noted that a second marriage after the death or divorce of the first wife (serial monogamy) is not infrequent among these tribes.

Widow inheritance in any form is prohibited by the people. The usual mode of acquiring a mate is through negotiation, but marriage by mutual consent and elopement is fairly frequent among them. Two hundred respondents from both the sexes and belonging to all the four groups have been interviewed in this regard. Their responses have been presented in Table IV.8. It will be seen from the table that around 47.00% of the respondents had their spouses by mutual consent and elopement. Table IV. 9. records the reaction of the parents/guardian towards a marriage by mutual consent and elopement. The table reveals that in the majority of the cases in all the groups the parents' responses are favourable. It will be interesting to note that the unfavourable attitude is expressed relatively more by the women respondents.

Nevertheless, it seems, now-a-days, the marital union among the younger generation, by and large, has been becoming more a personal affair than an affair of the families and the relatives.

While choosing a spouse, it seems, some factors are considered by the people. The responses in this regard have been presented in Table no. IV. 10. The majority (61.00%) of the respondents look for the reputation of the family of the prospective spouse. There are around 20.00 % of the respondents who give a weightage to the personality factor. There are however, some inter-group and inter-sex variations in the responses. Thus, for example, the vast majority (78.00%) of the Tantis give priority to family reputation, whereas the women respondents by and large give relatively more weightage to the personality factor. In this context, it may be noted that as far as possible, the people prefer to select spouses from their own ethnic as well as religious group.

Data with regard to the married couples under study reveals that more than 50.00% of the couples, having offsprings are yet to perform the social functions connected with marriage. This is a very common practice in almost all the communities working as tea plantation labourers in Assam. The union, and the offsprings, born out of the same seem to have provisional recognition in the society. The couples however, are required to perform the social functions before they give their children in marriage. Identical observations were also made by Kar (1981:176) in his study among the Savaras working in tea gardens in Assam.

Thus, marriage, among the people is not considered as a pre-condition for the establishment of a family. The concept, as a matter of fact, may operationally be used to indicate the common residence of a male-female exercising sexual rights and recognizing the children born out of them. The marriage formalities are observed conveniently at a later period. In practice, the formalities involve (i) throwing a feast for the friends and relatives, and for the important

Table No. IV.8. Distribution of the respondents according to the mode of acquiring mate (n=200) (Dhelakhat and Dirial Tea Estates)

Sl. No	Mode	Christian Munda			Non-Christian Munda			Parjah			Tanti			Total		
		Male	Female	Total	Male	Female	Total	Male	Female	Total	Male	Female	Total	Male	Female	Total
1	2	3	4	5	6	7	8	9	10	11	12	13	14	15	16	17
1	Mutual consent & elopment	11 (22.00)	15 (30.00)	26 (52.00)	15 (30.00)	7 (14.00)	22 (44.00)	13 (26.00)	7 (14.00)	20 (40.00)	18 (36.00)	7 (14.00)	25 (50.00)	57 (28.50)	36 (18.00)	93 (46.50)
2	Negotiation	14 (28.00)	10 (20.00)	24 (48.00)	10 (20.00)	18 (36.00)	28 (56.00)	12 (24.00)	18 (36.00)	30 (60.00)	7 (14.00)	18 (36.00)	25 (50.00)	43 (21.50)	64 (32.000	107 (53.50)
3	Total	25 (50.00)	25 (50.00)	50 (100.00)	25 (50.00)	25 (50.00)	50 (100.00)	25 (50.00)	25 (50.00)	50 (100.00)	25 (50.00)	25 (50,00)	50 (100.00)	100 (50.00)	too (50.00)	200 (100.00)

A sub-Divided showing the distribuiton of the respondnets according to the mode of acquiring mate

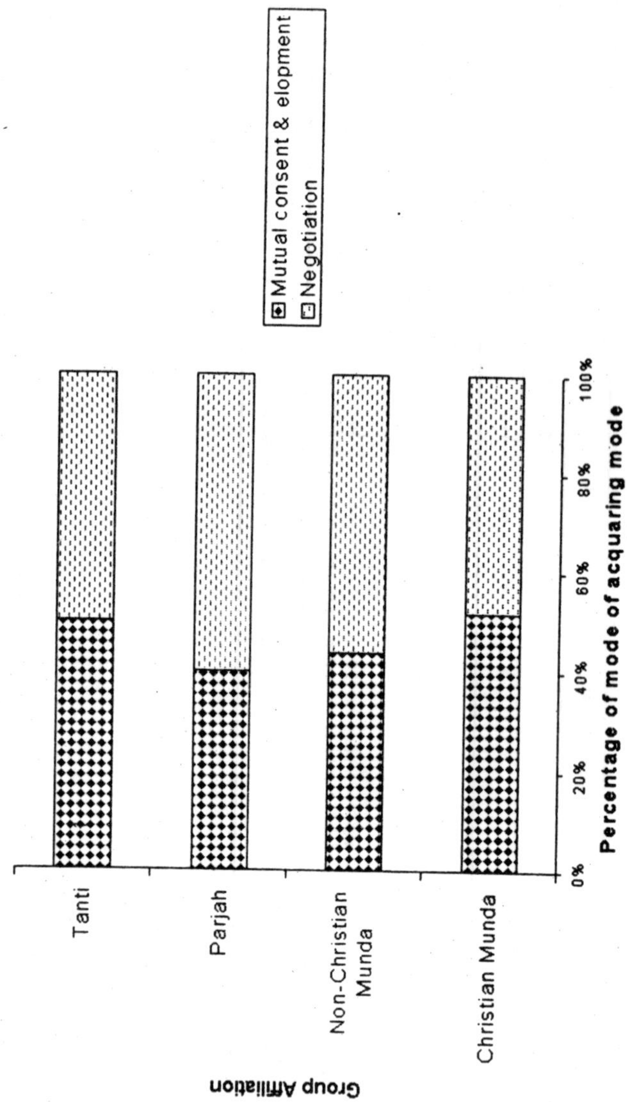

Figure No. IV.4.

Table No. IV.9. Reaction of the Parents/Guardians to Marriage by mutual consent and elopement (n=200) (Dhelakhat and Dirial Tea Estates)

Sl. No	Reac-tion	Christian Munda			Non-Christian Munda			Parjah			Tanti			Total		
		Male	*Female*	*Total*	*Male*	*Female*	*Total*	*Male*	*Female*	*Total*	*Male*	*Female*	*Total*	*Male*	*Female*	*Total*
1	2	3	4	5	6	7	8	9	10	11	12	13	14	15	16	17
1	Favou-rable	10 (38.46)	4 (15.38)	14 (53.84)	15 (68.18)	3 (13.63)	18 (81.81)	10 (50.00)	5 (25.00)	15 (75.00)	16 (64.00)	1 (4.00)	17 (68.00)	51 (54.83)	13 (13.97)	64 (68.8 1)
2	Unfav-ourable	0 (3.84)	11 (42.30)	11 (46.15)	-	4 (18.18)	4 (18.18)	3 (15.00)	2 (10.00)	5 (25.00)	2 (8.00)	6 (24.00)	8 (32.00)	6 (6.45)	23 (24.73)	29 (31.18)
3	Total	10 (42.30)	15 (67.69)	25 (100.00)	15 (68.18)	7 (31.81)	22 (100.00)	13 (65.00)	7 (35.00)	20 (100.00)	18 (72.00)	7 (28.00)	25 (100.00)	57 (61.29)	18 (38.70)	93 (100.00)

Table No. IV.10. Factors influencing the choice of a spouse (n=200)
(Dhelakhat and Dirial Tea Estates)

Sl. No	Factor	Christian Munda			Non-Christian Munda			Parjah			Tanti			Total		
		Male	Female	Total	Male	Female	Total	Male	Female	Total	Male	Female	Total	Male	Female	Total
1	2	3	4	5	6	7	8	9	10	11	12	13	14	15	16	17
1	Reputation of the family	21 (42.00)	11 (22.00)	32 (64.00)	15 (30.00)	8 (16.00)	23 (46.00)	20 (40.00)	8 (16.00)	28 (56.00)	25 (50.00)	14 (28.00)	39 (78.00)	81 (40.50)	41 (20.50)	122 (61.00)
2	Wealth	–	–	–	–	–	–	–	–	–	–	–	–	–	–	–
3	Personality	3 (6.00)	11 (22.00)	14 (28.00)	7 (14.00)	5 (10.00)	12 (24.00)	1 (2.00)	1 (2.00)	2 (4.00)		11 (22.00)	11 (22.00)	11 (5.50)	28 (14.00)	39 (19.50)
4	Nothing special	1 (2.00)	3 (6.00)	4 (8.00)	3 (6.00)	12 (24.00)	15 (30.00)	4 (8.00)	16 (32.00)	20 (40.00)	-	-	-	8 (4.00)	31 (15.50)	39 (19.50)
5	Total	25 (50.00)	25 (50.00)	50 (100.00)	25 (50.00)	25 (50.00)	50 (100.00)	25 (50.00)	25 (50.00)	50 (100.00)	25 (50.00)	25 (50.00)	50 (100.00)	100 (50.00)	100 (50.00)	200 (100.00)

members of the community as well as of the labour community of the garden and (ii) making some presentations to some selected leaders; and to close consanguineal and affinal relatives.

The frequent incidence of unmarried couples among the people may have resulted from (i) weakening of the control of the traditional social forces and (ii) economic constraints to bear the expenses, needed to perform all the social formalities in completion of the wedding.

Case IV. 11.

Kishkol Povi Guria is 54 years old and is working in Dirial tea plantation as a permanent labourer. He is an illiterate person and belongs to the Munda community. His wife Berta is 53 years old. She too is an illiterate woman working permanently in Dirial tea plantation. They have seven children.

They started living together as husband and wife through courtship some 24 years back; and could not celebrate their marriage ceremony due to economic constraints. When their elder daughter, too, ran away with a man, they had to settle their own marriage before settling their daughter's marriage. Their marriage ceremony was celebrated during the period of the present investigation(1999). The ceremony is locally known as *Sindhur* ceremony in which the wife receives *sindhur* (vermilion) as a sign of her marital commitment. Their relatives and other important persons were invited on the occasion.

Marital Composition

Distribution of the population, as a whole, according to age, sex and marital status has been presented in Table no. IV.11.

It will be seen from the table that none of the boys and girls below 15 years of age have been found to be married. In other words, child marriage is not practised among the people.

All the age-groups being considered, it is seen that around 60.00% of the people are unmarried and 4.00% widowed. Among the unmarried persons, the males are more in number (31.04%) as compared to the females (28.66%).

Among the married ones, the maximum number (6.38%) falls in the age group "35-39 years".

The table further reveals that there is a tendency towards late marriage in both the sexes; and there are a few men and women who seem to have decided against entering into marital relations for this or that reason.

The community-wise distributions of the people by age, sex and marital status have been presented in Table nos. IV. 12 to 15. It will be seen from the tables that in all the four groups the highest incidence of married people (men and women) falls in the age range 35-39 years. No boy or girl below the age of 15 years has been found to be married, whereas people above 35 years of age, by and large, do not remain unmarried. The age of the husband is generally more than that of the wife. The age difference between the spouses is around 5 years.

It is relevant to note here that the age at marriage and the age difference between the husband and wife do play a certain role in moulding the relationship between the members of a family. A girl, for example, if married during childhood, is expected to obey her parent's/guardian's decision in this regard. Further, she is likely to be relatively more loyal to her husband and in-laws. Similar is the expectation when a wife is younger than the husband.

Divorce, though permitted, has not been reported from the population under investigation. However, 3 cases of separation have been reported from among the Parjahs. The reasons leading to separation include misunderstanding, quarrel and sickness.

Case IV. 12.

Chanu Hikoka, aged 34 years is a temporary worker in Dhelakhat tea estate. He belongs to the Parjah community. He is an illiterate person. He got married at the age of 28 with Nisoda, who, too, belongs to the same community and was working in the same tea garden as a temporary labourer. She is also an illiterate woman. Nisoda bore one daughter and a son. During the time of investigation they were 5 and 4 years old respectively. After the birth of the second child, very often there were quarrel between Chanu and Nisoda. At this time, Nisoda developed a friendly affair with another man named Kisok, who, too, was a co-worker in the same garden. On a convenient day, at an opportune moment, Nisoda ran away with him, leaving behind her husband and children. Chanu did not marry again because of his two children.

Case IV. 13.

Musri Hikoka is 50 years old. He belongs to the Parjah community and is an illiterate person. Earlier, he was working in the tea plantation as a permanent worker. As he developed leprosy he was unable to continue his work in the tea plantation. His wife Bina (45 years old) belongs to the same community. She is also an illiterate woman and was working in the same garden temporarily. They have four children (2 sons and 2 daughters). Due to Musri's leprosy, some three years back, Bina left him and her children; and went away with another man who works in the same tea garden. Since then they have been living together. Musri is looked after by his children. As a matter fact, Bina went to stay with his next door neighbour, belonging to the same community. He was a bachelor and Bina had a friendly relationship with him.

Inter-ethnic Marriage

Inter-ethnic marital alliances in all the groups are traditionally considered to be a serious offence. In their natal home, in many cases, the offenders were subjected to public humiliation, heavy fines and sometimes ex-communication.

In the present setting too, the people, by and large, maintain group endogamy. However, it seems at present there has been some liberal attitude in this regard. In the population under study, at least 17 such cases have been reported. Data this regard has been presented in table IV. 16. It will be seen from the table that the majority of the cases (13) have been reported from the Christian Mundas. On the other hand no such episode has been reported from their Non-Christian counterpart. The Tantis share 3 cases whereas among the Parjah one marriage has taken place with an Assamese spouse. The other non-tea labour spouse involved in the marriage of a Tanti boy hails from the Nepali community.

Case IV. 14.

Philip Munda, aged 50 years is a permanent worker in Dhelakhat tea plantation and is a Christian. He studied up to class I. Through mutual consent he got married at the age of 25 years with Rita Oraon who was 15 years old and was a Christian. She works in Dhelakhat tea plantation as a permanent labourer. She is illiterate. Though in the initial stage the parents disapproved of their act, since the spouses had the same religious background, they finally settled their marriage within two months and the society also accepted the union.

Case IV. 15.

Farncis Munda (45 years) was born in Dhelakhat tea estate. He is Christian by religion and works as a permanent labourer. When he was 28 years old, he fell in love with Jacinta Parjah, who was then 24 years old. She is also a Christian girl, illiterate and a temporary labourer in the same plantation. Through mutual consent they started living together as husband and wife. Though the parents and the relatives initially disapproved of the relationship, within a year the two ceremonially married with the approval of the society.

Case IV. 16.

Birospatia Tanti, aged 30 years is Hindu by religion. He is working in Dhelakhat tea estate permanently. He was born and brought up in the same plantation and read up to class X. He fell in love with Purnima at the age of 28 years. She belongs to the Nepali community and is working temporarily in the same plantation. She is an illiterate Hindu girl. Though his father was against this marriage, through mutual consent they have been living together as husband and wife. Their marriage ceremony is yet to be performed.

Case IV. 17.

Gutuloi Tanti (23 years) was born in Dirial tea estate. He is Hindu by religion and is temperarily working in the same plantation. He is an illiterate person. At the age of 19 years he fell in love with Budini Munda, aged 21 years. She is also a Ḥindu, illiterate girl and works in the same garden as a temporary labourer. Because of disapproval of the parents, they started living together independently as husband and wife. At present they have two sons. Their marriage ceremony is yet to be performed.

Similar accommodating attitudes towards inter-ethnic alliances have also been reported by Bhadra (op.cit) in her study among the tea garden labourers in North Bengal. However, such a marriage always involves the imposition of a cash penalty on the couple. A part of this amount is given to the parents of the girl and the rest is taken by the community leaders who are instrumental in according social approval to such a union. The penalty is considered to be a token of social sanction. It may be noted here that the system of payment of bride price (a token one) is prevalent in all the communities.

Sex and Marriage

Sex and marriage in all the communities go together. Pre-marital sex relation and pregnancy is looked down upon by the people, if it does not end up in marital union.

During the present investigation, at least two such cases of pre-marital sex relationship leading to pregnancy have been reported. In one case, the outcome was marital union, and in the other case it was not.

Case IV. 18.

Miliani Munda, aged 19 years is a Christian girl. She read up to class V. She was born and brought up in Dhelakhat tea estate and is a temporary labourer. She fell in love with Joseph Munda, aged 22 years who was also a Christian boy. He too is working in the same garden. They had premarital sex relations and Miliani became pregnant. This came to her parent's knowledge. The parents then took the initiative and finally compelled the boy to marry her. The marriage was an arranged one.

Case IV. 19.

Thaddeus Soi, aged 24 years is a Christian Munda and is an lliterate Person from Naharkatia. He came to stay with his uncle in Dhelakhat tea estate and was looking for an employment. He was working as a temporary labourer. During the course of his work, he met Rita, aged 21 Years, who too was working in the same plantation as a temporary labourer. She too was a Christian belonging to the Santal tribe and was an illiterate girl. Their friendship led to pre-marital sex which ultimately resulted in Rita's pregnancy. When Thaddeus' parents were informed about the incident, they immediately took steps to arrange the marriage. But Rita's parents vehemently opposed the match and as such it did not materialise. Thaddeus finally left for his home town, Naharkatia, where he married another girl. Rita during the time of investigation was still unmarried.

Widowhood

Widowhood differs greatly for men and women. The ratio of widows to widowers is high everywhere, generally due to men's higher rates of re-marriage, older age at marriage and shorter life expectancy. As a result most of the elderly men are found to be married, whereas many elderly women live as widows.

In the sample population under investigation, the figure for widows is 51 (5.25%) and that for widowers is 35 (3.48%). The group and sex-wise distribution of these 86 individuals is as follows: Christian Munda male-8 (1.65%), female - 13 (2.68%); Non-Christian Munda : male - 8 (1.38%), female -12 (2.07%); Parjah : male - 13(2.35%), female -13 (2.35%); and Tanti: male - 6 (1.69%), female- 13 (3.66%).

Table No. IV.11. Distribution of the Population by age, sex and marital status (Dhelakhat & Dirial Tea Estates)

Sl. No	Age group in years	Population			Unmarried			Married			Widowed		
		Male	Female	Total	Male	Female	Total	Male	Female	Total	Male	Female	Total
1	2	3	4	5	6	7	8	9	10	11	12	13	14
1	0-4	150 (7.59)	138 (6.99)	288 (14.58)	150 (7.59)	138 (6.99)	288 (14.58)	– –	– –	– –	– –	– –	– –
2	5-9	123 (6.23)	113 (5.72)	236 (11.95)	123 (6.23)	113 (5.72)	236 (11.95)	– –	– –	– –	– –	– –	– –
3	10-14	129 (6.53)	144 (5.77)	273 (13.82)	129 (6.53)	144 (7.29)	273 (13.82)	–	–	–	–	–	–
4	15-19	127 (6.43)	114 (5.77)	241 (12.20)	120 (6.07)	98 (4.96)	218 (11.03)	7 (0.35)	16 (0.81)	23 (1.16)	–	–	–
5	20-24	72 (3.65)	77 (3.90)	139 (7.03)	45 (2.28)	35 (1.77)	80 (4.05)	17 (0.86)	42 (2.13)	59 (2.99)	–	–	–
6	25-29	70 (3.54)	78 (3.95)	148 (7.49)	28 (1.42)	29 (1.47)	57 (2.89)	41 (2.08)	49 (2.48)	90 (4.56)	1 (0.05)	–	1 (0.05)
7	30-34	52 (2.63)	42 (2.13)	94 (4.76)	9 (0.46)	5 (0.25)	14 (0.71)	41 (2.08)	36 (1.82)	77 (3.90)	2 (0.10)	1 (0.05)	3 (0.15)
8	35-39	59 (2.99)	87 (4.41)	146 (7.39)	6 (0.30)	2 (0.10)	8 (0.40)	48 (2.43)	78 (3.95)	126 (6.38)	5 (0.25)	7 (0.35)	12 (0.61)

(Contd...)

Table No. IV.11 (Contd...)

Sl. No	Age group in years	Population			Unmarried			Married			Widowed		
		Male	Female	Total	Male	Female	Total	Male	Female	Total	Male	Female	Total
1	2	3	4	5	6	7	8	9	10	11	12	13	14
9	40-44	52 (2.63)	56 (2.84)	108 (5.47)	–	2 (0.10)	2 (0.10)	50 (2.53)	49 (2.48	99 (5.01)	2 (0.10)	5 (0.25)	7 (0.35)
10	45-49	61 (3.09)	39 (1.97)	100 (5.06)	1 (0.05)	–	1 (0.05)	58 (2.94)	35 (1.77)	93 (4.71)	2 (0.10)	4 (0.20)	6 (0.30)
11	50.54	40 (2.03)	25 (1.27)	65 (3.29)	1 (0.05)	–	1 (0.05)	38 (1.92)	19 (0.96)	57 (2.89)	1 (0.05)	6 (0.30)	7 (0.35)
12	55-59	33 (1.67)	17 (0.86)	50 (2.53)	1 (0.05)	–	1 (0.05)	38 (1.42)	19 (0.66)	57 (2.08)	1 (0.20)	6 (0.20)	7 (0.40)
13	60 & above	46 (2.33)	41 (49.16)	87 (4.41)	–	–	–	28 (1.42)	17 (0.86)	45 (2.28)	18 (0.91)	24 (1.22)	42 (2.13)
Total		1004 (50.84)	971 (49.16)	1975 (100.00)	613 (31.04)	566 (28.66)	1179 (59.70)	356 (18.03)	354 (17.92)	710 (35.95)	35 (1.77)	51 (2.58)	86 (4.35)

Table No. IV.12. Distribution of the Christian Mundas by age, sex and marital status (Dhelakhat & Dirial Tea Estates)

Sl. No	Age group in years	Population			Unmarried			Married			Widowed		
		Male	Female	Total	Male	Female	Total	Male	Female	Total	Male	Female	Total
1	2	3	4	5	6	7	8	9	10	11	12	13	14
1	0-4	31 (6.39)	24 (4.95)	55 (11.34)	31 (6.39)	24 (4.95)	55 (11.34)	-	-	-	-	-	-
2	5-9	21 (4.33)	24 (4.95)	45 (9.28)	21 (4.33)	24 (4.95)	45 (9.28)	-	-	-	-	-	-
3	10-14	34 (31.49)	31 (6.39)	65 (13.40)	34 (7.01)	31 (6.39)	65 (13.40)	-	4	4	-	-	-
4	15-19	43 (8.87)	28 (5.77)	71 (14.64)	41 (8.45)	28 (5.77)	69 (14.23)	2 (0.41)	-	2 (0.41)	-	-	-
5	20-24	24 (4.95)	25 (5.15)	49 (10.10)	20 (4.12)	16 (3.30)	36 (7.42)	4 (0.82)	9 (1.86)	13 (2.68)	-	-	-
6	25-29	20 (4.12)	27 (5.57)	47 (9.69)	15 (3.09)	20 (4.12)	35 (7.22)	4 (0.82)	7 (1.44)	11 (2.27)	1 (0.20)	-	1 (0.21)
7	30-34	11 (2.27)	9 (1.86)	20 (4.12)	3 (0.62)	3 (0.62)	6 (1.24)	8 (1.65)	6 (1.24)	14 (2.89)	-	-	-
8	35-39	13 (2.68)	20 (4.12)	33 (6.80)	2 (0.41)	1 (0.20)	3 (0.62)	10 (2.06)	17 (3.51)	27 (5.56)	1 (0.20)	2 (0.41)	3 (0.62)

(Contd...)

Table No. IV.12 (Contd...)

Sl. No	Age group in years	Population			Unmarried			Married			Widowed		
		Male	Female	Total	Male	Female	Total	Male	Female	Total	Male	Female	Total
1	2	3	4	5	6	7	8	9	10	11	12	13	14
9	40-44	12 (2.47)	10 (2.06)	22 (4.54)	-	-	-	11 (2.27)	8 (1.65)	19 (3.92)	1 (0.20)	2 (0.41)	3 (0.62)
10	45-49	10 (3.97)	15 (3.09)	25 (5.15)	-	-	-	10 (2.06)	14 (2.89)	24 (4.95)	-	1 (0.20)	1 (0.21)
11	50-54	13 (2.68)	11 (2.27)	24 (4.95)	1 (0.20)	-	1 (0.21)	12 (2.47)	7 (1.44)	19 (3.92)	-	4 (0.82)	4 (0.82)
12	55-59	11 (2.27)	4 (0.82)	15 (3.09)	-	-	-	10 (2.06)	4 (0.82)	14 (2.89)	1 (0.20)	-	1 (0.21)
13	60 & above	9 (1.86)	5 (1.03)	14 (2.89)	-	-	-	5 (1.03)	1 (0.20)	6 (1.24)	4 (0.82)	4 (0.82)	8 (1.64)
14	Total	252 (51.96)	233 (48.04)	485 (100.00)	168 (36.64)	147 (30.37)	315 (64.95)	76 (15.67)	73 (15.05)	149 (30.72)	8 (1.65)	13 (2.68)	21 (4.33)

Table No. IV.13. Distribution of the Non-Christian Mundas by age, sex and marital status (Dhelakhat & Dirial Tea Estates)

Sl. No	Age group in years	Population			Unmarried			Married			Widowed		
		Male	Female	Total	Male	Female	Total	Male	Female	Total	Male	Female	Total
1	2	3	4	5	6	7	8	9	10	11	12	13	14
1	0-4	38 (7.75)	37 (7.23)	75 (14.97)	38 (7.75)	37 (7.23)	75 (14.97)	-	-	-	-	-	-
2	5-9	45 (4.33)	42 (4.95)	87 (9.28)	45 (4.33)	42 (4.95)	87 (9.28)	-	-	-	-	-	-
3	10-14	49 (8.43)	44 (7.57)	93 (16.01)	49 (8.43)	44 (7.57)	93 (16.01)	-	4	4	-	-	-
4	15-19	30 (5.16)	37 (6.37)	67 (11.53)	27 (4.65)	29 (4.99)	56 (9.64)	3 (0.52)	8 (1.38)	11 (0.41)	-	-	-
5	20-24	13 (2.24)	17 (2.93)	30 (5.16)	8 (1.38)	7 (1.20)	15 (2.58)	5 (0.86)	10 (1.72)	15 (2.58)	-	-	-
6	25-29	16 (2.75)	21 (3.61)	37 (6.37)	2 (0.34)	3 (0.52)	5 (0.86)	14 (2.41)	18 (3.10)	32 (5.51)	-	-	-
7	30-34	11 (1.89)	7 (1.20)	18 (3.10)	1 (0.17)	1 (0.17)	2 (0.34)	10 (1.72)	6 (1.03)	16 (2.71)	-	-	-
8	35-39	12 (2.06)	28 (4.81)	40 (6.89)	-	-	-	12 (2.07)	27 (4.65)	39 (6.71)	-	1 (0.17)	1 (0.17)

(Contd...)

Table No. IV.13 (contd...)

Sl. No	Age group in years	Population			Unmarried			Married			Widowed		
		Male	*Female*	*Total*	*Male*	*Female*	*Total*	*Male*	*Female*	*Total*	*Male*	*Female*	*Total*
1	2	3	4	5	6	7	8	9	10	11	12	13	14
9	40-44	20 (3.34)	23 (3.96)	43 (7.40)	-	-	-	19 (3.27)	22 (3.79)	41 (7.06)	1 (0.17)	1 (0.17)	2 (0.62)
10	45-49	26 (4.48)	14 (2.41)	40 (6.89)	-	-	-	26 (4.48)	13 (2.24)	39 (6.71)	-	1 (0.17)	1 (0.17)
11	50-54	9 (1.55)	4 (0.69)	13 (2.24)	-	-	-	9 (1.55)	4 (0.69)	13 (2.24)	-	-	-
12	55-59	7 (1.20)	4 (0.69)	11 (1.89)	-	-	-	6 (1.03)	2 (0.34)	8 (1.38)	1 (0.17)	2 (0.34)	3 (0.52)
13	60 & above	13 (2.24)	14 (2.41)	27 (4.65)	-	-	-	7 (1.20)	7 (1.20)	14 (2.41)	6 (1.03)	7 (1.20)	13 (2.24)
14	Total	289 (49.74)	292 (50.26)	581 (100.00)	170 (29.26)	163 (28.05)	333 (57.31)	111 (19.10)	117 (20.14)	228 (39.24)	8 (1.38)	12 (2.07)	20 (3.44)

Table No. IV.14. Distribution of the Parjahs by age, sex and marital status (Dhelakhat & Dirial Tea Estates)

Sl. No	Age group in years	Population			Unmarried			Married			Widowed		
		Male	Female	Total	Male	Female	Total	Male	Female	Total	Male	Female	Total
1	2	3	4	5	6	7	8	9	10	11	12	13	14
1		0-4 (9.21)	51	47 (8.48)	98 (17.69)	51 (9.21)	47 (8.48)	98 (17.69)	-	-	-	-	-
2	5-9	38 (6.86)	31	69 (5.60)	38 (12.45)	31 (6.86)	69 (5.60)	- (12.45)	-	-	-	-	-
3	10-14	28 (5.05)	46	74 (8.30)	28 (13.36)	46 (5.05)	74 (8.30)	- (13.36)	-	-	-	-	-
4	15-19	31 (5.60)	30 (5.41)	61 (11.01)	29 (5.23)	26 (4.69)	55 (9.93)	2 (0.36)	4 (0.72)	6 (1.08)			
5	20-24	17 (3.07)	20 (3.61)	37 (6.68)	14 (2.53)	to (1.81)	24 (4.33)	3 (0.54)	10 (1.81)	13 (2.34)			
6	25-29	20 (3.61)	21 (3.79)	41 (2.40)	8 (1.44)	5 (0.90)	13 (2.35)	12 (2.17)	16 (2.89)	28 (15.05)	-	-	-
7	30-34	20 (3.61)	18 (3.25)	38 (6.86)	3 (0.54)	1 (0.18)	4 (0.72)	15 (2.71)	16 2.89	31 (5.42)	2 (0.36)	1 (0.18)	3 (0.54)
8	35-39	22 (3.97)	20 (3.61)	42 (7.58)	4 (0.72)	-	4 (0.72)	15 (2.71)	18 5	33 (5.96)	3 (0.54)	2 (0.36)	5 (0.90)

(Contd...)

Table No. IV.14 (contd...)

Sl. No	Age group in years	Population			Unmarried			Married			Widowed		
		Male	Female	Total	Male	Female	Total	Male	Female	Total	Male	Female	Total
1	2	3	4	5	6	7	8	9	10	11	12	13	14
9	40-44	14 (2.53)	13 (2.35)	27 (4.87)	-	2 (0.36)	2 (0.36)	14 (2.53)	10 (1.81)	24 (4.33)	-	1 (0.18)	1 (0.18)
10	45-49	10 (1.81)	7 (1.26)	17 (3.07)	-	-	-	10 (1.81)	6 (1.08)	16 (2.89)	-	1 (0.18)	1 (0.18)
11	50-54	10 (1.81)	5 (0.90)	15 (2.71)	-	-	-	10 (1.81)	4 (0.72)	11 (1.81)	2 (0.36)	2 (0.36)	4 (0.72)
12	55-59	9 (1.62)	6 (1.08)	15 (2.71)	-	-	-	7 (1.26)	3 (0.54)	9 ~1.62)	6 (1.08)	5 (0.90)	11 (1.96)
13	60 & above	12 (2.17)	8 (1.44)	20 (3.61)	-	-	-	6 (1.08)	3 (0.54)	9 (1.62)	6 (1.08)	5 (0.90)	11 (1.96)
14	Total	282 (50.90)	272 (49.10)	554 (100.00)	175 (31.59)	168 (30.32)	343 (61.91)	94 (16.97)	91 (16.43)	185 (32.85)	13 (2.35)	13 (2.35)	26 (4.69)

Table No. IV.15. Distribution of the Tantis by age, sex and marital status (Dhelakhat & Dirial Tea Estates)

Sl. No	Age group in years	Population			Unmarried			Married			Widowed		
		Male	Female	Total	Male	Female	Total	Male	Female	Total	Male	Female	Total
1	2	3	4	5	6	7	8	9	10	11	12	13	14
1	0-4	30 (8.45)	30 (8.45)	60 (16.90)	30 (8.45)	30 (8.45)	60 (16.90)	-	-	-	-	-	-
2	5-9	19 (5.35)	16 (4.51)	35 (9.86)	19 (5.35)	16 (4.51)	35 (9.86)	-	-	-	-	-	-
3	10-14	18 (5.07)	23 (6.48)	41 (11.55)	18 (5.07)	23 (6.48)	41 (11.55)	-	-	-	-	-	-
4	15-19	23 (6.48)	19 (5.35)	42 (11.83)	23 (6.48)	15 (4.23)	38 (10.70)	-	4 (1.23)	4 (1.23)	-	-	-
5	20-24	8 (2.25)	15 (4.23)	23 (6.48)	3 (0.85)	2 (0.56)	5 (1.41)	5 (1.41)	13 (3.66)	18 (5.07)	-	-	-
6	25-29	14 (3. 4)	9 (2.54)	23 (6.48)	3 (0.85)	1 (0.28)	4 (1.13)	11 (3.10)	8 (2.25)	19 (5.35)	-	-	-
7	30-34	10	8 (2.82)	18 (2.25)	2 (5.07)	(0.56)	2 (0.56)	8 (2.25)	8 (2.25)	16 (4.51)	-	-	-
8	35-39	12 (3.38)	19 (5.35)	31 (8.73)	-	1 (0.28)	1 (0.28)	11 (3.10)	16 (4.51)	27 (7.61)	1 (0.28)	2 (0.56)	3 (0.85)
9	40-44	6 (1.69)	10 (2.82)	16 (4.51)	-	-	-	6 (1.69)	9 (2.54)	15 (4.23)	-	1 (0.28)	3 (0.85)

(Contd...)

Table No. IV.15 (contd...)

Sl. No	Age group in years	Population			Unmarried			Married			Widowed		
		Male	Female	Total	Male	Female	Total	Male	Female	Total	Male	Female	Total
1	2	3	4	5	6	7	8	9	10	11	12	13	14
10	45-49	15 (4.23)	3 (0.85)	18 (5.07)	1 (0.28)	-	1 (0.28)	12 (3.38)	2 (0.56)	14 (3.94)	2 (0.56)	1 (0.28)	3 (0.85)
11	50-54	8 (2.25)	5 (1.41)	13 (3.66)	-	-	-	7 (1.97)	4 (1.23)	11 (3.10)	1 (0.28)	1 (0.28)	2 (0.56)
12	55-59	6 (1.69)	3 (0,85)	9 (2.54)	1 (0.28)	-	1 (0.28)	5 (1.41)	3 (0.85)	8 (2.25)	-	-	-
13	60 & above	12 (3.38)	14 (3.94)	26 (7.32)	-	-	-	10 (2.82)	6 (1.69)	16 (4.51)	2 (0.56)	8 (2.25)	10 (2.82)
14	Total	181 (50.99)	174 (49.01)	355 (100.00)	100 (28.17)	88 (24.79)	188 (52.95)	75 (21.13)	73 (20.56)	148 (41.69)	6 (1.69)	13 (3,66)	19 (5.35)

Table IV. 16. Distribution of the Population according to inter-group marriages (Dhelakhat & Dirial Tea Estates)

Sl. No.	*Ethnic Group*	*Married with*									
		Santal	*Saora*	*Gorh*	*Parjah*	*Oraon*	*Oriya*	*Assamese*	*Nepali*	*Tanti*	*Total*
1	2	3	4	5	6	7	8	9	10	11	12
1	Christian Munda	1	1	1	3	5	1	-	-	1	13
2	Parjah	-	-	-	-	-	-	1	-	-	1
3	Tanti	-	-	-	1	1	-	-	1	-	3
	Total	1	1	1	4	6	1	1	1	1	17

Widowhood, in fact, is a problem even among the tea labourers. Almost 50.00% of the widows belong to the age group of 60 years and above.

Remarriage is socially permitted after the death of one of the spouses in all the groups under study. In the sample population, however, none of the widows remarried. Of the 51 widows, 18 have been found to be heading the households. Commumty-wise distribution of such households has been shown in the Table IV 17. It will be seen from the table that barring the Christian Munda, where it is 3.00%, in all the other three groups the incidence of such families ranges between 1.00% and 2.00%.

In the patriarchal society, no married or unmarried woman, has been found to head a family. Normally, in the event of the death of the husband, leaving behind minor children, the widow takes up the responsibility and command of the family and continues to head the family until a son attains adulthood, either to assist or substitute her. This arrangement has been accepted by the respective communities and the woman head does not seem to face any disability in discharging her day-to-day activities in running the family matters. Incidentally, all the woman heads have been found to be permanent workers in the plantation.

Table No. IV. 17. Community - wise Distribution of Women-headed Households (Dhelakhat and Dirial Tea Estates)

Sl.No.	*Community*	*No. of House holds (%)*	*Remarks, if any*
1	2	3	4
1	Christian Munda	7 (3.00)	
2	Non-Christian Munda	3 (1,03)	
3	Parjah	5 (1.84)	
4	Tanti	3 (1.72)	
	Total	18 (0.91)	

A Pie diagram showing the community-wise distribution of women-headed house holds

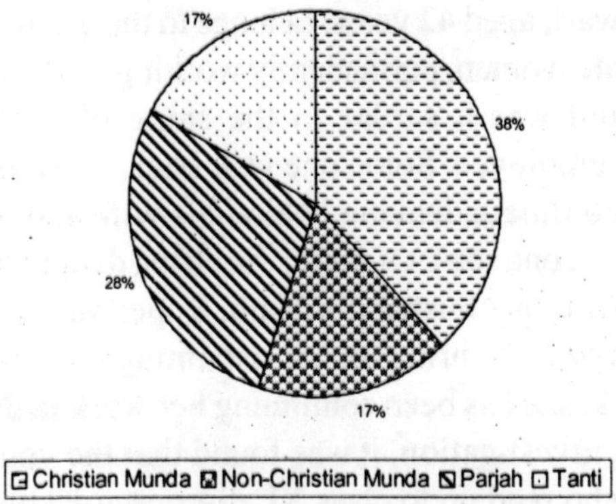

Figure No. IV.5.

In the caste community (the Tanti) it has been observed that the widows have restricted diet, dress and demeanour, etc. Besides, many of them have very little access to or support from extended family networks. Customary rules often restrict their options of residence, inheritance and social interactions etc. Despite lots of other difficulties, most of them remain widows, so that they can look after their children properly.

Case IV.20.

Lakhi, a permanent worker in Dhelakhat tea plantation is 38 years old. She belongs to the Parjah community. She is an illiterate woman. Her husband was a permanent worker in the garden. Some five years back, he suddenly died of cardiac failure. She became a young widow with four children (three daughters and a son). Though young enough to look for a second husband, she decided to remain alone for the proper up-bringing of the children. During the time of investigation her youngest son was 8 years old. As a lone widow she sometimes faces problems from some alcoholic neighbours, but by and large, she is maintaining her children and herself reasonably well.

Case IV.21.

Rupeswari, aged 42 years, belongs to the Tanti community. She is an illiterate woman, permanently working in Dirial tea plantation. Her husband was a sardar in the same plantation and was a permanent employee. Some one year back, he suddenly died of an undiagnosed illness, leaving behind his wife and three children (2 daughters and one son). Of these, the eldest daughter married before his death. After her husband's death, Rupeswari decided to remain a widow in order to bring up her remaining two children properly. Though sick, she has been continuing her work in the plantation. At the time of investigation, it was found that the youngest son, aged 18 years, who read up to class XI, discontinued his studies to take garden employment on compassionate grounds. Being a widow of a caste community, she continues to have restricted diet and dress, etc. Notwithstanding all the obvious hurdles, it seems she has been maintaining her family quite well.

Intra-Family Relationship

The fundamental role of the family has undergone a change with a change in the traditional mode of production to a new type of production relation in the plantation economy. Work in the plantation has changed their economic activity from self-supporting agriculturists to wage earners. The family thus has changed from a unit of production to a unit of consumption. Traditionally, joint living was essential to support the family economy. But under the present system joint living, as noted elsewhere in this chapter, to some extent deprives the workers of some of their due benefits from the garden authorities. Though there is a predominance of nuclear families, generally a close relationship with other prmiary and secondary relatives is maintained. Here, the kinsmen who live side by side in the nuclear families often help one another in times of need. In this respect a close kinship inter-dependence exists between the members. The intimate social interaction of the family members is for most part centered in the home, with the members of the nuclear family.

Every society has its own behavioural patterns and every member is expected to follow these norms. This reciprocal intra-family relationship contributes a lot to knit the family members together.

In the following pages, an attempt has been made to describe some of the observed behavioural patterns among the different members of the family in the studied groups.

Between Husband & Wife

A good marital adjustment is the ability of the husband and the wife to relate emotionally to each other and to give and receive love. The husband and the wife who do not have the habit of expressing affection will have difficulty in establishing a warm and close relationship, because each interprets the other's behaviour as an indication of 'not caring' (Hurlock, 1981:306).

Among the people under investigation the husband-wife relationship is very cordial and open. Normally, the husband is older than the wife and the wife, though a co-worker in the industry is loyal and obedient to the husband. The wife talks to her husband freely and shares their mutual feelings. This could be seen among all the groups. However, a Tanti woman respects her husband to the extent that she is not allowed to address him by name. They are not allowed to utter the husband's name even after the latter's death.

Case IV.22.

Puthi, a Tanti widow, aged 62 years, is a resident of Dhelakhat tea estate. She is an illiterate woman who was working in the plantation and is now retired. During an interview with her she was asked to tell her husband's name. At that time she was alone in the family. So she called a boy from the neighbourhood to tell her husband's name. Being asked to tell the reason for such relationship between a couple, she maintained that their tradition does not allow her to utter the husband's name as he is considered to be a god *(Devata)*.

The husband and the wife have equal responsibilities in the welfare of the family and upbringing of the children. Though there is a broad division of labour in the household activities and most of these are allotted to females, in case of necessity both work together.

However, most of the free time of a wife seems to be spent in household activities and in the midst of her independent friends circle. This may be a probable reason for the observation that very rarely do a couple go out together for recreation or visiting others.

The husband-wife relation is of love and affection along with due in respect and responsibilities towards each other. Both spend their earnings in the smooth running of the family. But, in most of the cases, the husband's decision dominates the course of events; and it seems, the wives by and large, accept this domination as a matter of fact. Most of them acknowledge that the husband's responsibilities are relatively more in running the affairs of the family. Some women respondents are of the view that, if their husbands do not control them they cannot have discipline in themselves. It may be noted here that as a tradition, the major decisions in the family are generally taken by the husband. The wife has also got used to this practice and as such she normally does not take any offence at his prerogative.

In fact, one of the indicators of the status of women is whether they can play an active and effective role in the decision- making process in the family. A randomly chosen sample of 100 women respondents (with proportionate representation from all the groups) were interviewed in this regard. Around 73.00% of the respondents maintain that they do not have any perceptible role in the decision-making process in the family. In most of the cases it is the husband who decides the issue either independently or having the final say on the matter. A further query was made as to their reconciliation to the state of affairs. It seems, barring the Non-Christian Munda and the Tanti respondents, others have, by and large, accepted the trend. Around 50.00% of the Non-Christian Munda and 30.00% of the Tanti women have expressed their unhappiness over the prevailing manner of the decision-making process.

Nevertheless, it may be noted here that in certain vital issues in the family, like marriage and education of children, etc., both the husband and the wife do discuss together. Generally, a wife does take the major decisions regarding day-to-day family expenditure and domestic activities, etc. As an earning wife spends all her wages for maintenance of the family, she has a greater say in the day-to-day affairs of the family. A good number of husbands spend a substantial part of their earnings in drinking rice-beer *(haria)*.

With regard to the unpleasant manifestation of disagreement between husband and wife, around 80.00% of the respondents replied in the affirmative. Sometimes they disagree with one another even in the ordinary issues of the family. But in such circumstances, generally the wife gives up and accommodates the ideas of her husband. But, there are some wives (around 14.00%) who generally do not yield to their husbands easily. In such cases, the husbands at times, quarrel with their wives to the extent of beating and using abusive words. On the other hand, around 6.00% of the respondents reported that they had never had any disagreement with their husbands.

Despite all these odds here and there, on the whole, it may be said that the relationship between husband and wife, is by and large, pleasant and harmonious.

Among the other members of the family

With marriage, every adult acquires a whole new set of relatives, especially the in-laws. These are people of different ages ranging from babies to the elderly ones, who, often have different interests and values and sometimes have markedly different educational, cultural and social backgrounds. Both the husbands and the wives must learn to adjust with their in-laws if they are to avoid any strained relationship with their spouses.

It is not at all uncommon, particularly when the married couple is young and inexperienced, for the in-laws to try to exert some control over their lives, especially if they are partially or totally dependent on their support; but when the couple is older, experienced and financially independent, in-law interference is less likely to occur. In-law trouble is especially serious during the early years of marriage and is one of the most important causes of marital breakup during the first year (cited in Hurlock, 1981).

Certain factors have been found to contribute to good in-law adjustments. These include approval of the marriage by the parents of both the spouses, opportunities for the parents to meet and become acquainted before the marriage, and friendliness on the part of both the families when they meet. In-law problems are also eased if : (i) the marriage is between persons of the same religion; (ii) the relationship between the grand parents and the grand children is good; (ill) in-laws have a similar pattern of social activities; (iv) the in-laws and the young couples are happily married; and above all, if the husband and the wife accept each other's family as their own (cited in Hurlock, 1981).

In the plantation setting, the relationship between the in-laws seems to be positive as most of the spouses and their families are already known to one another, and are very often friendly with one another. In many cases, marriages take place between persons of the same religious background, though their ethnic affiliation may differ. Besides, their overall activities, too, are similar. In case of inter-ethnic and inter-religious marriages, generally the parents' approval becomes an initial problem. But, this is generally settled by the community leaders in a socially approved manner.

With the birth of a child, the intimacy of the husband-wife relationship transforms from a dyad to a triad relationship (Russel,1974). Both the husband and the wife gradually learn to play family-centred roles rather than a dual-centred one.

The mother is the centre of the family. The infant and the mother establish a close emotional relationship with each other soon after the baby's birth, but the world of the infant soon expands to include others in the family. Both the parents establish love-ties with their children. However, the parental roles combine both authority and intimacy. The parent or the child may each get his own way through love, but each is expected to be called back to socially approved norms by their own needs (Kar, 1981:103).

The status of the mother and that of the children implies certain roles that every mother and child is expected to play. In many societies the role of the mother involves protecting and emotionally supporting the child, while the role of the child involves displaying obedience and affection towards the mother. A 'good' mother is one whose actual behaviour closely conforms to the role expectation. In real life the mother and the child may attempt to avoid performing certain aspects of their roles or may engage in bargaining about the manner in which their respective roles are to be played (Beals & Hoijer, 1977 : 424).

In conformity with the classical psychoanalytic view, a young child generally concludes his infancy period by becoming emotionally attached to the parent of the opposite sex. That is, the boy is more involved emotionally with his mother, while the daughter becomes more attached to her father. The relationship seems to give pleasure to both the partners. Thus, both the parents establish a close relationship with their children and fulfill their needs so as to enable the children reach maturity harmoniously.

As an adolescent moves into adulthood, he/she constantly threatens the authority of the parents by the simple process of maturation. The son and the daughter are to be given in marriage, usually arranged by the parents. But, as noted elsewhere in the chapter, the frequent selection of a spouse by the adult himself/herself appears to have become the usual deviation from the traditional norm in the present context. Though, in most cases the marriages are regularised and approved by the parents, the strain sometimes continues to remain.

The daughter, even after marriage keeps contact with the parents regularly. Around 53.00% of the women respondents maintain that they enjoy complete liberty to visit their parents whenever they desire to do so. The rest however, report that the husband's consent is needed for the visit. The parents also regularly visit their married daughters and extend help and cooperation whenever necessary.

The daughter-in-law-Parents-in-law relation is generally comparable to a parents-daughter relationship, however, there is certain degree of reservation in frequent interaction and manner of approach which, again is more rigid in respect to the father-in-law.

With regard to the relationship among the siblings, it has been found to be very friendly and affectionate. The elder siblings are generally given some respect by the younger ones; and they claim a certain degree of authority over the others. In the absence of the parents, they look after the younger ones in all spheres as demanded by the situation. The elder siblings deem it to be their moral obligation to take on the responsibility for the younger ones in case the parents are dead, invalid or otherwise unable to discharge their role in this regard.

Finally in respect of the relationship between the members in a joint family it has been found that though there are occasions of minor outbursts, the relation between the various members is more or less cordial and accommodating. The head of the household with the assistance and contribution of the other earning members, manages and controls the family purse. He is respected and obeyed by the junior members of the family.

Daily Life

Although the day-to-day activities of the people vary from season to season, yet basically the flow of life is the same throughout the year. Most of the adult members of both the sexes are wage earners. During the peak plucking season as well as in the agricultural season, they are busier than at any other season. A major section of the unemployed youths is also engaged during the plucking season as temporary (*faltu*) labourers.

The people generally rise early in the morning before the sun rises. The adult members, both men and women, leave the rooms before the others. Whether in industry, service or agriculture, women and men by and large have different responsibilities and activities. After attending to nature's call, both the men and the women engage themselves in various activities. After their personal cleaning, the men who possess cattle bring them out of the shed, give them fresh fodder and water; and milk them. The cattle are then driven out for grazing and are looked after by a cow-man who is paid by the authorities. Later, the watering of the plants in the kitchen garden and planting of new items, etc., are done by the male adults. They also help in some domestic work if necessary. Normally, breakfast is over by 7.30 a.m.

During the agricultural season the menfolk get up from bed earlier and go to the paddy field to till the land. They have to go to their duties in the garden at 8.00 a.m. So, they return home before that time and after having their breakfast report to the workplace by 8.00 a.m.

After returning from work, the menfolk are generally free. After a bath they go to other places, generally with some of their friends, to take *haria* (home-made rice beer) or *chulai* (country liquor), made out of molasses. During the agricultural season, they go to the agriculture field for the second time in the afternoon and come back at around dusk. They usually take their night meal between 8.00 and 8.30 p.m. and retire to bed early.

Most of the unmarried and unemployed boys get up late in the morning and spend the day in roaming about and gossipping.

For most women, family and work are constantly tied together. Whether employed or not, a woman has the major responsibility for the household chores and the care of the children and other family members. The women-folk generally get up from bed before dawn and normally earlier than the men-folk. After finishing their wash, toilet, etc., they clean the kitchen (particularly the place where the hearth is located) and also the utensils. Normally they do not wash the utensils in the night, as they believe that the leftover food should not be thrown away , but should be given to the animals in the morning. Thereafter, they engage themselves in the daily routine work. They sweep their houses and courtyards and prepare the morning meal, which generally consists of either *rooti* or rice with some cooked vegetables; sometimes they take leftover *dal* (pulses) of the previous night in their morning meal. If there are non-working females in the family, they help to prepare the meal for all the members of their household. When the breakfast is ready, they prepare tiffin for the working people, serve breakfast to all the inmates and after having eaten themselves and kept aside food for their children, they leave for work. Black tea is served for all the labourers in their work places during the short break.

After returning from their work, a woman normally prepares black tea, serves it to all the inmates and then has a bath. Just after dusk they start cooking the night meal. Normally, the night meal consists of rice and *dal* with or without vegetables. Fish and meat are prepared only occasionally. On the day of payment they sometimes purchase fish from the garden market that is organised only on that (payment) day. During the rainy season many of them indulge in individual fishing by using nets and rods in the nearby drains as well as rivers. Between 8.00 and 8.30 p.m. most of them retire to bed.

In a few cases the young boys and girls generally look after their infant and toddler brothers and sisters during the day time if their mothers are employed. Most of the unemployed young boys spend their time in gossippmg. Young unemployed girls however, generally do all the household works. Non-working women also clean the house and cowshed after sending all the male and female members to work. They smear the walls and floors with mud and cowdung diluted in water, and then they have a bath and continue their household chores.

On Sundays and other holidays, working women also smear the walls and floors of the house, bathe their children and wash their clothes, etc. Many of them also sell home- made rice beer on Sundays and holidays at home. Even the retired elderly women spend their time and earn their living by preparing and selling rice beer.

Sometimes, the young boys go to Tinsukia to enjoy a movie. If a nearby family has television, most of the neighbours assemble there to watch the programmes during the free time.

The foregoing discussion thus makes it apparent that women generally do not get much leisure time in the Midst of their domestic, material and job preoccupations. From early morning till night, they remain very busy with their work at home as well as in tea the gardens, in addition to the child care and child-rearing activities. There seems to be no time for leisure. In response to a query, around 70.00% of the women expressed the feeling that they do not get sufficient time even to take care of their children. Many of the mothers realise the necessity of proper maternal care for the healthy upbringing of the children; and as such, suffer from a guilt-feeling as if they were neglecting their duties towards the children.

Hard and monotonous work associated with this sense of guilt very often results in mental tension which they themselves acknowledge. About 80.00% of the respondents say that they feel tense now and then whereas 18.00% are always in the grip of tension, mainly because of paucity / non-availability of leisure time.

Paradoxically, however, during the annual leave the same women-folk wonder how to spend their leisure time usefully as they have got used to the strict regimen of their working lives. They seem to have got so used to this routine mechanical life that most of them, during the holidays say that they prefer to be in the tea beds than to be at home all the day having plenty of leisure time.

5

HEALTH AND EDUCATION

Health and education may be considered as two sides of the same coin. Wherever people are educated, their health consciousness also increases. They become relatively more conscious about personal cleanliness, proper sanitation, and the necessary preventive, curative and promotive health measures. A good number of recent studies in India have also revealed that the literate mothers are relatively more health conscious, which is reflected in the declining death rates of their infants (Gonglah, 1996). Thus health and education cannot be separated from each other, and both are very important parameters in deciding the social well-being of a community.

Health refers to a state of complete physical, mental and social well-being. As a social issue, health depends on a society's technology and distribution of resources. Culture shapes both the definitions of health as well as the responses to illness.

Education on the other hand, is a major social institution for transmitting knowledge and skills as well as cultural norms and values. In pre-industrial societies, education used to be imparted informally within the family and other social institutions (eg. Youth dormitory). Industrialised societies, by contrast, have developed the formal system of schooling.

Besides an immediate positive correlation between education and health, literature is replete with the fact that women's education has a positive impact on the overall health of the family and children's education with special reference to the education of the girl children. Table V.I. provides a clearer picture in this regard.

It may contextually be noted here that in Africa and Southern Asia illiteracy rates among adult women are still over 50 percent, and total fertility rates are still over 5 births per woman. In Latin America and the Caribbean and in eastern and southeastern Asia, illiteracy rates among women are largely under 20 per cent and fertility rates are less than 4 births per woman, often even less (Digumarti & Digumarti, 1998).

With regard to the mother's education and the rate of child survival, Digumarti & Digumarti (1998) report that in Ghana, women with no education are twice as likely to lose the children as mothers with primary schooling, and four times as likely as mothers with secondary education. Similarly, in Indonesia, mothers who have not received any education are three times more likely to lose children under five than mothers with some schooling.

Besides, education helps women overcome social prejudice, take control of their lives and assume a status and identity beyond child-bearing, thereby allowing them to participate more fully in the public life of their community. It opens up wider horizons, creates new opportunities and, most importantly, empowers women with choice. Education is the single most important weapon to combat sexual stereotype discriminatory attitudes towards women. Against this backdrop, an attempt has been made in this chapter, to have a brief understanding of the health and educational status of the people with special reference to the women under investigation.

Health

Health, in general, may be defined as the quality of life that enables an individual to live a full and rewarding life. It is the state in which the mental and physical activities of the body are adjusted satisfactorily to the environment (Bedi, 1980). In the preamble of the charter for Health and Development signed by India on 15th February, 1980, it has been stated that a nation's greatest asset is its

Table V.1. Impact of Women's Education on Family, Health, Children and Girl child's Education

Impact on the health of the family	*Impact on Education of children*	*Impact on the education of girls*
1	2	3
Highly educated parents produce healthier pre-school children	Families with higher levels of literacy have children who learn to read better	The Mother's education is positively related to higher aspirations for participation in education by their daughters
Educating women reduces child mortality.	Parents educated in the ways of school spend more time reading story books to the children and have more frequent contact with regard to home work, assignments and other schooling matters.	The Mother's educational aspiration for their daughters exceeds that of fathers.
Educating women reduces fertility.	Mother's education influences children's propensity to stay at school.	
Mother's education is important in determining how many children will be in the household.	Mother's education is important for children in later grades of school where more difficult assignments make demands on mother's knowledge for help with home work. Mother's education has strong effects on achievements in academic skills. The effects may persist into adulthood.	

Sources : Sticht t. and B.A. Macdonald (1990). *Teaching the mother and reach the child.* Geneva : International Bureau of Education.

Summers, 1. (1964). *Investing in all the people educating women in developing* countries. Washington: Education Development Institute of the World Bank.

people, who are endowed with good health which promotes them to creativeness, dynamism and determination . Health is a basic requirement of human aspiration and happiness.

The standard of health and well-being varies very much with the environment which varies enormously among the population, or even among the sub groups. It has been observed by the social scientists that there is a close relationship between health problems and socio-economic and environmental conditions of the people. These factors could often pose as barriers in obtaining adequate medical care. Sometimes, it is also seen that while being aware of modern medical care, the people also retain some of their old customs, beliefs and practices with regard to health and sickness.

Again, as cited by Sharma (1992:3) health is a composite and cumulative effect of a host of factors including availability of food, food habits, safe drinking water, hygienic living conditions, improved purchasing capacity and above all education; and not just immunity against communicable diseases.

In the following few pages, an attempt has been made to depict in brief some of the factors, like housing, sanitation, food and drink, ailment episodes and medical facilities, that have a strong bearing on the general health of the tea garden workers, particularly of the women workers.

Housing

Housing is an important part of health and welfare scheme. Being the basic human need, housing conditions play an integral part in the maintenance of one's health. It is needless to expand upon the ill effects of poor housing on the health, efficiency and welfare of the workers, and the social problems it creates. Home is a place of pleasure, relaxation and peace for a worker. A reasonably housed worker can work with maximum efficiency.

Section 16 of the Assam Plantation Labour Rules, 1956 along with the Plantation Labour Act, 1951 as amended by Act No. 58 of 1981 prescribe the provisions for housing facilities in the garden.

Rule 58 of the section 16 stipulates that every employer shall provide for a worker and his family residing in a plantation, housing accommodation as near as possible to the place of work.

Rule 60 provides sites for housing accommodation :

(1) The housing accommodation shall be provided on dry well-drained land which is consistent with the requirement regarding distance from the plantation and has a supply of wholesome drinking water within a reasonable distance. The houses shall be provided at a safe distance from the swamps and marshes and above the highest flood level.

(2) Adequate lighting arrangements shall be provided in and around the area in which the housing accommodation is provided.

(3) The employer shall maintain in good condition the approach roads and paths to the area where houses are located and all sewers and drains in that area.

(4) The employer shall not deny to the public free access to those parts of the plantation where the workers are housed.

Apart from these, the maintenance requirements of houses are incorporated in Rule 63. These are as follows:

(1) The employer shall at his expense maintain all houses provided for accommodation of workers in a fit and safe condition and execute annual and other repairs as may be necessary from time to time.

(2) A worker occupying a house may, and an Inspector appcinted under the Act shall, bring to the notice of the employer any defect in the condition of the house which makes it dangerous to the health and safety of the worker. Where an Inspector brings any such defects to notice, it shall be the duty of the employer to rectify the same with the least possible delay.

(3) The employer shall get all the houses lime washed at least once every year and all the doors, windows and other

wooden structures varnished and painted once in three years. A record of dates on which lime washing or painting was carried out shall be maintained in register in Form No. 5.

(4) If any employer fails to comply with the requirements of sub rules (1), (2), (3), the Chief Inspector may cause repairs, etc., to be done and realise the cost thereof from the employer as arrears of land revenue. The rule further explains that the above provisions shall be applicable to all houses whether built prior to the enforcement of the Rules or subsequently, in accordance with the Housing scheme and conforming to the standards and specifications as approved by the Government.

And according to Rule 64 no rent shall be charged by any employer for the housing accommodation provided to the workers and their families within the plantation.

With this background of the various existing clauses intended for proper housing of the tea labour, it is important to note the ground reality with regard to the housing and other associated facilities enjoyed by the people under investigation.

The permanent labourers along with their families of Dhelakhat and Dirial tea plantations are provided with housing facilities by the management under the provision of the Plantation Labour Act (PLA), within the plantation boundary. Different types of houses have been observed in different residential clusters in the field during the time of investigation. These can be classified into three categories based on the quality and content of construction. They are (1) *pucca* houses, (2) semi *pucca* houses, and *kutcha* houses. The *pucca* houses are built of brick walls with cement plaster (only inner side), the floor is unpaved , the roof is made of asbestos sheet with bamboo ceiling. The semi *pucca* houses consist of two living rooms with one kitchen and a front *verandah*. The walls up to a height of 3' from the floor are made of brick, sand and cement and the rest is made of bamboo with mud plaster. With regard to the *Kutcha* house, its roof is made of thatch resting on bamboo walls with mud plaster.

It has been observed that these do not conform to any uniform plan and are relatively more unhygienic.

It may be noted here that without any official approval of the management, many of the labour quarters have been extended by bamboo and thatch construction to cope with the increased size of the family. These unplanned extensions in many cases have made the home environment unhygienic and thereby have contributed negatively to the health and welfare of the people. Even otherwise, the provision of the ventilation in *pucca* and semi *pucca* houses cannot be considered as sufficient because the rooms, even during the day time remain dark and the floor damp. With regard to the maintenance and repairing of the houses, it seems Rule 63 of the PLA has by and large been violated by the management. Most of the houses are in a dilapidated condition. During the rainy season, at times through the rotten roof, water enters within the house. Lime washing, painting and varnishing according to the provisions of the rule are also not done.

The bathing enclosures, too, are provided by the garden authority. Some of these are twinned, some are single. These enclosures are made of bricks and cement plastered walls and floors. Some of these have no roofs. During the time of investigation, however, most of the enclosures showed broken floors containing lots of moss here and there. These make the floor very slippery, unhygienic and also insecure.

Apart from this, the drainage system of the two plantations under investigation seem to be very poor. During the rainy season the *Kutcha* by-lanes of the Divisions become water logged and filled with mud. The entrances of the houses become slippery with mud causing inconvenience and hindering easy accessibility.

Besides, cowsheds, are generally built attached to the dwelling houses. Even if these are built independently, the distances from the dwelling houses are very negligible. The manner of keeping the domestic animals too seem to have some adverse effects on the health of the people.

Food and Drink

Food stuff contains substances known as nutrients that perform various functions in the body. These include proteins, fats, carbohydrates, vitamins and mineral salts. Proteins, fats and carbohydrates are also sometimes called "proximate principles". Human beings require a sufficient amount of proximate principles, vitamins and minerals to enable them to live and thrive. A well balanced diet should contain all these factors in correct proportion and in adequate amount.

However, dietary habits in different areas have been determined mainly by the local availability of food items. Prescriptions and prohibitions of various items are also guided by cultural values and practices.

During the present investigation, it has been found that the basic diet of the people consists of rice, wheat (*atta*), vegetables and black tea with salt. Sometimes *dal* is also added to their food but not always.

Rice is the staple food; wheat (*atta*) is also taken regularly by the people. A reasonably large variety of vegetables, pumpkin, brinjal, ginger, onion, chilli, the flower of plantain and bamboo shoots, etc., are included in the diet. Meat, fish and eggs are taken occasionally. Fish is sometimes caught in the paddy fields, drains and ditches for domestic consumption. They eat pork, mutton or chicken once in a while when it is killed and sold in a *line* at very low price. The market price is substantially higher than that of the *line*. So, meat is very rarely purchased from the market by the people . The adults, irrespective of sex, working in the tea garden take principal meals twice a day; one meal before going to their duty and the other after returning from their duty. The children however, take their meals several times during the day.

Black tea with salt is also taken with two principal meals. Similarly, the labourers are provided with black tea with salt by the management also during their working hours.

Haria (locally made rice beer) is also taken throughout the day by the members of both the sexes. In this regard Roy (1975) observes that undistilled rice or millet beer usually has a high nutritive value and half a litre of rice beer supplies 5 to 10 percent of daily requirement of calories, proteins, iron, calcium and vitamin B_2. Yet, continuous excess intake of *haria* and other alcoholic drinks can lead one to alcoholism.

As a matter of fact, alcoholism is by and large considered a disease. Very often it affects the proper functioning of the brain. It provides a lot of empty calories without any nutritive value whatsoever. It is a depressant drug and slows down the activities of the brain.

In the context of tea garden workers Karotemprel, (1990: 398) observes, probably very rightly, " Alcoholism is a major social evil to be reckoned with. It leads to considerable absenteeism from work, poor productivity, family break down, and neglect of care of children, etc. Thoughtless spending, especially at the time of *Durga Puja*, impoverishes many families and reduces them to total misery".

During the present investigation, it has been observed that the people, irrespective of their sex, by and large are in the habit of taking alcoholic drinks, especially the locally fermented *haria*, more or less regularly. Some of them get so much addicted to it that they spend a major part of their earnings, very often at the cost of their basic needs, on *haria*. This affects not only their basic economic condition and health, but also the peace and tranquillity of the family. It may often lead to quarrels between husband and wife, sometimes leading to physical abuse of the wife. Incidentally, there are some extreme cases where the husbands entire income is spent on *haria*; and the wife has to manage the family expenditure from her own wages.

Case V. 1.

Hikoka was a permanent worker in Dhelakhat tea garden. He is an illiterate person and belongs to the Parjah community. He has five children. His wife, too, is a permanent worker in the same garden. Being very strongly addicted to alcohol, he frequently absented himself from work. As a result the management removed him from his job which was then offered to his wife on compassionate grounds. When he does not have enough money, he demands money from his wife for buying liquor.When she refuses to oblige him, it very often leads to violence including physical assault.

Case V.2.

Mundu is 40 years old and his wife is 38 years old. Both of them are illiterate and are working in Dirial tea garden. They have four children, one boy and three girls. The couple drink regularly, especially on payment days. On payment day they buy for the family, the minimum necessities and the rest of their earnings is spent on alcohol. During the present investigation, on a payment day it was found that the couple drank heavily and got intoxicated for a prolonged period of more than 15 hours. On the following day, in the morning, the 11 years old eldest son had to prepare food for his younger siblings. On enquiry, it was found that almost the entire amount was spent on alcohol and a meagre amount of only Rs. 40 was left behind. The wife said that she drank to oblige her husband, otherwise she would have been physically tortured.

Case V.3.

Maharati Tanti belongs to the Tanti community. He is 46 years old. He studied upto primary level and is working as a permanent labourer in Dirial tea garden. He has five children. His wife too is a permanent labourer. He drinks heavily and regularly. He never makes any financial contribution towards the maintenance of the family. None of his children are sent to school. With the meagre income of the wife, somehow she can manage only the minimum requirements for the survival of the family inmates.

Case V. 4.

Ramu is 42 years old and is a permanent labourer. He belongs to the Munda community. He studied upto class VIII. He has four children, two boys and two girls. He spends all his money on drinking.

His wife too is a permanent worker in the same garden. Often he fights and quarrels with his wife and beats the children when he is drunk. He also absents himself from work. The management has already warned him about his absence.

Case V.5.

Sankar aged 52 years is a temporary worker in Dirial tea estate. He is illiterate and belongs to the Munda community. He has three sons and one daughter. Though of age, none of them have yet married. Whatever he earns, he drinks and does not take care of his family. At the time of investigation, one evening at around 7.30 p.m, as he returned home intoxicated,, he started fighting with his wife and children. He used abusive words. As a result, his wife and children asked him to go away from the house, since the quarter belonged to the wife. They took out all his belongings and put them out of the house. But the following morning, he again returned home. As reported by the neighbours, similar episodes are recurrent features in Sankar's family.

Case V.6.

Sombari, aged 14 years, works as a temporary labourer in Dirial tea estate. She is illiterate. She also goes out daily, outside the garden in search of work during her off-days in the garden. She has three other sisters and one brother. Her father, aged 38 years, too, works in the garden. Whatever he earns he spends on alcohol. Her mother is a permanent worker. But she is unable to meet the entire expenditure of the family. As a result, Sombari, though young, has been compelled to explore earning sources to help her mother make ends meet in the family.

Health Scenario of Women

With regard to women's health, it may be noted that along with other usual factors like food and drink, personal hygiene and environmental sanitation, etc., reproductive performance and the nature of care taken during the reproductive activities are also important determinants.

In the following paragraphs, an attempt has been made to portray an overall qualitative idea about the health scenario of the womenfolk under investigation.

The women workers of the tea plantation often remain busy with their work in the tea beds for a larger part of the year. After the day's work, when they return to their homes, they have to perform almost every household chore. There is very limited time to take care of themselves. On the whole, the women workers, by and large, do not get time for recreation and relaxation. The situation however, is not identical with the menfolk. After finishing their work in the plantation, they generally spend the evening without any definite work to do.

This continuous excessive strain, coupled with an imbalanced and under-nutritious food habit, may probably have contributed towards the frequent incidence of a number of diseases among the women.

Most of the women workers have been found to suffer from diseases like backache, chest pain, knee pain, gastritis, cough and cold, etc. Interestingly, most of the respondents have taken these ailments as part and parcel of their working life, and as such, they generally do not go for any kind of treatment for the same.

As noted earlier, the nature of care taken during the reproductive activities is an important determinant of women's health. Necessary modification in the dietary habit is an important health care measure. It is a well known fact that the dietary behaviour of the mother during pregnancy has a profound effect on the nutrition of both the mother and the foetus. While some cultural factors forbid the intake of some food items, it is advised to increase the consumption of certain other things. However, the diet during pregnancy should be provided with a slightly higher level of proteins, calories, minerals and vitamins than is usually required for a woman.

During the present investigation, it has been observed that the people by and large, do not provide any special nutrient food to a woman, neither during pregnancy nor after the child-birth. They have also not been found to increase the quantity of food intake. It seems the people are not aware of the necessity of effecting dietary changes for the mother during pre-natal and post natal times.

In order to have an idea about their level of awareness of the necessity of better nutrient food during pregnancy and lactation, 100 women respondents were interviewed. The results reveal that more than 95 percent of the women are not aware of the fact that an expectant mother needs some extra care in respect of diet. They are, by and large, not aware of the fact that an expectant mother takes food not only for herself , but also for the foetus. Similarly, they do not seem to be well informed about the importance of the special care and attention needed for a nursing mother.

With regard to the fertility performance and health, it may be noted that the fertility rate of the mother has a direct bearing on her health. A large number of well- known scientists who carried out research in fertility and related issues, have pointed out that the general tendency among the women of developing countries is to have a large number of children. As it has been seen, one of the basic reasons behind this motive is that the women are not sure how many children will survive till the old age of the mother. Infant and child mortality is comparatively high in the developing countries due to inadequate care taken of a child. The studies conducted on fertility rate and survival rate among the Indian women show that in the rural areas nearly 1/4 to 1/3 of the children born are eliminated before they reach the reproductive age, only half of the children surviving till the old age of the parents (cited in Deka & Patojoshi, 1978).

Tables V.2, V.2.a, V.2.b, V.2.c and V.2.d. provide us with an overall idea about the number of live-births per mother in the population as a whole; and also those for each group separately.

It will be seen from Table No.V.2 that the average number of live-births in the population is 3.75. The distribution in the different groups however, is not uniform. It ranges from 2.89 (The Tanti) to

4.48 (the Christian Munda). The figure stands at 3.55 for the Non-Christian Munda and 4.03 for the Parjah.

The tables further show that the highest number of live-births in all the groups are observed among the mothers, in the age group 40 years and above'.

As reported by the medical practioners as well as by the elderly people of the plantations, pregnancy wastage due to abortion and still birth is very negligible in the population. But however, infant and child mortality is not very infrequent among them.

With regard to the child-birth, it may relevantly be noted here that the people, by and large, have been found to prefer home - delivery. In the hospital there are facilities for the safe and secure delivery, but the people prefer to have it at home with the assistance of untrained but experienced *dais* (midwives) hailing from among the tea labour community. Their reluctance to go to hospital for child-birth, seems mainly to be conservatism and shyness rather than any objective reason. As a result, in many cases, there arise complications that probably could have been avoided if the venue of delivery would have been the hospital.

Home delivery at times can lead not only to infant mortality, but also maternal death. During the course of the present investigation, incidentally, there was a home delivery which led to maternal death.

Case V. 7.

Rahil, aged 22 years, belonged to the Munda community. She was illiterate and was a temporary labourer in Dhelakhat tea estate. Rahil was keeping good health during the pregnancy period. Delivery took place at home. Her mother-in-law was a *dai budi* (mid-wife). She was reported to be an experienced woman and had handled many delivery cases successfully among the tea garden labourers. In fact, the birth of Rahil's child was normal. But after the delivery, the placenta did not fall. Immediately, seeing the danger, they sent for the ambulance of the garden. Though late, Rahil was taken to the civil hospital, 8 km. away from the garden in a very critical condition at around mid-night. The infant too was carried with her. Seeing such serious condition and due to the immediate non-availability of the physician at that odd hour, the inexperienced nurses asked the people to take her to another hospital. Meanwhile, Rahil expired, though the infant survived.

Before concluding our discussion on the health scenario of the women under investigation, it will probably be relevant to have an idea about the maternity benefits that a woman receives from her employer.

Under the Maternity Benefit Act, 1944, every woman who has worked directly under the employer for a period of 12 months preceding the date on which the notice was given by the expectant mother, is to be provided with maternity benefit in the form of leave for a maximum period of 12 weeks i.e. 4 weeks upto the day of delivery and 8 weeks mimediately following that day at the average rate of wage.

Table V. 2. Average Number of Live-Births per Mother in Different Age Groups

Age Group (years)	*Number of Children born alive*									*Total no. of mothers*	*Average no. of live-birth per mother*
	1	2	3	4	5	6	7	8	9		
1	2	3	4	5	6	7	8	9	10	11	12
15-19	2	3								5	1.6
20-24	10	12	6	1		1				30	2.07
25-29	3	10	11	10	3	1				38	3.08
30-34	3	3	10	11	2	4	3			36	3.83
35-39	4	10	17	21	12	6	3	3		76	3.95
40-44	2	3	9	11	10	5	4	1		45	4.33
45 & above	11	12	6	14	17	9	7	5	2	83	4.28
Total	35	53	59	68	44	26	17	9	2	313	3.75

Table V. 2.a Average Number of Live-Births per Mother in Different Age Groups (Christian Munda)

Age Group (years)	*Number of Children born alive*									*Total no. of mothers*	*Average no. of live-birth per mother*
	1	2	3	4	5	6	7	8	9		
1	2	3	4	5	6	7	8	9	10	11	12
15-19	-	1								1	2.00
20-24	3	4	1	-	-	-	-	-	-	8	1.75
25-29	-	1	-	1	2	-	-	-	-	4	4.00
30-34	1	-	1	2	-	2	1			7	4.43
35-39	1	-	4	4	3	3	2	-	-	17	4.47
40-44	-	-	1	3	2	2	-	-	-	8	4.63
45 & above	-	2	3	1	7	3	5	3	1	25	5.52
Total	5	8	10	11	14	10	8	3	1	70	4.48

Table V. 2.b Average Number of Live-Births per Mother in Different Age Groups (Non-Christian Munda)

Age Group (years)	*Number of Children born alive*									*Total no. of mothers*	*Average no. of live-birth per mother*
	1	2	3	4	5	6	7	8	9		
1	2	3	4	5	6	7	8	9	10	11	12
15-19	-	-	-	-	-	-	-	-	-	-	-
20-24	3	1	1	-	-	-	-	-	-	5	1.60
25-29	1	3	3	5	-	-	-	-	-	12	3.00
30-34	-	-	1	3	-	-	1	-	-	5	4.40
35-39	1	5	6	4	5	2	-	1	-	24	3.75
40-44	1	1	3	5	6	1	1	-	-	18	4.17
45 & above	5	6	-	10	6	2	-	-	-	29	3.41
Total	11	16	14	27	17	5	2	1	-	93	3.35

Table V. 2.c Average Number of Live-Births per Mother in Different Age Groups (Parjah)

Age Group (years)	Number of Children born alive 1	2	3	4	5	6	7	8	9	Total no. of mothers	Average no. of live-birth per mother
1	2	3	4	5	6	7	8	9	10	11	12
15-19	1	1	-	-	-	-	-	-	-	2	1.5
20-24	1	4	2	1	-	-	-	-	-	8	2.37
25-29	2	5	4	2	1	2	-	-	-	16	3.06
30-34	2	-	6	3	2	2	1	-	-	16	3.81
35-39	2	-	2	8	4	-	1	2	-	19	4.37
40-44	1	-	2	-	1	2	3	1	-	10	5.30
45 & above	2	2	-	1	4	3	2	2	1	17	5.12
Total	11	12	16	15	12	9	7	5	1	88	4.03

Table V. 2.d Average Number of Live-Births per Mother in Different Age Groups (Tanti)

Age Group (years)	Number of Children born alive 1	2	3	4	5	6	7	8	9	Total no. of mothers	Average no. of live-birth per mother
1	2	3	4	5	6	7	8	9	10	11	12
15-19	1	1	-	-	-	-	-	-	-	2	1.50
20-24	3	3	2	-	-	1	-	-	-	9	2.33
25-29	-	1	4	2	-	-	-	-	-	7	3.14
30-34	-	3	2	3	-	-	-	-	-	8	3.00
35-39	-	5	5	5	-	1	-	-	-	16	3.19
40-44	-	2	3	3	1	-	-	-	-	9	3.33
45 & above	4	2	3	2	-	1	-	-	-	12	2.58
Total	8	17	19	15	1	3	-	-	-	63	2.89

The Maternity Benefit Act, 1961, as a matter of fact, applies to every establishment, be it a factory, or mine or a plantation except those factories or establishments to which the provision of Employee's State Insurance Act, 1948 applies. All the Maternity Benefit Acts provide maternity benefits to women workers on conditions prescribed under the Act.

The period of qualifying services to avail of maternity benefits in Assam is 150 days. The Assam Act merely provides for free medical aid during the period of confinement. Subject to the provision of the Act, maternity benefit shall be granted to woman workers which will include a daily cash allowance and the usual food concession during the period of 4 weeks preceding the day of delivery and 4-8 weeks after the date of delivery.

Any woman, entitled to maternity benefit under this Act, may give notice of her expected confinement to her employer orally or in writing either herself or by any of her relations. On receipt of such notice the employer shall record it in writing if the notice was received orally and enter the particulars of each case in the register in form B appended to the Maternity Benefit Rules and record his comments as to whether he admits the claim and also the probable date of confinement after getting the woman examined medically, if necessary. The employer shall obtain the medical certificate from the medical practioner and shall file it with the record.

An employer may not dismiss a woman during this period for which she is entitled to be absent from work under provision of the Act, and if a notice of dismissal is given without sufficient cause within a period of six months before her delivery, she shall be entitled to maternity benefits.

No employer shall knowingly employ a woman in any employment during the 4 weeks preceeding the day of her delivery, save upon such light work as may be endorsed by the medical practitioner.

With regard to the nature and extent of implementation of Maternity Benefit Act as well as other provisions of medical facilities, the observations during the present investigation are of mixed nature. In both the plantations, an expected mother is generally provided with leave for 12 weeks (4 weeks before; and 8 weeks after the birth of a child) with full wage. Besides, free medical services are also provided to the pregnant women. They are examined in the plantation hospitals at regular intervals, and are administered with requisite antitetanus injections, vitamins and iron tonic, etc. It has however, been observed that the Dirial Central Hospital has relatively better health care facilities as compared to those in the Dhelakhat Hospital.

With a view to having an idea about the level of satisfaction of the beneficiaries with the available health care services, one hundred respondents were interviewed to share their feelings in this regard.

The answers were confined to two alternatives, viz "satisfactory" and "not satisfactory" services. The opinions have been presented in Table no.V.3. It is apparent from the table that the majority of the respondents (63.00%) are not satisfied with the services. Besides the dearth of proper infrastructural. facilities (in terms of instruments etc.) for examining the patients (particularly in Dhelakhat hospital), they maintain that proper medicines are not provided for various diseases. Interestingly, many of the respondents are of the opinion that the same medicine is administered for different types of ailments. From Table V.3 it is also seen that 72.00% of the Non-Christian Munda respondents have paradoxically expressed satisfaction with the prevailing medical services. Probably they are not aware of the better facilities that they could receive from the management. 'Satisfaction' also could be due to the acceptance of the situation in which they are living.

Table V. 3. Distribution of the respondents according to their opinions regarding the medical services

Responses	*Number of respondents*				*Total*
	Christian	*Non-Munda*	*Parjah Christian Munda*	*Tanti*	
1	2	3	4	5	6
Satisfactory	3	18	6	10	37
Not Satisfactory	22	7	19	15	63
Total	25	25	25	25	100

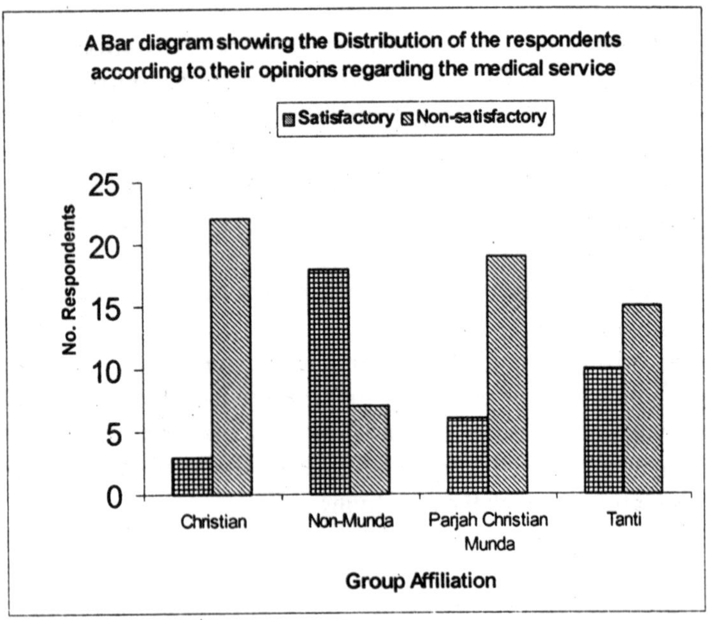

Figure No. V.1.

Education

Education has always been considered to be a very important dimension of any agenda for development programmes in a society. With the socio-economic and the political evolution of mankind and its growth in consciousness, education has been gradually recognized as a "human right."

The 1966 International Covenant on Economic, Social and Cultural Rights adds, among other things, that education shall enable all persons to participate effectively in a free society and that the secondary and higher education, on the basis of capacity, shall be made accessible to all by every appropriate means, and in particular by the progressive introduction of free education (Desrochers, 1987).

The Constitution of India, too, acknowledges the right of all to education (Art.4 1) and set up the target of universal elementary education by 1960. "The state shall endeavour to provide, within a period of ten years . . . , for free and compulsory education for all children until they complete the age of 14 years" (Art.45). The Constitution also desires the state to "promote with special care the educational and economic interests of the weaker section of the people, and, in particular, of the SCs and the STs" (Art 46 and 15.4).

Notwithstanding all these constitutional provisions, it seems, illiteracy is one of the most crucial problems of development faced by many developing countries including India. Asia has the largest number of illiterates. In absolute terms in 1970 there were 540 million illiterates; in 1980 there were 599 million and in 1990 there were 654 million illiterates (cited in Digniurti and Digmurti, 1998).

According to the 1991 census the illiteracy percentage was 47.79 (Men: 3 5.80, women : 60.8 1). The tremendous increase in population has contributed to the increase in the number of illiterates. The apparent shocking reality is that over 50 million children in India do not go to school, and of those who do, nearly 40% drop out along the way (Singh and Rajya Lakshmi, 1993).

The situation is still gloomier especially among the backward classes including the tea labourers. As revealed by the data, generated from the field, in the following pages, an attempt has been made to have an idea about the level of education among the people under investigation, with special reference to women.

Educational Attainment of the People

Data on educational attainment of the people as a whole has been presented in Table no. V.4.

Table V.4. A comparative Analysis of Literacy Rate of the Population under Investigation

Sl. No	Ethnic/ Religious Group	Men	Literate	%*	Women	Literate	%	Total	Literate	%
1	2	3	4	5	6	7	8	9	10	11
1	Christian Munda	252	144	57.14	233	80	34.33	458	224	46.19
2	Non - Christian Munda	289	58	20.07	292	21	7.19	581	79	13.60
3	Sub total	541	202	37.34	525	101	19.24	1066	303	28.42
4	Parjah	282	62	21.99	272	34	12.5	554	96	17.33
5	Tanti	181	76	41.99	174	33	18.97	355	109	30.70
6	Grand Total	1004	340	33.86	971	167	17.20	1975	507	25.67

* Percentage calculation in this table has been made sex-wise.

It will. be seen from the table that the literacy rate for the entire group is 25.67% (Men: 33.86%, Women: 17.20%). The table further shows that the two Munda groups (The Christian and the Non-Christian) have both the highest and the lowest literacy rates. It is 46.19% (Men : 57.14% Women: 34.33%) among the Christian, and 13.60% (Men: 20.07%, Women: 7.19%) among the NonChristian Mundas. If the two groups are taken together, the percentage stands at 28.42 (Men : 37.34%, Women : 19.24%) which is slightly less than that of the Tantis which stands at 30.70% (Men: 41.99%,

A 3-D column Bar diagram showing a comparative analysis of Literacy Rate of the population under investigation

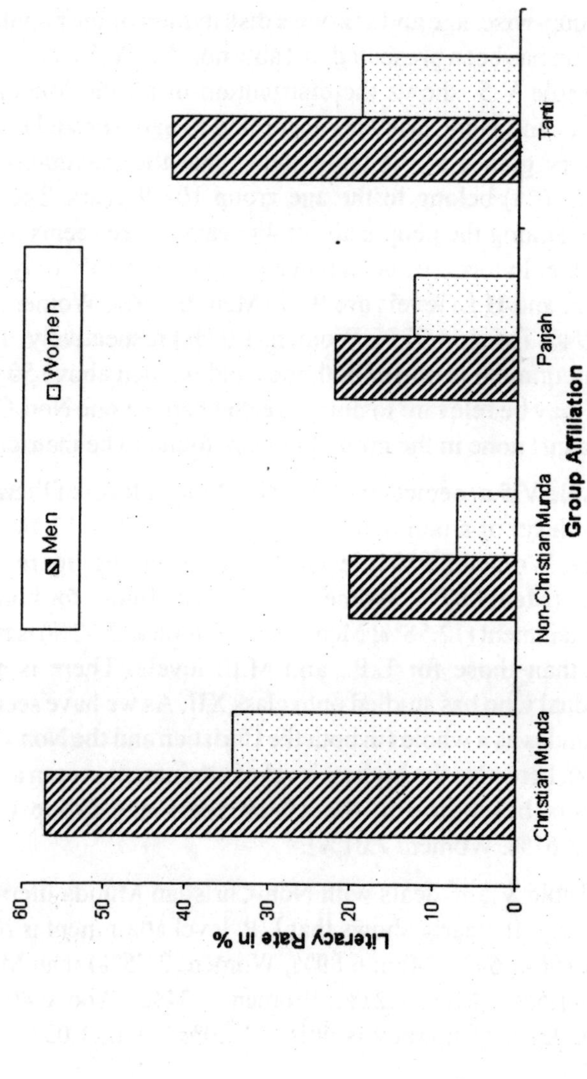

Figure No. V.2.

Women : 18.97%). The Parjah's literacy rate is 17.33% (Men : 21.90%, Women: 12.50%) which is slightly above that of the Non-Christian Munda.

Group-wise, age and sex-wise distribution of the population by education has been presented in Table nos. V.5,V.5a,V.5b,V5c and V5d. Table V.5. shows the distribution of all the Mundas (both Christian and NonChristian) according to age, sex and education. A cursory glance at the table shows that the maximum number (136,12.76%) belong to the age group 10-19 years. The level of literacy among the people above 40 years of age seems to be very negligible. In terms of percentage it stands at 3.85% only. Figures for M.E. and H.E. levels are 9.01 (Men: 6. 10%, Women: 2.91%) and 6.94% (Men: 4.97%, Women: 1.97%) respectively. The H.E. level attainment is nil for both men and women above 50 years of age. It may be relevant to note here that barring one Non-Christian Munda girl none in the group has been found to be matriculate.

Table V.5.a. depicts the Christian Munda level of literacy. The highest level of attainment of literacy is in M.E. (17.94%; Men : 11.96%, Women:5.98%) level. At L.P. level, the figure stands at 15.67% (Men:9.07%, Women-6.60%) The figure for high school level attainment (12.58%; Men: 8.66%, Women: 3.92%) is relatively lower than those for L.P., and M.E. levels. There is also one individual who has studied upto class XII. As we have seen among the Mundas as a whole (in both the Christian and the Non-Christian groups), here also the highest level of attainment is seen among the members belonging to the 10-19 years age group (20.62%; Men:13.61%, Women: 7.01%).

Table V.5.b. deals with Non-Christian Munda literacy level separately. It clearly shows that L.P. level attainment is relatively higher (56-9.64%; Men: 6.89%, Women: 2.75%) than M.E. level one (5-1.55%; Men: 1.21%, Women: 0.34%). Above 40 years of age the level of literacy is only 7-1.20% (Men: 1.03%, Women: 0.17%).

Table V.5.c. depicts the level of literacy among the Parjah. Here too, we find that the majority of the literates are in L.P. standard (50-9.03%; Men:5.60%, Women: 3.43%). It will be interesting to note here that in the M.E. level of literacy, the percentages of the members of both the sexes are more or less at par (Men : 3.25%, Women : 2.7 1 %). Again, as has been observed among the Mundas, the maximum number of literates among the Parjahs also belong to the age group 10-19 years. The table also reveals that barring two men and a woman, none of the people above 45 years of age (total no. 67) is literate.

Table V5.d. shows the literacy level of the Tantis. As is observed in the other groups, the majority of the literates (12.96%; Men : 8.45%, Women:4.51%) belong to the L.P. standard. Numerical strengths of the members attaining M.E. and H.E. levels of education are relatively insignificant. The figure for M.E. is 9.02% (Men : 5.92%, Women : 3. 10%) and that for H.E. is 9.30% (Men: 7.32%, Women: 1.98%). The table further shows that in this group too, the highest level of attainment is observed among the members belonging to the age group 10-19 years of age.

While making a group-wise probe of the data, it is seen that the level of the caste group (i.e. the Tanti) literacy is relatively better than those of the tribes (i.e. the Mundas and the Parjahs). When a comparison is made between the two tribes only, it is seen that the Mundas are relatively in an advantageous position as compared to the Parjahs. Within the Mundas again, there is a conspicuous difference between the Christians and the NonChristians. It is 13.60% for the Non-Christians, whereas it is 46.19% for the Christians. Thus, the Non-Christian Mundas and the Parjahs seem to be more or less at par in this regard. This variation between these two groups seem to be in conformity with the observations made in this regard among many other Indian tribes where Christianity predominates. Thus, for example, the literacy rate among the Naga tribes, the Mizos and the Khasis which is around 40.00% is much higher than the national average for ST population which is 23.63% (Kar, 1996 : 384).

Table V. 5. Distribution of the Munda Population by Sex, Age and Education

Sl. No.	Age Group (in yrs)	All ages			L.P			M.E.			H.E.			All Levels Total		
		Male	Female	Total	Male	Female	Total	Male	Female	Total	Male	Female	Total	Male	Female	Total
1	2	3	4	5	6	7	8	9	10	11	12	13	14	15	16	17
1	0-4	69 (6.47)	61 (5.72)	130 (12.20)	-	-	-	-	-	-	-	-	-	-	-	-
2	5-9	66 (6.19)	66 (6.19)	132 (12.38)	23 (2.16)	15 (1.41)	38 (3.56)	1 (0.09)	-	1 (0.09)	-	-	-	24 (2.25)	15 (1.41)	39 (3.66)
3	10-14	83 (7.79)	75 (7.04)	158 (14.82)	24 (2.25)	16 (1.50)	40 (3.75)	16 (1.50)	5 (0.47)	21 (1.97)	5 (0.47)	2 (0.19)	7 (0.66)	45 (4.22)	23 (2.16)	68 (6.38)
4	15-19	73 (6.85)	65 (6.10)	138 (12.95)	10 (0.94)	4 (0.38)	14 (1.31)	23 (2.16)	11 (1.03)	34 (3.19)	13 (1.22)	7 (0.66)	20 (1.88)	46 (4.32)	22 (2.06)	68 (6.38)
5	20-24	37 (3.47)	42 (3.94)	79 (7.41)	3 (0.28)	1 (0.09)	4 (0.38)	7 (0,66)	5 (0.47)	12 (1.13)	13 (1.22)	5 (0.47)	18 (1,69)	23 (2.16)	11 (1.03)	34 (3.19)
6	25-29	36 (3.38)	48 (4.50)	84 (7.88)	1 (0.09)	2 (0.19)	3 (0.28)	5 (0.47)	5 (0.47)	10 (0.94)	5 0.47)	5 (0.47)	10 (0.94)	11 (1.03)	12 (1.13)	23 (2.16)
7	30-34	22 (2.06)	16 (1.50)	38 (3.56)	2 (0.19)	2 (0.19)	4 (0.48)	-	2 (0.19)	2 (0.19)	5 (0.47)	-	5 (0.47)	7 (0.66)	5 (0.47)	12 (1.13)

8	35-39	25 (2.35)	48 (4.50)	73 (6.85)	4 (0.38)	2 (0.19)	6 (0.56)	3 (0.28)	1 (0.09)	4 (0.38)	7 (0.66)	1 (0.09)	8 (0.75)	14 (1.31)	4 (0.38)	18 (1.69)
9	40-44	32 (3.00)	33 (3.10)	65 (6.10)	-	1 (0-09)	1 (0.09)	3 (0.28)	-	3 (0.28)	2 (0.19)	-	2 (0.19)	5 (0.47)	1 (0.09)	6 (0.56)
10	45-49	36 (3.38)	29 (2.72)	65 (6.10)	2 (0.19)	1 (0.09)	3 (0.28	1 (0.09)	1 (0.09)	2 (0.19)	3 (0.28)	1 (0.09)	4 (0.36)	6 (0.56)	3 (0.28)	9 (0.84)
11	50-54	22 (2.06)	15 (1.41)	37 (3.47)	3 (0.28)	3 (0.28)	6 (0,56)	3 (0.28)	1 (0.09)	4 (0.38)	-	-	-	6 (0.56)	4 (0.38)	10 (0.94)
12	55-59	18 (1.69)	8 (0,75)	26 (2.44)	7 (0.66)	-	7 (0.66)	2 (0.19)	-	2 (0.19)	-	-	-	9 (0.84)	-	9 (0.84)
13	60 and above	22 (2.06)	19 (1.78)	41 (3.85)	5 (0.47)	1 (0.09)	6 (0.56)	1 (0.09)	-	1 (0.09)	-	-	-	6 (0.56)	1 (0.09)	7 (0.66)
14	Total	541 (50.75)	525 (49.25)	1066 (100.00)	84 (7.88)	48 (4.50)	132 (12.38)	65 (6.10)	31 (2.91)	96 (9.01)	53 (4.97)	21 (1.97)	74 (6.94)	202 (18.95)	101 (9.47)	303 (28.42)

Table V. 5.a Distribution of the Christian Munda Population by Sex, Age and Education

Sl. No.	Age Group (in yrs)	All ages			L.P			M.E.			H.E.			All Levels Total		
		Male	Female	Total	Male	Female	Total	Male	Female	Total	Male	Female	Total	Male	Female	Total
1	2	3	4	5	6	7	8	9	10	11	12	13	14	15	16	17
1	0-4	31 (6.39)	24 (4.95)	55 (11.34)	-	-	-	-	-	-	-	-	-	- -	-	-
2	5-9	21 (4.33)	24 (4.95)	45 (9.28)	11 (2.27)	10 (2.06)	21 4.33	1 (0.21)	-	1 (0.21)	-	-	-	12 (2.47)	10 (2.06)	22 (4.53)
3	10-14	34 (7.01)	31 (6.39)	65 (13.40)	10 (2.06)	9 (1.85)	19 (3.92)	15 (3.09)	5 (1.03)	20 (4.12)	5 (1.03)	1 (0.21)	6 (1.24)	30 (6.19)	15 (3.09)	45 (9.28)
4	15-19	43 (8.87)	28 (5.77)	71 (14.64)	7 (1.44)	3 (0.62)	10 (2.06)	20 (4.12)	to (2.06)	30 (6.18)	9 (1. 85)	6 (1.24)	15 (3.09)	36 (7.42)	19 (3.92)	55 (11.34)
5	20-24	24 (4.95)	25 (5.15)	49 (10.10)	1 (0.21)	1 (0.21)	2 (0.41)	6 (1.24)	4 (0.82)	10 (2.06)	11 (2.27)	5 (1.03)	16 (3.30)	18 (3.71)	10 (2.06)	28 (5.77)
6	25-29	20 (4.12)	27 (5.57)	47 (9.69)	-	1 (0.21)	1 (0.21)	4 (0.82)	5 (1.03)	9 (1.85)	4 (0.82)	5 (1.03)	9 (1.86	8 (1.65)	11 (2.27)	19 (3.92)
7	30-34	11 (2.27)	9 (1.85)	2 (4.12)	1 (0.21)	2 (0.41)	3 (0.62)	-	2 (0.41)	2 (0.41)	4 (0.82)	-	4 (0.82)	5 (1.03)	4 (0.82)	9 (1.85)

8 35-39	13 (2.68)	20 (4.12)	33 (6.80)	2 (0.41)	1 (0.21)	3 (0.62)	2 (0.41)	1 (0.21)	3 (0.62)	5 (1.03)	1 (0.21)	6 (1.24)	9 (1.85)	3 (0.62)	12 (2.47)
9 40-44	12 (2.47)	10 (2.06)	22 (4.53)	-	1 (0.21)	1 (0.21)	3 (0.62)	-	3 (0.62)	2 (0.41)	-	2 (0.41)	5 (1.03)	1 (0.21)	6 (1.24)
1045-49	10 (2.06)	15 (3.09)	25 (5.16)	1 (0.21)	-	1 (0.21)	1 (0.21)	1 (0.21)	2 (0.41)	2 (0.41)	1 (0.21)	3 (0.62)	4 (0.82)	2 (0.41)	6 (2.06)
11 50-54	13 (2.68)	11 (2.27)	24 (4.95)	3 (0.62)	3 (0.62)	6 (1.24)	3 (0.62)	1 (0.21)	4 (0.82)	-	-	-	6 (1.24)	4 (0.82)	10 (0.26)
1255-59	11 (2.27)	4 (0.82)	15 (3.09)	6 (1.24)	-	6 (1.24)	2 (0.41)	-	2 (0.41)	-	-	-	8 (1.69)	-	8 (1.69)
13 60 & above	9 (1.85)	5 (1.03)	14 (2.88)	2 (0.41)	1 (0.21)	3 (0.62)	1 (0.21)	-	1 (0.21)	-	-	-	3 (0.62)	1 (0.21)	4 (0.82)
14 Total	252 (51.95)	233 (48.04)	485 (100.00)	44 (9.07)	32 (6.60)	76 (15.67)	58 (11.96)	29 (5.98)	87 (17.94)	49 (8.66)	19 (3.92)	61 (12.58)	145 (29.900)	80 (16.49)	255 (46.39)

Table V. 5.b Distribution of the Non-Christian Munda Population by Sex, Age and Education

Sl. No.	Age Group (in yrs)	All ages			L.P			M.E.			H.E.			All Levels Total		
		Male	Female	Total	Male	Female	Total	Male	Female	Total	Male	Female	Total	Male	Female	Total
1	2	3	4	5	6	7	8	9	10	11	12	13	14.	15	16	17
1	0-4	38 (6.54)	37 (6.37)	75 (12.91)	-	-	-	-	-	-	-	-	-	-	-	-
2	5-9	45 (7.75)	42 (7.23)	87 (14.97)	12 (2.07)	5 (0.86)	17 (2.93)	-	-	-	-	-	-	12 (2.07)	5 (0.86)	17 (2.93)
3	10-14	49 (8.43)	44 (7.57)	93 (16.01)	14 (2.41)	7 (1.20)	21 (3.61)	1 (0.17)	-	1 (0.17)	-	1 (0.17)	1 (0.17)	15 (2.58)	8 (1.38)	23 (3.96)
4	15-19	30 (5.16)	37 (6.37)	67 (11.53)	3 (0.52)	1 (0.17)	4 (0.69)	3 (0.52)	1 (0.17)	4 (0.69)	4 (0.69)	1 (0.17)	5 (0.86)	10 (1.72)	3 (0.52)	13 (2.24)
5	20-24	13 (2.24)	17 (2.93)	30 (5.16)	2 (0.34)	-	2 (0.34)	1 (0.17)	1 (0.17)	2 (0.34)	2 (0.34)	-	2 (0.34)	5 (0.86)	1 (0.17)	6 (1.03)
6	25-29	16 (2.75)	21 (3.61)	37 (6.37)	1 (0.17)	1 (0.17)	2 (0.34)	1 (0.17)	-	1 (0.17)	1 (0.17)	-	1 (0.17)	3 (1.52)	1 (0.17)	4 (0.69)
7	30-34	11 (1.89)	7 (1.21)	18 (3.10)	1 (0.17)	-	1 (0.17)	-	-	-	1 (0.17)	-	1 (0.17)	2 (0.34)	1 (0.17)	3 (0.52)

8 35-39	12 (2.07)	28 (4.82)	40 (6.89)	2 (0.34)	1 (0.17)	3 (0.52)	1 (0.17)	-	1 (0.17)	2 (0.34)	-	2 (0.34)	5 (0.86)	1 (0.17)	6 (1.03)
9 40-44	20 (3.34)	23 (3.96)	43 (7.40)	-	-	-	-	-	-	-	-	-	-	-	-
10 45-49	26 (4.26)	14 (2.41)	40 (6.89)	1 (0.17)	1 (0.17)	2 (0.34)	-	-	-	1 (0.17)	-	1 (0.17)	2 (0.34)	1 (0.17)	3 (0.52)
11 50-54	9 (1.55)	4 (0.69)	13 (2.24)	-	-	-	-	-	-	-	-	-	-	-	-
12 55-59	7 (1.20)	4 (0.69)	11 (1.89)	1 (0.17)	-	1 (0.17)	-	-	-	-	-	-	1 (0.17)	-	1 (0.17)
13 60 and above	13 (2.24)	14 (2.41)	27 (4.65)	3 (0.52)	-	3 (0.52)	-	-	-	-	-	-	1 (0.17)	-	1 (0.17)
14 Total	289 (49.74)	292 (50.26)	581 (100.00)	40 (6.89)	16 (2.75)	56 (9.64)	7 (1.21)	2 (0.34)	9 (1.54)	11 (1.89)	2 (0.34)	13 (2.24)	52 (9.98)	21 (3.61)	79 (13.60)

Table V. 5.c Distribution of the Parjah Population by Sex, Age and Education

Sl. No.	Age Group (in yrs)	All ages			L.P			M.E.			H.E.			All Levels Total		
		Male	Female	Total	Male	Female	Total	Male	Female	Total	Male	Female	Total	Male	Female	Total
1	2	3	4	5	6	7	8	9	10	11	12	13	14	15	16	17
1	0-4	51 (9.21)	47 (8.48)	98 (17.69)	-	-	-	-	-	-	-	-	-	-	-	-
2	5-9	38 (6.86)	31 (5.59)	69 (1145)	6 (1.08)	3 (0.54)	9 (1.62)	-	1 (0.18)	1 (0.18)	-	-	-	6 (1-08)	4 (0.72)	10 (1.81)
3	10-14	28 (5.05)	46 (8.30)	74 (13.35)	10 (1.81)	9 (1.62)	19 (3.43)	4 (0.72)	6 (1.08)	10 (1.81)	1 (0.18)	-	1 (0.18)	15 (2.71)	15 (2.71)	30 (5,40)
4	15-19	31 (5.60)	30 (5.41)	61 (11.01)	1 (0.18)	4 (0.72)	5 (0.90)	8 (1.44)	3 (0.54)	11 (1.98)	4 (90.72)	-	4 (0.72)	13 (2.35)	7 (1.26)	20 (3.61)
5	20-24	17 (3.07)	20 (3.61)	37 (6.68)	2 (0.36)	2 (0.36)	4 (0.72)	1 (0.18)	2 90.36)	3 (0.54)	1 (0.18)	-	1 (0.18)	4 (0.72)	4 (0.72)	8 (1.44)
6	25-29	20 (3.61)	21 (3.79)	41 (7.40)	4 (0.72)	-	4 (0.72)	1 (0.18)	1 (0.180	2 90.36)	2 (0.360	1 (0-18)	3 (0.54)	7 (1,26)	2 90.36)	9 (1.62)
7	30-34	20 (3.61)	18 (3.25)	38 (6.86)	-	-	-	2 (0.36)	2 (0.36)	4 (0.72)	4 (0.72)	-	4 (0.72)	6 (1.08)	2 (0.36)	8 (1.44)

8	35-39	22 (3.97)	20 (3.61)	42 (7.58)	3 (0.54)	1 (0.18)	4 (0.712)	1 (0.18)	-	1 (0.18)	-	-	-	4 (0.72)	1 (0.18)	5 (0.90)
9	40-44	14 (2.53)	13 (2.35)	27 (4.88)	3 (0.54)	-	3 (0.54)	-	-	-	1 (0.18)	-	1 (0.18)	4 (0.72)	-	4 (0.72)
10	45-49	10 (1.81)	7 (1.26)	17 (3.07)	-	-	-	1 (0.18)	-	1 (0.18)	-	-	-	1 (0.18)	-	1 (0.18)
11	50-54	10 (1.81)	5 (0.90)	15 (2.71)	2 (0.36)	-	2 (0.36)	-	-	-	-	-	-	2 (0.36)	-	2 (0.36)
12	55-59	9 (1.62)	6	15 (1.08)	-	-	-	-	-	-	-	-	-	-	-	-
13	60 and above	12 (2.17)	8 (1.44)	20 (3.61)	-	-	-	-	-	-	-	-	-	-		
14	Total	282 (50.90)	272 (49.10)	554 (100.00)	31 (5.60)	19 (3.43)	50 (9. 3)	18 (3.25)	15 (2.71)	33 (5.96)	13 (2.35)	1 (0.18)	14 (2.53)	62 (11.19)	35 (6.32)	97 (17.51)

Table V. 5.d Distribution of the Tanti Population by Sex, Age and Education

Sl. No.	Age Group (in yrs)	All ages			L.P			M.E.			H.E.			All Levels Total		
		Male	Female	Total	Male	Female	Total	Male	Female	Total	Maie	Female	Total	Male	Female	Total
1	2	3	4	5	6	7	8	9	10	11	12	13	14	15	16	17
1	0-4	30 (8.45)	30 (8.45)	60 (16.90)	2 (0.56)	-	2 (0.56)	-	-	-	-	-	-	2 (0.56)	-	2 (0.56)
2	5-9	19 (5.35)	16 (4.51)	35 (9.86)	4 (1.13)	7 (1.97)	11 (3.10)	-	-	-	-	-	-	4 (1.13)	7 (1.97)	11 (3.10)
3	10-14	18 (5.07)	23 (6.48)	41 (11.55)	1 (0.28)	8 (2.25)	9 (2.54)	6 (1.69)	2 (0.56)	8 (2.25)	3 (0.85)	1 (0.28)	4 (1.13)	10 (2.82)	11 (3.10)	21 (5.92)
4	15-19	23 (6.48)	19 (5.35)	42 (11.83)	5 (1.41)	-	5 (1.41)	4 (1.13)	3 (0.85)	7 (1.97)	5 (1.41)	3 (0.85)	8 (2.25)	14 (3.94)	6 (1.69)	20 (5.63)
5	20-24	8 (2.25)	15 (4.23)	23 (6.48)	-	-	-	-	3 (0.85)	3 (0.85)	4 (1.13)	3 (0.85)	7 (0.47)	4 (1.13)	6 (1.69)	10 (2.82)
6	25-29	14 (3.94)	9 (2.54)	23 (6.48)	3 (0.85)	-	3 (0.85)	4 (1.13)	-	4 (0.85)	3 (1.13)	-	3 (0.85)	11 (3.10)	-	11 (3.10)
7	30-34	10 (2.82)	8 (2.25)	18 (5.07)	2 (0.56)	-	2 (0.56)	-	1 (0.28)	1 (0.28)	2 (0.56)	-	2 (0.56)	4 (1.13)	1 (0.28)	5 (1.41)

8	35-39	12 (3.38)	19 (5.35)	31 (8.73)	3 (0.85)	-	3 (0.85)	3 (0.85)	-	3 (0.85)	1 (0.66)	-	1 (0.28)	7 (1.97)	-	7 (1.97)
9	40-44	6 (1.69)	10 (2.82)	16 (4.51)	1 (0.28)	1 (0.28)	2 (0.56)	-	-	-	2 (0.56)	-	2 (0.56)	3 (0.89)	1 (0.28)	4 (1.13)
10	45-49	15 (4.23)	3 (0.85)	18 (5.07)	3 (0.85)	-	3 (0.85)	3 (0.85)	-	3 (0.85)	4 (1.13)	-	4 (1.13)	10 (2.82)	-	10 (2.82)
11	50-54	8 (2.25)	5 (1.41)	13 (3.66)	2 (0.56)	-	2 (0.56)	1 (0.28)	-	1	-	-	-	3 (0.85)	-	3 (0.85)
12	55-59	6 (1.69)	3 (0.85)	9 (2.56)	2 (0.56)	-	2 (0.56)	-	1 (0.28)	1 (0.28)	1 (0.28)	-	1 (0.28)	3 (0.85)	1 (0.28)	4 (1.13)
13	60 and above	12 (3.38)	14 (3.94)	26 (7.32)	2 (0.56)	-	2 (0.56)	-	1 (0.28)	1 (0.28)	1 (0.28)	-	1 (0.28)	3 (0.85)	1 (0.28)	4 (1.13)
14	Total	181 (50.99)	174 (49.01)	355 (100.00)	30 (8.45)	16 (4.51)	46 (12.96)	21 (5.92)	11 (3.10)	32 (9.02)	26 (7.32)	7 (1.97)	33 (9.30)	77 (21.69)	33 (9.30)	110 (30.99)

With regard to the positive influence of Christianity on the level of literacy, it may be noted that the Christian labourers have a better exposure to the wider world. Not only do they receive instructions on qualitative importance of education, but also the religious leaders interact with them at regular intervals and impress upon them the need of formal education. Even in other spheres like health, hygiene, etc., also they seem to lead a better life as compared to their Non-Christian counterparts.

It may also be noted here that many boys also do not go to school or discontinue going to school any time after their enrolment. On enquiry, it has been found that in some cases, the very infrastructural facilities in the garden schools fail to motivate the students to continue the formal education; and in many other cases the family environment acts as a negative factor.

Case V.8

George, aged 20 years, belongs to the Munda community. He is a permanent worker in Dirial tea garden. He read upto class VIII. His father who was working as a permanent worker in the same garden, was asked to resign due to his heavy drinking habit, which resulted in frequent absenteeism. As a result, George was forced to discontinue his studies so as to take up the work in the garden in his father's place.

Case V.9

Kumar is 18 years old. He is a temporary worker in Dhelakhat tea garden. He belongs to the Parjah community. He read up to class II and discontinued his studies because of his lack of interest. He says that by going to school, he does not gain anything. But if he works, he can earn something. His parents too did not encourage him to continue his study.

Case V.10.

Govind, aged 26 years, belongs to the Tanti community. He is illiterate and works as a permanent labourer in Dhelakhat tea garden.

His parents also work in the same tea garden. His parents strongly desired him to study, as he was the eldest son in the family. They got him admitted into class I. He attended the school only for a month and then discontinued his studies. The reason, as stated by him is that the school environment was not encouraging. His parents, however, tried their best to make him continue his studies, but without success.

Case V.11.

Narendra, aged 21 years, belongs to the Tanti community. He is the only son of the family. He studied up to class X1. At present he is working as a permanent worker in Dirial tea garden. Despite his sincere desire to continue further studies, he had to take up the garden job because of the premature death of his father. Some one year back his father died. As a result, he was compelled to enter into garden work in order to maintain the family consisting of his mother and two younger siblings.

Thus, sometimes, because of the premature death of the father, a son is to take responsibility of the family by being employed in the garden on compassionate grounds. In such situations,even boys who would like to study, sometimes cannot continue formal schooling.

While conducting group interviews on the issue, a good number of people stated that the authorities in the garden hardly provide even the minimum facilities for education. As a general convention, a plantation, by and large, has provision only for an L.P. school within its jurisdiction. But here, too, the minimum infrastructural facilities are not available. Sometimes, the location of the school creates a problem for the small children. The young children are very often not able to cover a distance of around two km on foot to reach the school. This difficulty increases during the rainy season, when the road is bad and slushy. As reported by many of the respondents, they can't send their children even to the L.P. school because of these conditions.

In Dhelakhat tea estate, most of the Parjahs reside at the extreme end of the garden, where the level of the land is very low. During the rainy season, the entire area gets flooded and the children are unable to continue their studies for almost three to four months. This is a recurring disrupting factor for their children' s education.

Women & Education

An educated woman almost always has more value and status in the eyes of her family and her community. She is more likely to share in family decisions about how many children to have, how to bring them up, how to spend money, how to organise domestic affairs, etc. Educating a woman has great social benefit and has enormous economic advantages as well. She can raise a healthier family. She not only knows about nutrition, but may help in responding to health-related emergencies. Education, thus, is considered to be essential in order to raise the status of women in the family and society, as well as to improve the quality of family and social life.

According to Digmurti & Digmurti, (1998) educating women is a high return investment in socio-economic development for society as a whole since by educating a woman, one is in effect enriching an entire family. Again, the Zambian Declaration on Girl Child Education states that the high levels of adult illiteracy represent profound personal privations for the large number of people who are not able to read, write or make simple numerical computations. Their state of illiteracy also has a bearing on the education of the next generation.... In particular, mothers who cannot read and write, or who are basically non-numerate, may not show great concern if their daughters do not find a place in school and may readily agree to their withdrawal once they reach marriageable age.

Realising the importance of women's education, the University Education Commission, 1948-49 stated, "There cannot be educated people without educated women. If general education had to be limited either to men or to women, that opportunity should be given to women, for then, it would most surely be passed on to the next generation" (Cited in Rath, 1999).

The importance of women's education can be pronounced by quoting the words of Mahatma Gandhi : "You educate a man, you educate an individual; educate a woman, you educate a family". (Cited in Veeramani and Ravi, 1999: 58)

Women's education is thus considered to be one of the crucial factors in the development of family and society, yet the access to education for women is very limited. Women's illiteracy is one of the most characteristic features of developing countries, including India.

Notwithstanding the fact that there has been an increase in the awareness of the importance of women's education, and also the fact that greater numbers of girls are entering school, the fact remains that the illiteracy rate among women workers is very high.

In all the groups under discussion, it has been seen that the literacy level of the females is much below that of their male counterparts.

With regard to the observed difference in the literacy rates among the male and the female tea garden workers, it seems a number of factors play their roles either independently or in collaboration with one another. First of all, the traditional attitude such as "education is not very important for girls", still exists in the tea garden. In the opinion of the workers, it is more important for girls to learn their roles and domestic duties so as to get prepared for their future married life. In their childhood, primary importance is given to domestic training. They are supposed to get up early in the morning, clean the house, and help their mothers in the kitchen and outside works.

In most of the families in a plantation, both the father and the mother are generally employed as wage earners. As a result, a girl child is to look after her younger siblings; and also to take care of the domestic chores during the working hours of her parents. Thus, in many families it has been found that the girls of school-going ages are not sent to school.

Case V.12.

Dulai, aged 17 years, belongs to the Munda community. She is employed as a temporary worker in Dhelakhat tea estate. she is illiterate and is the second eldest offspring in the family. Her parents are permanent workers in the same tea plantation. She has four brothers and two sisters. Her elder brother as well as the other brothers of school-going age were sent to school. But Dulai was denied this opportunity, because she was required to stay at home to look after her brothers and sisters. In being asked why Dulai was not sent to school, her mother said that girls did not need to go to school since they would later be married and would go to another house. She further added that a girl's education did not in anyway benefit the family. But a boy, according to her, should receive education as he is to look after the family in due course of time.

In order to have an idea about the women's attitude/interest towards formal education, 100 respondents were interviewed in a 3-point scale : "very much interested", "interested" and "not interested". The responses have been presented in Table no. V.6.

It is interesting to note that barring only two respondents, all of them have expressed interest in receiving education. At least 12% have shown their extreme interest. Most of them maintain that despite their interest, they have not been provided with proper opportunities for education as they are girls. Denial of opportunities has been considered by most of the respondents as one of the major obstacles to women's education.

It is a well known fact that education is one of the important indices of the social status of an individual in a society. It is not only an insurance for women in times of need, but also an assurance for the full-fledged development of their personalities. Thus, the education of women ultimately contributes towards the building of a family and the society as a whole.

Table V.6. Distribution of the Respondents according to their level of interest in education

Responses	*No. of Respondents*				*Total*
	Christian Munda	*Non-Christian Munda*	*Pariah*	*Tanti*	
1	2	3	4	5	6
Very much interested	1	-	11	-	12
Interested	24	25	12	25	86
Not interested	-	-	2	-	2
Total	25	25	25	25	100

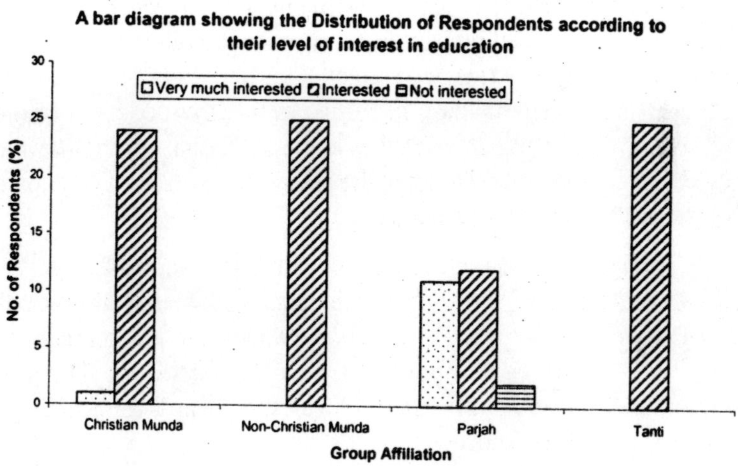

Figure No. V.3.

6

ECONOMIC FILE

Employment of women in non-traditional gainful activities is considered as the critical entry point to the development of a society. The total female working population in India accounts for approximately 100 million in the year 1988; and around 2 million women are added to the labour force every year. Again with the growing industrialisation , the share of women in the organised sector has increased from 8.00 per cent in 1981 to 13.03 per cent in 1988 (cited in Tripathy,1999:132).

Access to the different types of paid works is however , by and large, not equal for women and men. With regard to the division of labour between the members of the two sexes vis-a-vis the status of women, Quinn,, (1977:187) observes, "Whatever be the evolutionary history behind men's greater size, strength and energy, writers have considered that these characteristics suit men for heavy labour and thus help explain the near universal exclusion of women from such tasks as tree felling, ploughing and operation of heavy agricultural machinery as well as hunting and warfare. And the resulting division of labour between the sexes has been argued by some to initiate far-reaching effects on the status of women".

However, whatever outdoor work women may do, they also have the major responsibility for most of the household work, including the care of children and other family members. These dual responsibilities, termed respectively *productive* and *reproductive* by social scientists, have always played a vital role in human economic activity. Women not only contribute significantly to economic life everywhere, but also, to the proper maintenance of family life through bearing, rearing and upbringing of children as well as by carrying out other household activities.

Several scholars (e.g Lowie, 1929; Parsons,1954; Sullerot,1971; Thompson, and Finalyson, 1953) have dealt with the issue of women's gainful employment and the related matters. Different authors have made their observations in different spheres. Thus, eg; Thompson and Finalyson (*op.cit*) have seriously questioned the compatibility of women's employment with a proper psychological development of children. They have also argued that the domestic responsibility of women workers adversely affects the quantity, quality and duration of their work. Sullerot (*op.cit*), on the other hand,restricts his observations to some other aspects. He argues that women have become increasingly aware that the surest way of raising their social status and their position in the families is to become earners. According to him, by working, women gain a new sense of power.

Keeping these facts and observations in mind, in the present chapter, an attempt has been made to understand the nature and content of the gainful activities of the women and their position in the work place as well as in the family and the society.

Tea Plantations and Women Workers

Tea is one of the few industries which mainly depend upon woman labourers to work in the tea beds. Surveys show that the entire North East India has as much as 60.00% women workers and in the case of Assam alone 45.00% women are employed in the tea plantations. The probable factors that contribute towards having such a large number of women workers in the plantations are: a) the plantation work is only a special kind of agricultural work and is, therefore, familiar to Indian women, the vast majority of whom live in rural areas; b) facilities have been given to male workers to settle in, or in the vicinity of the plantations and to have their wives and families with them ; c) under the old system, labour contract was based on the principle of utilisation of the able bodied persons of the family of a labourer and fixing the wage rates accordingly; and d) many women had to seek employment in order to balance the family budget. Although the contract system has been abolished, the wage system and the need for supplementary earnings still remain (ILO,1938:35-36).

Before taking up a discussion on the various aspects of women's economic pursuits and the related issues, it will be probably prudent to have a general idea about the nature of the different types of activities in a tea plantation.

In a plantation, which is mostly a productive unit, there are basically two types of activities. These are a) the activities connected with growing and collection of tea leaves; and b) processing of tea leaves.

Growing, Plucking and Processing of Tea leaves

(i) Growing: Generally, the activities connected with the growing of tea leaves are undertaken by male labourers. Such activities are as follows:

1. Preparing the tea beds
2. Preparing seedlings and maintaining the nursery
3. Transplanting seedlings and tipping
4. Pruning and forking
5. Weeding and digging
6. Manuring
7. Spraying and pest control.

(ii) Plucking : Collection or plucking of tea leaves is generally better suited to female labourers. It is an important operation, because the quality of the manufactured tea depends upon the care and attention with which the plucking is done. The proper plucking constitutes "two leaves and a bud". Anything less than this is considered as "fine plucking" and inclusion of more leaves as "coarse plucking".Proper plucking may be considered as a skilful art that demands tremendous patience on the part of the plucker. May be for this reason, the task is believed to be more suitable to women. In India, plucking is done by hand and women are largely employed in the operation. Plucking wages are generally dependent on the weight of the leaves plucked, and as such, coarse plucking by increasing the amount of the crop provides increased remuneration to the plucker. Therefore, very often there is a temptation to resort to coarse plucking. In Assam, in most of the areas, the bushes are usually plucked once every 7 or 8 days during the season. The plucking season here usually extends from February/March to October/November.

(iii) Processing: The operations undertaken in a factory have been briefly described as follows by Carter (1951:5299). "After plucking, the leaf is placed on withering lofts where it remains for 18 to 24 hours until it becomes completely flaccid. It is then ready for the second process and is sent to the rollers where a twist is imparted to the leaf. From the rollers the tea is sent to the fermenting room where it is spread thinly, either on floors or on racks.It remains there for 3 to 4 1/2 hours, while certain chemical changes take place in the leaf. From the fermenting room, the tea goes to the firing machines, where it is dried. The object of this operation is to drive off all moisture; and during this process, the tea takes on its traditional black appearance. After firing, the tea is sorted out into the various grades required by the trade and is then packed into chests and despatched for sale"(cited in Kar,1981).

The labourers working in the factory are mostly males. Sometimes female labourers, are engaged for carrying the leaves from one place to another, and also in helping the male labourers in packing the leaf in the chests.

Besides these regular phases of work directly connected with the growing, plucking and processing of tea leaves, there are a good number of essential services in the plantation. Each labour *line* has one *chowkidar* who works as the head man and each establishment (office, factory, hospital and bungalows of the executive staff, etc.)

has a *chowkidar* who works as a care taker; then there are *Sardars* (gang leaders)who, supervise the labour force at work; there are employees in various cadres in school hospital and office; there are also drivers, carpenters, and people for preparing and repairing fences in the garden; some labourers are engaged in distributing drinking water and raw tea-liquor to the labour force actively engaged in the outdoor work connected with the growing and plucking of tea leaf. Further, there are sweepers, peons, and bearers, etc., in different units of a plantation.

As noted earlier, the participation of women in the tea plantation is much higher than that in any other sector. Sometimes, it is seen that the women workers outnumber their men counterparts.

An overall idea about the total population under study versus total working population is provided in table no. VI. 1. It will be seen from the table that out of the total population of 1975, the effective labour force in the plantation consists of 891 (45.11%) individuals. As anticipated, the numerical strength of the woman workers (454 : 50.95%) is more than that of their male counterpart (437: 49.04%). However, the difference in the representation of both the sexes is not a significant one.

The table further reveals that, barring the Non-Christian Mundas, where woman workers are reasonably more in number, the other three groups, by and large, show equitable distribution of the sexes in this regard.

Barring one, engaged in teaching, the entire workforce is directly or indirectly involved in growing, plucking or processing of tea leaves. Except for a very few skilled ones, most of them are unskilled labourers and are generally engaged in different types of work at different points of time. In this connection Tripathy (*op.cit*) observes, "Since a majority of woman workers lack any technical knowledge or proper education, technological advancement has forced them to opt for unskilled and semi-skilled jobs with low wages".

Table No. VI.I. Working Population versus the Total Population by Sex and Group Affiliation

Sl. No.	Category of populatin	Group Affiliation														
		Christian Munda			*Non-Christian Munda*			*Parjah*			*Tanti*			*Total*		
		Male	*Female*	*Total*	*Male*	*Female*	*Total*	*Male*	*Female*	*Total*	*Male*	*Female*	*Total*	*Male*	*Female*	*Total*
1	2	3	4	5	6	7	8	9	10	11	12	13	14	15	16	17
1	Working Population	112 (12.57)	112 (12.57)	224 (25.14)	112 (12.57)	138 (15.49)	250 (28.06)	132 (14.81)	127 (14.25)	259 (29.07)	81 (9.09)	77 (8.64)	158 (17.73)	437 (49.04)	454 (50.95)	891 (100.00)
2	Total Population	252 (12.75)	233 (11.80)	485 (24.56)	289 (14.69)	292 (14.78)	581 (29.42)	282 (14.28)	272 (13.77)	554 (28.05)	181 (9.16)	174 (8.81)	355 (17.97)	1004 (50.84)	971 (49.16)	1975 (100.00)

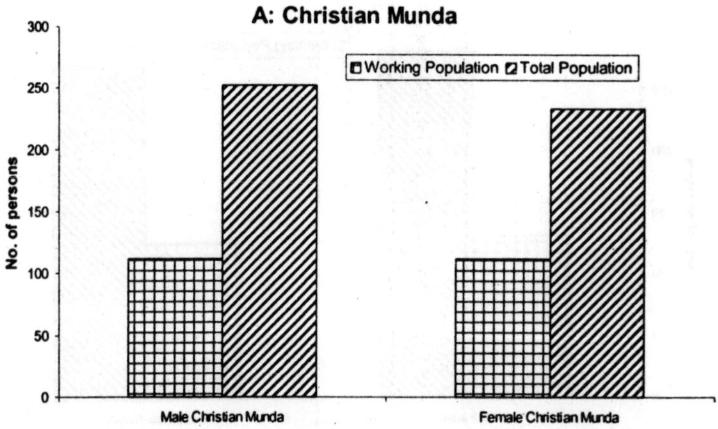

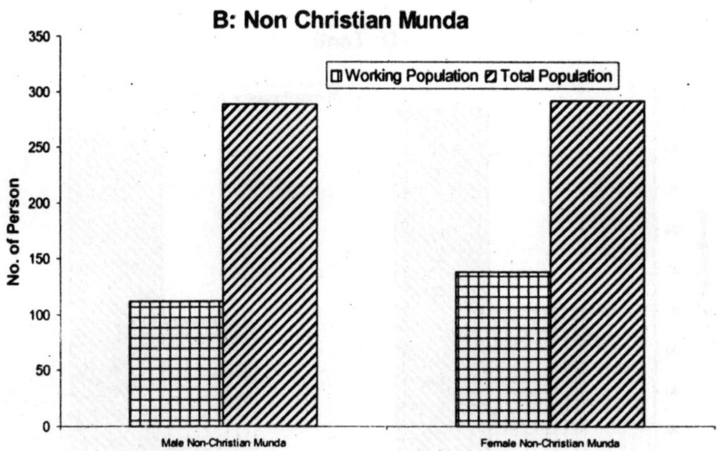

Figure No. VI.1.

Bar showing the working population versus total population of different group affiliation

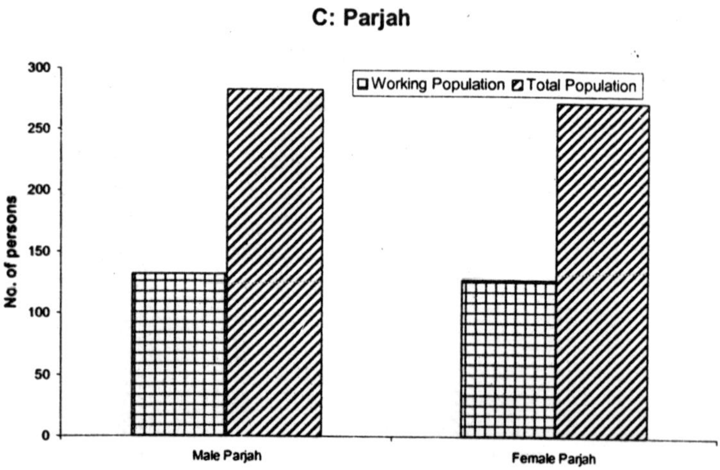

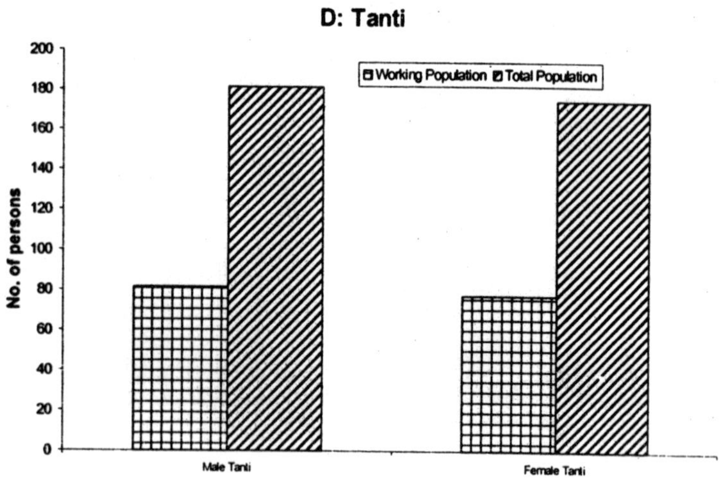

Figure No. VI.1.

Bar showing the working population versus total population of different group affiliation

It may however, be emphasized that women workers are always preferred in plucking operation that demands patience which, it is believed the woman workers do possess better than their male counterparts.

Distribution of the population according to various specific occupations during the time of investigation is presented in table VI.2. It will be seen from the table that most of the members of the working population (92.8 1 %) are engaged in outdoor work, basically plucking, cutting and cleaning. More than 50.00% (450:50.50%) of the woman workers belong to this category. As a matter of fact, only four of them are employed in other pursuits, viz; primary school teacher (one), *Sardarin* (one) and hospital attendant (two).

Group-wise distribution of the working population is shown in the Table nos. VI.2.a, b, c, d, while Table VI. 2.a depicts the distribution of the Christian Munda working population. Among the females there are two workers who are employed in the hospital as attendants. Table VI.2.b. reveals the details about the non-Christian Munda working population. Among them one is employed as a teacher in the garden primary school. She has completed her higher secondary courses. It is a rare opportunity for a woman member of a tea labour family to be a member of the teaching staff. The table further reveals that 54.00% of the female members are engaged in outdoor activities.

Table Vl.2.c shows the position of the Parjah working population. Almost 98.00% of them are engaged in the outdoor work in the garden.

In case of the Tanti (Table VI.2.d.),there is one woman who works as a *Sardarin*. In the entire garden there is only one female who works as a *Sardarin* (female *sardar*). The rest of the *sardar* posts are occupied by male incumbents. The *Chowkidars* and the *sardars* belong to the supervisory staff, they are better paid and also enjoy a better status. As noted earlier, most of these posts are generally occupied by the males. For a general unskilled tea labourer

Table VI.2. Distribution of the Population by Occupation

Sl. No.	*Occupation*	*Male*	*Female*	*Total*
1	2	3	4	5
1	Teacher	--	1 (0.11)	1 (0.11)
2	*Sardar/Sardarin*	4 (0.44)	1 (0.11)	5 (0.55)
3	*Line chowkidar*	2 (0.22)	--	2 (0.22)
4	Plantation *chowkidar*	5 (0.55)	--	5 (0.55)
5	Night *Chowkidar*	2 (0.22)	--	2 (0.22)
6	Electrician	2 (0.22)	--	2 (0.22)
7	Carpenter	2 (0.22)	--	2 (0.22)
8	Driver	1 (0.11)	--	1 (0.11)
9	Hospital (Unskilled)	4 (0.44)	2 (0.22)	6 (0.66)
10	Factory (Unskilled)	18 (2.02)	--	18 (2.02)
11	Outdoor work (including plucking)	397 (44.56)	450 (50.50)	847 (95.05)
12	Grand Total	437 (49.05)	454 (50.95)	891 (100.00)

Table V1.2.a Distribution of the Christian Munda. Population by Occupation

Sl. No.	*Occupation*	*Male*	*Female*	*Total*
1	2	3	4	5
1	Teacher	--	--	--
2	*Sardar/Sardarin*	--	--	--
3	Garden *Chowladar*	2 (0.89)	--	2 (0.89)
4	*Line Chowkidar*	--	--	--
5	Night *Chowkidar*	2 (0.89)	--	2 (0.89)
6	Electrician	2 (0.89)	--	2 (0.89)
7	Carpenter	--	--	--
8	Driver	--	--	--
9	Hospital (Unskilled)	1 (0.45)	2 (0.89)	3 (1.34)
10	Factory (unskilled)	9 (4.02)	--	9 (4.02)
11	Outdoor work (including plucking)	95 (42.86)	110 (49.11)	205 (91.97)
12	Total	111 (49.77)	112 (50.23)	223 (100.00)

Table VI.2.b Distribution of the Non-Christian Munda Population by Occupation

Sl. No.	*Occupation*	*Male*	*Female*	*Total*
1	2	3	4	5
1	Teacher	--	1 (0.40)	1 (0.40)
2	*Sardar/Sardarin*	--	--	--
3	Line *Chowladar*	--	--	--
4	*Garden Chowkidar*	2 (0.80)	--	2 (0.80)
5	Night *Chowkidar*	--	--	--
6	Electrician	--	--	--
7	Carpenter	--	--	--
8	Driver	--	--	--
9	Hospital (Unskilled)	2 (0.80)	--	2 (0.80)
10	Factory (unskilled)	1 (0.40)	--	1 (0.40)
11	Outdoor work (including plucking)	107 (42.80)	137 (54.80)	244 (96.40)
12	Total	112 (44.80)	138 (55.20)	250 (100.00)

Table VI.2.c Distribution of the Parjah Population by Occupation

Sl. No.	*Occupation*	*Male*	*Female*	*Total*
1	2	3	4	5
1	Teacher	--	--	--
2	*SardarlSardarin*	--	--	--
3	*Line Chowkidar*	1 (0.39)	--	1 (0.39)
4	Garden *Chowkidar*	1 (0.39)	--	1 (0.39)
5	Night *Chowkidar*	--	--	--
6	Electrician	--	--	--
7	Carpenter	--	--	--
8	Driver	--	--	--
9	Hospital (Unskilled)	--	--	--
10	Factory (unskilled)	1 (0.39)	4	1 (0.39)
11	Outdoor work ('including plucking)	129 (49.80)	127 (49.03)	255 (98.45)
12	Grand Total	132 (50.96)	127 (49.03)	259 (100.00)

Table VI.2.d Distribution of the Tanti Population by Occupation

Sl. No.	*Occupation*	*Male*	*Female*	*Total*
1	2	3	4	5
1	Teacher	--	--	--
2	*Sardar/Sardarin*	4 (2.53)	1 (0.63)	5 (3.16)
3	*Line Chowkidar*	1 (0.63)	--	1 (0.63)
4	Garden *Chowkidar*	--	--	--
5	Night *Chowkidar*	--	--	--
6	Electrician	--	--	--
7	Carpenter	2 (1.27)	--	2 (1.27)
8	Driver	1 (0.63)	--	1 (0.63)
9	Hospital (Unskilled)	1 (0.63)	--	1 (0.63)
10	Factory (unskilled)	7 (4.43)	--	7 (4.43)
11	Outdoor work (including plucking)	65 (41.13)	76 (48.10)	141 (89.24)
12	Grand Total	81 (51.26)	77 (48.73)	158 (100.00)

the scope for promotion is almost non-existent. The very few posts of *Sardars* and *Chowkidars* are their ultimate aspiration, and as such, there is keen competition for these posts. With regard to a woman worker, it may be emphasized that the opportunity for a promotion is extremely rare, and stagnation in the work place is the characteristic feature.

Bhadra (1997) in the context of the plantation labourers in North Bengal also made a similar observation when she states that in the plantation industry upward occupational mobility is extremely difficult and in the case of women it hardly exists.

The tables taken together (Table VI.3) reveal that the representation in the workforce is by and large equal for the members of both the sexes.It is almost identical for the Christian Mundas whereas it is relatively a little more favourable (55.20%) with regard to women for the Non-Christian Mundas. In case of the other two groups it is slightly favourable for the male members.

The table further reveals that the Tanti and the Christian Munda labourers have an edge over the other two groups in respect of occupying supervisory posts. As noted earlier, it must be emphasized here that for a tea labourer the scope of promotion is very limited and this is even more so in the case of a woman member.

While dwelling more on the different activities in a tea plantation, it may be noted that the people, by and large, show relatively less preference for the outdoor activities and the least preferred one is the job of plucking. Any work within the factory or associated with it is preferred by most of the people. Association with the factory or some technical activities, they believe provides them with a better status. As noted earlier, women are by and large engaged in plucking operations, and as such, their felt status in the society is obviously relatively inferior.

It may, however, be pointed out in this context that the management generally provides the women, especially the aged or sickly labourers, with relatively lighter tasks.

Table No. VI.3. Distribution of the Population by Occupation & Group Affiliation
Group Affiliation

Sl. No	*Occupation*	*Christian Munda*			*Non-Christian Mmunda*			*Parjah*			*Tanti*			*Total*		
		Male	*Female*	*Total*	*Male*	*Female*	*Total*	*Male*	*Female*	*Total*	*Male*	*Female*	*Total*	*Male*	*Female*	*Total*
1	2	3	4	5	6	7	8	9	10	11	12	13	14	15	16	17
1	Teacher	-	-	-	-	1 (0.40)	1 (0.40)	-	-	-	-	-	-	-	1 (0.11)	
2	*Sardar*	-	-	-	-	-	-	-	-	-	4 (2.53)	1 (0.63)	5 (3.16)	4 (0.44)	1 (0.11)	5 (0.55)
3	Garden *Chokidar*	2 (0.89)	-	2 (0.89)	2 (0.80)	-	2 (0.80)	1 (0.39)	-	1 (0.39)	-	-	-	5 (0.55)	-	5 (0.55)
4	Line *Chowkidar*	-	-	1	-	I	-	1	1	1	2	2				
5	Night *Chowkidar*	2 (0.89)	-	2 (0.89)	-	-	-	-	-	-	-	-	-	2 (0.22)	-	2 (0.22)
6	Electrician	2 (0.89)	- (0.89)	2	-	-	-	-	-	-	-	-	-	2 (0.22)	-	2 (0.22)
7	Carpenter	-	-	-	-	-	-	-	-	-	2 (1.27)	-	2 (1.27)	2 (0.27)	-	2 (0.22)

8	Driver	-	-	-	-	-	-	-	-	-	1 (0.63)	-	1 (0.63)	1 (0.11)	-	2 (0.11)
9	Hospital (unskilled)	1 (0.45)	2 (0.89)	3 (1.34)	2 (0.80)	-	2 (0.80)	-	-	-	1 (0.63)	-	1 (0.63)	4 (0.44)	2 (0.22)	6 (0.66)
10	Factory unskilled	9 (4.02)	-	9 (4.02)	1 (0.40)	1 (0.39)	1 (0.40)	1 (0.39)	-	1 (0.39)	7 (4.43)	-	7 (4.43)	18 (2.02)		18 (2.02)
11	Outdoor work Including	95 (42.86)	110 (49.11)	205 (91.97)	107 (42.80)	137 (54.80)	244 (96.40)	129 (49.80)	127 (49.03)	255 (98.45)	65 (41.13)	76 (48.10)	141 (89.24)	397 (44.56)	450 (50.50)	847 (95.05)
12	Total	111 (49.77)	112 (50.23)	223 (1 00.00)	112 (44.80)	138 (55.20)	250 (100-00)	132 (50.96)	127 (49.03)	259 (100.00)	81 (51.26)	77 (48.73)	158 (100.00)	437 (49.05)	454 (50.96)	891 (100.00)

Case V1. 1.

Christina Guria, aged 48 years, belongs to Dhelakhat tea estate. She belongs to the Munda tribe and is a permanent labourer in the plantation (1999). Sometime back she suffered from some physical disabilities, and as such, was not in a position to carry out all types of work. She was unable to carry out any heavy work, especially that of carrying the plucked leaves to the factory. As per the recommendation of the doctor of the plantation hospital, the mangement relieved her of the plucking task in favour of some lighter job like planting seeds in the nursery.

Despite the care and concern shown most of the women feel that by working in the plantation, it will not be possible to improve their economic standard.

During the present investigation, an opinion survey was made of a sample of 100 woman respondents as to the feasibility of improving their living standard while continuing to work in the plantation. 25 respondents were chosen from each group under investigation. The responses have been presented in Table No.VI.4.

Table. VI. 4. Distribution of the Respondents according to their opinion about the improvement possibilities of Economic condition

Sl.No.	*Opinions*	*Christian Munda*	*Non-Christian Munda*	*Parjah*	*Tanti*	*Total*
1	2	3	4	5	6	7
1	Possible	1 (4.00)	4 (16.00)	8 (32.00)	-	13
2	Highly Possible	-	13 (52.00)	-	-	13
3	Impossible	7 (28.00)	-	14 (56.00)	2 (8.00)	23
4	Highly Impossible	17 (68.00)	8 (32.00)	3 (12.00)	23 (92.00)	51
5	Total	25 (100.00)	(100.00)	25 (100.00)	25 (100.00)	25 100

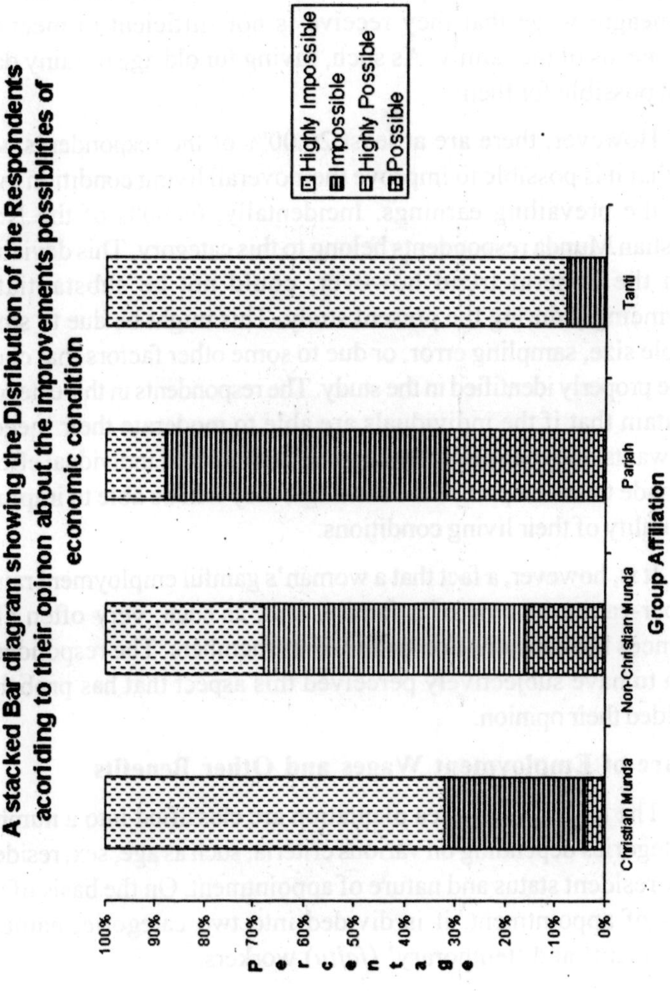

Figure No. VI.2.

It will be seen from Table No.VI.4 that the majority of the respondents (74.00%) from all the groups, barring the Non-Christian Munda women, are of the opinion that it is not possible to improve the living standard in the present employment. They maintain that the meagre wage that they receive is not sufficient to meet the basic needs of the family. As such, saving for old age or rainy days is not possible for them.

However, there are at least 26.00% of the respondents who feel that it is possible to improve their overall living condition even with the prevailing earnings. Incidentally, 68.00% of the Non-Christian Munda respondents belong to this category. This deviation from the general trend however, could not be substantiated convincingly during the present study. This might be due to small sample size, sampling error, or due to some other factors that could not be properly identified in the study. The respondents in this category maintain that if the individuals are able to moderate their 'needs' and 'wants' they can probably improve their lives. If individual efforts are made to save a part of the earnings, they will be able to improve the quality of their living conditions.

It is, however, a fact that a woman's gainful employment raises the per-capita income of a family, and, as such, very often also enhances the consumption habits of its members. The respondents seem to have subjectively perceived this aspect that has probably moulded their opinion.

Nature of Employment Wages and Other Benefits

The labourers in a tea plantation are classified into a number of categories depending on various criteria, such as age, sex, resident or no-resident status and nature of appointment. On the basis of the terms of appointment, it is divided into two categories,namely, 'permanent' and 'temporary' (*faltu*) workers.

A permanent worker is one who resides inside the tea estate and whose name is entered in the estate roll of workers. It generally includes any person who has completed a probationary period of six month in the same or any other occupation in the industrial establishments, including breaks due to sickness, accidents, leave, lock out, strike (not illegal) or voluntary closure of the establishment.

With regard to the condition of work and social security benefits of the permanent workers, earlier Bengal Act III of 1863 (amended in 1865 to Bengal Act VI) prescribed minimum wages and limited hours of work. It laid down that contracts with an immigrant labourer must not extend beyond three years. Every estate was required to maintain a hospital. A protector and an Inspector of labour were appointed and empowered to visit gardens to supervise everything including the authority labour relation.

In Independent India a number of legislations were enacted from time to time to regulate the conditions of work of the labourers in tea plantations.

The Plantation Labour Act 1951, along with the Plantation Labour Rules, 1956, has defined many conditions of labour employment in clear terms, e.g.,

(i) Clause 30 of the Act provides that every worker shall be allowed leave with wages at the following rate;

  (a) One day for every twenty-two working days for an adult.

  (b) One day for every fifteen working days for a minor.

  (c) In case of sickness, sickness allowances, and

  (d) In case of woman workers maternity allowances are provided by this clause. Regulations provide that benefits must be paid for 12 weeks, i.e., four weeks before and eight weeks after confinement. Again, a woman is not allowed to perform arduous jobs during her pregnancy. In the event of a miscarriage certified by a doctor, a woman is entitled to two or three weeks leave.

(ii) Under clause 8, in every plantation effective arrangements shall be made by the employer to provide and maintain a sufficient supply of drinking water for all workers.

(iii) Clause 9 (I): There shall be provided separately for males and females in every plantation a sufficient number of latrines and urinals of prescribed types.

(iv) Clause 10 (i) : In every plantation there shall be provided and maintained free medical facilities for the workers and their families.

(v) Clause 15: The employer is to provide and maintain for every worker and his family residing in the plantation necessary housing accommodation.

(vi) Section 12 : The employer should provide creches for the children (below six years of age) of the working mothers.

(vii) Section 14 Facilities for education be provided to children below 12 years of age.

(viii) Section 13 The Employer should make provision in his plantation for recreational facilities for the workers and their children.

The Act also provides that an employer shall provide the workers with umbrellas, blankets, raincoats, slippers or other like amenities for the protection of the workers from rain and cold.

In the course of the present investigation, however, it has been observed that the labourers, by and large, in addition to their wages, are provided with the following benefits:

(i) Rent-free accommodation : The floor space covered by each standard type of house is 425 sq.ft., while the total area of the campus is 3000 sq.ft. (As per the plantation Act, the specifications for the twin quarters are as follows: Campus area - 5000 sq.ft. floor space - 894 sq ft.).

(ii) Contributory provident fund at the rate of 8 percent of wage. No provident fund accrues during the probation period (6 months).

(iii) Provision of paddy land subject to availability.

(iv) Free medical attention: In each plantation there is a hospital with its own attending staff.

(v) Leave with wages

(vi) Sickness allowance

(vii) Maternity benefits

(viii) Provision of fire wood: 228 cft; per year per family, 114 cft. per year per bachelor: - (I cft=8'x 6'x 4'6)

(ix) Subsidized ration and free tea leaf. 500 gm ricelatta per head per day Rs. 50.00 per quintal, and 500 gm tea leaf per month per family.

(x) Free cinema shows: 1 show in a month plus 4 shows during Durga/Kali *Puja*.

(xi) Bonus: Minimum is 8.33 percent of the annual wage.

(xii) Gratuity

(xiii) Drinking water

(xiv) Recreation club

(xv) Miscellaneous: (a) One apron in 2 years and (b) One pair of slippers in 2 years, (c) One umbrella in 2 years (d) One mosquito net and a blanket in 2 years and (e) Sunglass, gum-boots, jersey and hand glove for sprayers of pesticides and insecticides.

With regard to the permanent workers the wage rates for an adult and a minor are different. But there is no difference in wages on the basis of sex. As far as wage is concerned the status of man and woman seems to be at par.

However, the permanent workers are entitled to all the benefits mentioned above, such as, social security benefits and other fringe benefits. Apart from the permanent workers, there are also temporary workers who are engaged in the garden to work for a specific period.

A temporary appointment is limited to a maximum period of 150 working days. The period from May to November is generally regarded as the busy season in a tea plantation. During this peak plucking season there are quite a large number of temporary labourers who are employed for the plucking of the tea leaves.

The number of temporary workers varies from plantation to plantation depending on the plucking potentiality on the basis of the intensity of the flushing of the new leaves. It is thus implied that the *faltu* workers are the pluckers; and as such, the majority of them are women. If the volume of work demands, even the minor girls and others are also employed casually. The wage for the pluckers is always proportionate to the quantity of leaves, plucked by a labourer, irrespective of sex. Minimum wages of labour at present vary with age only (earlier sex also was a criterion), but the fringe and other social security benefits vary with the nature of the appointment. The temporary workers are not entitled to the benefits under serial numbers (i), (ii), (iii) and (xi) which have been mentioned earlier.

At present (2001), the minimum wage rates (per day) have been for Men: Rs.43.05 ; Women: Rs.43.05 (prior to 1985, the rate was Rs. 1.52 less than that of men); and Children: Rs.21.53.

During the present investigation, it has been found that the total number of the temporary workers under study is more or less equal to that of the permanent workers. Data in this regard has been presented in Table VI. 5. It will be seen from the table that there are 461 (51.74%) permanent workers and 430 (48.26%) temporary workers engaged in the present setting. The table further reveals that the female temporary workers outnumber their male counterparts. The total number of the female and the male temporary workers is 248 (27.883%) and 182 (20.43%) respectively. However, it may be noted here that out of the total woman workers, more than 50.00% have been found to be employed as casual (*faltu*) labourers.

Table VI.5. Distribution of the Population according to the Nature of Employment, Sex and Group Affiliations

Group Affiliation

Nature of Employ-ment	Christian Munda			Non-Christian Munda			Parjah			Tanti			Total		
	Male	Female	Total	Male	Female	Total	Male	Female	Total	Male	Female	Total	Male	Female	Total
1	2	3	4	5	6	7	8	9	10	11	12	13	14	15	16
Permanent	62 (6.95)	68 (7.63)	130 (14.59)	72 (8.08)	63 (7.07)	135 (15.15)	66 (7.41)	31 (3.48)	97 (10.89)	55 (6.17)	44 (4.94)	100 (10.11)	255 (28.62)	206 (23,12)	462 (51.74)
Temporary	50 (5.61)	44 (4.94)	94 (10.55)	40 (4.49)	75 (8.42)	115 (12.91)	66 (7.4)	96 (10.77)	162 (18.18)	26 (2.92)	33 (3.70)	59 (6.62)	182 (20.43)	248 (27.83)	430 (48.26)
Grand Total	!12 (12.57)	112 (12,57)	224 (25.14)	112 (12.57)	138 (15.49)	250 (28.06)	132 (14.81)	127 (14.25)	259 (29.07)	81 (9.09)	77 (8.64)	158 (17.73)	437 (49.05)	454 (5 0.95)	891 (100.00)

A Bar diagram showing the Distribution of the Population according to the nature of Employment and Group Affiliation

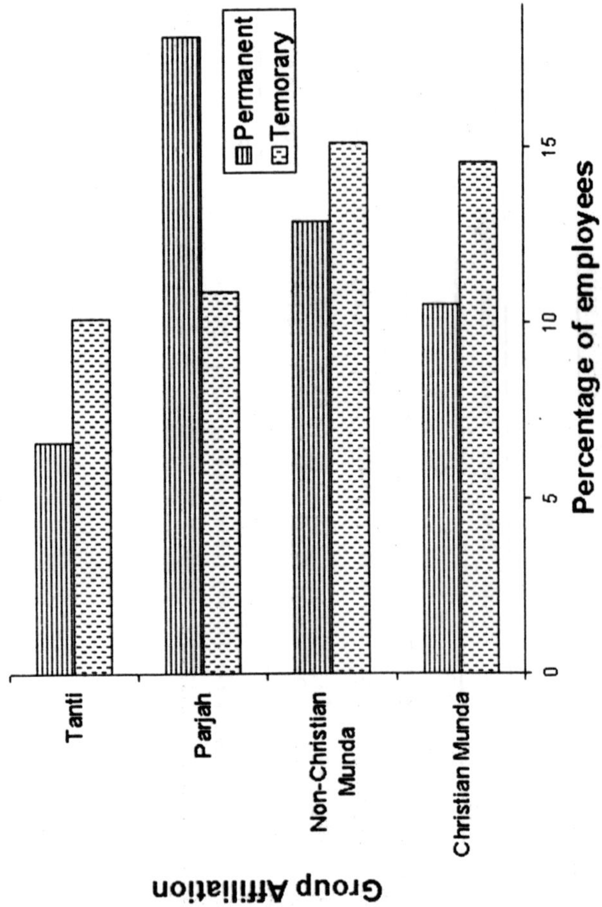

Figure No. VI.3.

It seems, that economic compulsion is the main driving force for this large number of women seeking employment in the tea plantation. Most of them spend whatever they earn in meeting the basic needs of the family. In other words, their income is by and large contributed to the common family fund. However, though an earning member, a woman worker very often does not enjoy absolute liberty in spending her income. In order to have a specific understanding in this regard, a sample of 100 respondents were interviewed during the study. The responses have been presented in Table VI.6.

It is apparent from the table that 16.00% of them hand over their income to their husbands who spend the cash as per their decision. The table also shows that 65.00% of the respondents are allowed to keep their own earnings with them. However, they require permission from their husbands to spend the amount. They are not allowed to spend the same as per their independent desires. In these families, normally the entire amount is spent to purchase food and other necessary commodities. Most of the women manage their family budget themselves. In some families, the husbands too hand over a part of their earnings to their wives for family expenditure. They generally decide together how to spend the entire amount. It can also be seen from the table that 19.00% of the women can keep their earnings with them and they can spend it as they wish. Their husbands do not question them or enquire about how they handle their earnings. In other words, these women can exercise their liberty in spending their own earnings.

A group-wise data in this regard reveals that the Non-Christian Munda and the Tanti women do not have the liberty to spend any of their earnings as they wish. They are, however, allowed to keep the cash with them, but it is their husbands who decide how and when to spend the amount. On the other hand, the Parjah women hand over their earnings to their husbands; and their husbands handle the same independently. It seems, the Christian Munda women are in an advantageous position with regard to the enjoyment of some liberty in handling their own income. It will be seen from the table

Table VI. 6. Distribution of the respondents according to their Freedom in handling their earnings (N=100)

Sl. No.	*Nature of handling*	*Christian Munda Munda*	*Non-Christian*	*Parjah*	*Tanti*	*Total*
1	2	3	4	5	6	7
1	Hands over the income to the head of the family husband	3 (12.00)	-	13 (52.00)	-	16 (16.00)
2	Can spend as one wishes	11 (44.00)	-	8 (32.00)	-	19 (19.00)
3	Can't spend11 without the permission of the husband/ head of the family	11 (44.00)	25 (100.00)	4 (16.00)	25 (100.00)	65 (65.00)
4	Total (10 .00)	25	25 (100.00)	25 100.00	25 (100.00)	100

A broken Pie diagram showing the Distribution of the Respondents according to their freedom in handling their earnings

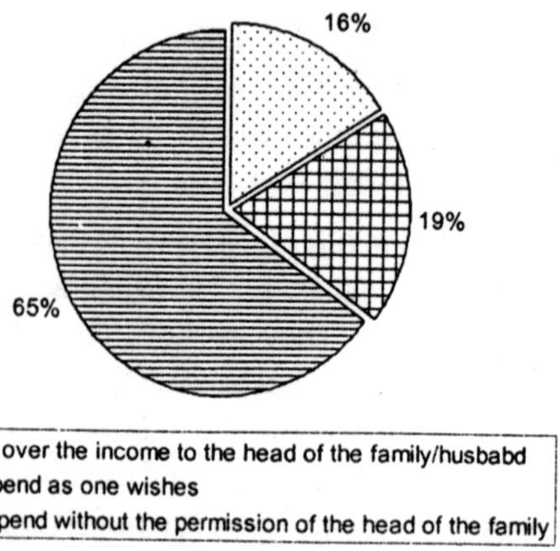

Figure No. VI.4.

that at least 44.00% of the Christian Munda women are able to keep their earnings themselves and are allowed to spend the money as they wish.

There are a few widows who however, manage the family budget themselves. It may be relevant to note here that there are a good number of families where the husbands spend their entire income on country liquor; and do not contribute anything to the family expenditure. In these families the basic needs are managed by the wives from their own income only.

Case V1.2.

Birospatia Bag is a permanent labourer in Dhelakhat tea estate. He is 32 years old. He is a Tanti. He is married and has three children - two sons and one daughter. His wife, aged 24 years is also a permanent worker in the same garden. Birospatia is an alcoholic. He drinks regularly, and usually exhausts his wage within a week of its receipt. As such, he borrows money from others for the rest of the month. On receipt of the next wage, he spends an amount for the repayment of the debt, and the rest in buying his regular drinks. Borrowing and repayment of the loan is a continuous process for him. Very often,after drinking to excess he beats his wife . Sometimes, he also quarrels with his neighbours. The entire family expenditure is borne by his wife. Due to financial hardship, she is unable to send her children to school.

Case V1.3.

Kishno Koya is 45 years old. He belongs to the Parjah tribe. He is a permanent labourer in Dhelakhat tea estate. He is married and has five children, of whom three are daughters and two sons. His wife too is a permanent labourer. He is an alcohol addict. He takes both *haria* and other varieties of drinks. Very often he remains absent from his work. Therefore, his wife has to bear the entire expense of supporting the family. Kishno not only spends his entire income on alcohol, but also sometimes takes some amount of his wife's income for the purpose. Their eldest daughter has attained marriageable age; and once it so happened that Kishno took some money from some aged person assuring him that they would arrange a marriage between their daughter. This, however, did not materialise due to the interference of his wife, daughter and other well wishers of the family.

Production and Reproduction Vis-A-Vis the Woman Workers

Most of the working women are burdened with a double work-load to dispense with one in the place of employment, and the other on the domestic front. Traditionally, a woman has to be a wife, mother and a home maker in the family. In the case of a working woman, alongside the reproductive and domestic responsibilities, she has to play a role in the productive activities too and as such, she confronts some problems that were hitherto unknown.

Evidence from several national surveys about how women feel about the double load of job and home- making have led to the following conclusion by Wright : " Evidence presented....... makes it reasonably plain that both work and house- keeping roles have costs and benefits attached to them. Working women enjoy an out-side income and some increase in independence as a result of it; they get out of the house and so on. But they also pay for these benefits in reduced free time for themselves, a more hectic pace, and a more complicated life. The life of a housewife, in contrast, is somewhat easier .... and almost certainly less hectic, than that of their employed counterparts" (cited in Hurlock,1981).

However, Hate (1969) maintains that the main problem of Indian working women is that of 'role-conflict' which stems from their dual responsibilities.

Role-conflicts occur when a person occupies two or more positions simultaneously and the expectations are not fulfilled properly. This is very evident in the life of a working woman. In her case, a new additional role is added to her existing role as a housewife and mother. Thus, she is subjected to plurality of role expectations which are mutually incompatible. In addition, they may also feel disturbed if they are too busy, or too tired when they return from work to take an active part in their children's interest. As a result of these feelings on the part of the working women, their home lives are far from satisfactory. This is tenable not only for the working woman, but also, for her entire family. In the following pages, an attempt is made to understand the constraints (in their family and at the work place) encountered by the woman workers under investigation.

As it has been stated earlier, a working woman has to bear a double work-load, unlike the working man who is considered to be the bread winner of the family, even though his wife may be an earning member. A working woman is expected to be competent in the household chores as well as in her responsibility outside the home. In this regard, Kapoor (1971) rightly observes, ".... the working wife, especially if she has children, will have to make in many instances, a little greater effort to keep things going and she actually needs more help than is commonly given to her" (cited in Jha, Mehta and Menon, 1998:132).

During the present study, it has been found that the woman workers of the tea plantation encounter a host of problems in this regard. The following concrete cases will provide an idea in this regard.

Case VI.4

Rukmoni Surin, aged 32 years, is a permanent worker in Dhelakhat tea plantation. She belongs to the Munda tribe. She is illiterate. She is married and has three children who are aged four years, two years and one year respectively. Rukmoni's husband also is a permanent labourer in the same garden. As per her daily schedule, she gets up early in the morning at 4.30 a.m. to do her household chores of preparing food and cleaning the house, etc. At around 8.00 a.m., she has to leave the house for her work. She carries packed tiffin with her. In case the working tea bed is close to her quarters, during the break she rushes back home to feed her young children. Very often she does not have her own food. After returning from the work in the evening at around 4.30.p.m., once again she continues her household chores. She has no time left to take care of herself and her children. At around 8.30 p.m., after preparing the food, she feeds her children and waits for her husband to return home. Then she takes her food and retires to bed at around 9.30 p.m. This cycle of activities is repeated every day with, however, some breathing gap on Sundays and holidays.

Case V1.5.

Sakuntala, aged 43 years, is a permanent worker in Diṛial tea estate. She is illiterate and belongs to the Parjah tribe. She is married and has four children. Their ages are six years, five years, three years , and two years respectively. Sakuntala's husband, too, is a permanent labourer.Their eldest son is a school-going boy who studies in class 1. In the morning she generally gets up from bed before any body else at around 4.00 a.m. She cleans the house and prepares food for the family. She serves food to her children and the husband, and also packs tiffin for her husband, the school-going son and also for herself. In addition, she has to prepare the meals for her children during the noon and the afternoon. She leaves for her work at around 8.00 a.m. Before leaving for the work-place, Sakuntala leaves the children in the Before leaving custody of one of the neighbouring families.

After returning from the tea bed, she takes a bath and also cleans her children before entering the kitchen to prepare the dinner. After providing meals to all the members of the family, she takes her own meal at around 8.30 p.m. Then again, some more time is needed for setting everything in order to have a convenient start of the daily cycle the following morning. She retires to bed at around 9.30.p.m.

It is apparent that the woman workers lead a very busy daily life with practically no time to have leisure and relaxation. As a matter of fact, they genuinely need some helping hand to provide relief from the burden of domestic chores. Incidentally, in the present study, the husbands, by and large, have not been found to assist the wives substantially on the domestic front. As such, women are generally overburdened with day-to-day routine activities. This is more so in the nuclear families. Again, because of the financial constraints they cannot afford to have paid helping hands in the family to share some of the work. In this context, Sethi rightly observes that employment of women does not necessarily lead to a change in the work pattern at home. The traditional role of a woman as a home maker and socializer of the young remains unaltered despite the addition of the role as an earner. Also, the mere fact of a woman making a financial contribution to the family income does not lead to a change in the existing role structure and ensuring power position within the family as manifested in her role in the decision-making process (cited in Jha, Mehta & Menon, *opcit*)

Similarly, the woman workers often have to experience some constraints outside the family too, i.e., the working environment which includes the physical environment as well as the relationship with the supervisors and the fellow workers . These constraints do have some impact on the maintenance of peace and tranquillity in the domestic sphere.

As stated earlier, though the Plantation Labour Act 1951, and the Plantation Labour Rules, 1956, have laid down many provisions in terms of working conditions, the prevailing physical conditions at work are, by and large not very satisfactory. Thus for example, facilities for proper drinking water, attending to nature's call, sheltering the kids (creche) and recreation, etc., are lacking in the workplace. Lack of toilet and creche facilities in many cases create acute problems for the woman workers.

Case VI.6.

Rajamoni Parjah, aged 43 years, has been working in Dirial tea estate. She is a permanent worker. She is married and has five children. According to her, the work environment is very hard and taxing. At around 8.30 a.m. she starts her work. At 12.00 noon there is half hour tiffin break. She is a lactating mother and as there are no creche facilities, during the break her son is brought to be breast fed. Often she does not even have time to take her tiffin since the work starts again at 12.30 p.m. During the working hours the garden *Sardars* are always supervising and so she must resume her work on time. Even if they stand to exchange a few words, they are reprimanded by the *sardar*. She has developed rheumatism, probably due to her long hours of standing work.

At their work place they lack drinking water and toilet facilities. At times they are unable to respond to nature's call due to lack of toilets near by. It has also been found that there is no canteen in the immediate neighbourhood.

Besides, the nature of the management-worker relationship is also of crucial importance for a worker at the work place. As noted earlier, the *Sardars* are supervisors at work; they are the defacto representatives of the management for a group of workers at work. So, the relationship that exists between a worker and the work-supervisor does have a lasting impression on the worker's motivation and morale. At times, it has been found that the *Sardars* deal with the women workers in a very unkind way.

Case V1.7.

Mariam Bhur, aged 38 years belongs to the Munda tribe. She is a permanent labourer in Dhelakhat tea estate. She is married and her husband Albius Bhur too is a permanent worker in the same garden. In the work place she is very often reprimanded by the *Sardar* on one pretext or the other. Sometimes she has to endure misbehaviour in the presence of other co-workers even if she talks with another woman worker. One day when the *Sardar* was chastising her for talking with a co-worker during plucking hours, Mariam just opened her mouth to defend herself. The *Sardar* got furious and refused to listen to her.

Over and above, he lodged a complaint with the manager about her alleged misbehaviour. The manager called her to his office and chastised her with a warning that any more complaints against her might cost her her job. She was not given any opportunity to defend herself. This is not the usual behaviour with a male worker even if one of them indulges in gossipping during the working hours.

To conclude, among the tea garden labourers, the women workers are normally more in number, and most of them are involved in the outdoor activities, especially in the plucking operation. A good number of woman workers are temporary labourers and they do not receive all the social security benefits as well as other fringe benefits. The physical facilities available in the working place do not seem to be very satisfactory. In other words all the provisions made in the PLA 1951, are not available to the workers. Some of these facilities (eg. creche & toilet) are genuinely needed for the women workers. In many instances, it has also been found that the women labourers are differently treated by the management, reflecting their relatively inferior status in the work place. In wage rate, however, they are treated at par with their male counterparts. Further, though engaged in gainful employment, barring a very few, they do not seem to enjoy any economic independence in their family life. It has been observed that most of them do not enjoy any relief in their traditional domestic preoccupations because of their outdoor employment.

7

COMMUNITY LIFE

Human beings, like other animals, have never been able to exist solely as individuals in isolation. They are social animals who live in interaction with others in families, tribes and communities as well as in the wider world. They build cities and nations; they form groups based on friendships, special interests, and hobbies etc (Perry & Perry, 1973).

It is only through interaction with others, that the individual gains an identity, takes on ideals, values and aspirations. An individual identity is obtained only through interactions and interpersonal relationship with others - the members of the primary and the secondary groups; and also those of the wider community.

Firth (1958:82), in this context, observes, "Life in a community means organisation of the interest of individuals, regulations of their behaviour towards one another, and grouping of them together for common action. The relationships thus created between them can be seen to have some kind of plan or system .... The way in which the relationships actually work, affecting the lives of individuals and the nature of the society, may be called their social function".

Human beings are social animals which means we have relationships with many other people. Some of these relationships intimate and some are formal. Similarly, some are close in certain situations only, while others are much more impersonal. But all these relationships form a web around us. The more we participate in the relationships the closer we weave ourselves into the web.

In other words, it may be said that the community life of a group of people invariably incorporates social interactions and relationships, patterns of social order, and shared cultural ideas.

"Wherever individuals interact with others through time, however, they become participants in the whole process of organization of the society. They may either create new relationships or join previously existing patterns of social order. In both cases they begin to change at least some of their action from those of a relatively independent social element to those of a relatively involved social part. The more extensive this shift in their action, the more deeply involved they become in the social organization" (Kar,1981:185).

Thus, a discussion on the community life of a group of people needs to focus on the patterns of relationships and interactions and also to provide an idea as to how individuals behave or exchange their views within an organisation. This calls for the observation and evaluation of who is expected to do what, in relation to whom, and following what socio-cultural norms.

Obviously, in such exercise, an individual's interaction is only the starting point, while an understanding of the context and the social relationships in which it is involved is regarded as the main focus of interest.

Keeping these facts and observations in mind, in the present chapter an attempt has been made to understand the nature and the content of the community life of the women workers under discussion inorder to have a better understanding of their role and status in the community as a whole.

The community life, or in other words, the socio-cultural life of the woman workers at the community level can probably best be viewed from a number of planes. It is, however, most that these sub-planes will not be mutually exclusive both in the wider perspective and also at certain levels of interactions within the supposed jurisdiction of these sub-communities. Nevertheless, these communities within the community are a major focus for a researcher initially.

In the context of the tea garden, an individual's interactions and relationships start from various angles. Under the umbrella of the tea garden community, first of all, the workers are identified as belonging to various tribes and caste groups. Each of these communities has its own ethnic-cultural identity as well as set norms for mutual interactions and establishing temporary or enduring relationships. Secondly, as stated earlier, they reside in different *lines* (i.e. residential clusters) that are generally shared by labourers with hetero-ethnic affiliations. Thus the immediate neighbourhood of a household, by and large, consists of fellow members belonging to different cultural and religious groups. Beyond all these, they belong to a larger community known as the tea labour community (can occupational group) based on many similarities and differences.

As noted earlier (cf. *Chapter Three*), the labourers, in Dhelakhat and Dirial tea plantations have been distributed in thirty six tribe and caste groups (Tribes 22 and Castes 14). It has also been noted earlier that the communities by and large are migrant ones; and they started migrating to Assam sometime during the mid-nineteenth century.

These heterogeneous groups, over the centuries, have preserved a distinctive style of life. In terms of the quality of life and cultural ethos, most of the tribes stand out in sharp contrast to the castes. Again, there are significant differences among the tribes themselves. They differ greatly in their tradition, economy and complexity of social organization, and there are wide variations in their customs and traditions. Their experiences with regard to various forms of economic exploitation, social discrimination and political isolation also show wide variations. However, over the years, since their migration to the present habitat, they have been exposed to a number of type-situations that have contributed towards altering the traditional model of inter-group relations as well as the quality and content of their world view. As a matter of fact, the respective ethnic identities, in the present setting, seem to have become dysfunctional for the people, at least in day-to-day life (Kar 1975 : 11-15). The social life of the various groups is not controlled by the traditional bodies and leaders. Community festivals have also been found to be equally shared by the members of all the ethnic groups. The festivals are also identified as tea labourers' festivals.

On the whole, in the overall day-to-day community life, there does not exist enough scope for the people to experience their independent ethnic identities in the present setting.

With regard to the distribution of the workers in the different residential clusters (*lines*) in the two plantations under intensive investigation, it has earlier been noted (cf. *Chapter Three*) that Dhelakhat has a total of six *lines* whereas in Dirial tea estate, the work force is distributed in seventeen *lines* (New Dirial - 11 and Old Dirial - 6).

In the present setting, beyond their familial context, the labourers relate themselves to their immediate neighbourhood, their ethnic group, as well as to the larger tea garden community. The immediate neighbourhood for them is the labour *lines* where the miscellaneous kinsmen along with wholly unrelated neighbours, (belonging to different tribes/castes) live as a community. The most operative sub-unit in the community life seems to be the *line* affiliation. The head of a *line* is the line *chowkidar*. The members identify themselves as belonging to their respective *lines*. In a *line*, the members of the various families are very familiar and friendly with one another. They do have a strong emotional attachment and a sense of belonging, to their respective *lines*.

In all matters of social organization and day-to-day affairs, each *line* exists as a distinct social community. When a household arranges a feast or some other function that demands menial help, mostly the neighbours from the *line* are called, assistance being specially taken from the next door neighbours. This preference is given irrespective of their ethnic affiliations. Similarly, on the occasion of some family level celebrations, if material items like utensils etc, are needed, these, too, are preferably taken from the neighbouring families. Most of the activities are, by and large, confined to the members of the respective *lines*.

Among the womenfolk, too, there exists a very intimate relationship between the members of the respective *lines*, irrespective of their other affiliations. On Sundays and holidays, the women belonging to the contemporary age group generally flock together in some common place or in someone's courtyard, to gossip about various interesting issues of common and mutual interest. Extension of mutual help and co-operation among the neighbours is almost a regular feature in a labour *line*.

Case VII.1.

Sukumoni, aged 42 years, belongs to the Parjah tribe. She is a permanent worker in Dirial tea estate. She is Hindu by religion, a married woman having four children, aged I I years, 9 years, 7 years and 5 years respectively. Catherine is her next-door neighbour. She is 44 years old and is working as a permanent labourer in the same garden. She belongs to the Munda tribe and subscribes to Christianity. She too is married and has six children. During the occasion of the marriage celebration of her eldest daughter Mariam (aged 19 years), in the second half of 1998, Catherine asked for assistance and help from Sukurnoni, her next-door neighbour (both of them are the residents of Pailabari *line*).

Notwithstanding their belonging to two different ethnic and religious groups, Sukumoni most willingly and generously extended her assistance for almost two days,leaving her household responsibilities with her eldest daughter who was only eleven years old.

Case VII.2.

Rajamoni, aged 48 years,, is a Tanti woman who works as a permanent labourer in Dhelakhat tea estate. She is married and has 5 children. Similarly, Sugandhi is also a permanent labourer in the same tea garden. Aged 43 years, Sugandhi is a Christian Munda.

She is married and has three children. Rajamoni and Sugandhi belong to *line* No. 2. During the time of Rajamoni's eldest sons wedding, the family needed extra utensils. So she approached Sugandhi for help. Immediately, and without any hesitation Sugandhi offered the utensils for the entire period of celebration.

Case V11.3.

Elizabeth, aged 23 years, belongs to the Munda tribe. She is a temporary labourer in Dhelakhat tea estate. She is illiterate, married and has a child who is one year old. Her husband Joachim, too, works in the same garden permanently. Elizabeth was pregnant and delivered a child in her own house. The *Dai Budi* was called to assist her. But after delivering the child the placenta did not fall and she was struggling with pain. Immediately, the neighbours rushed to the tea garden hospital with Elizabeth for help. The hospital failed to offer help since they did not have proper equipment. Again, they got the ambulance from the hospital and rushed her to the Tinsukia Civil hospital for treatment. Despite all these efforts, however, the patient could not be saved. During the entire exercise all the necessary help and co-operation were extended by the immediate neighbours only.

Thus, the relations between the members of the *lines* are very cordial and close. On every occasion, be it joyful or sorrowful, the members assist one another with mutual trust and affection. There exists even an emotional attachment towards one another. At the same time, they respect one another and do not interfere in one another's family affairs.

During the investigation, it has also been found that in any internal familial affair, especially when it is an unpleasant one, the neighbours generally do not come forward for any sort of voluntary help or interference. The following is an illustrative case of this.

Case VII.4.

Rajan, aged 48 years is a temporary labourer in Dirial tea estate. He is a Munda and is Hindu by religion. He is illiterate.

Rajan is married and has four children - three boys and one girl, aged 28 years, 25 years, 22 years and 20 years respectively. His wife Trishna also works in the same garden as a permanent labourer. She is 43 years old and she too is a Hindu Munda. On a payment day, during the present investigation, at around 8.30 p.m., Rajan arrived home after consuming alcohol (*haria*) heavily. Meanwhile the members of his family had already retired to bed. He entered the house and started shouting at his wife and children for going to sleep without waiting for him to return. Moreover, his eldest son was listening to the radio, which was playing at a high volume. This made Rajan still more angry. He shouted at everyone. Most of the neighbours could hear the high pitched quarrel in the family. Ultimately, his wife and children pushed him out through the door and shut it. Though every family in the neighbourhood was aware of the unpleasant incident in this particular family, no one came forward to interfere or to help the "aggrieved" ones.

It has, however, been reported by a number of respondents that earlier they used to volunteer their help on such occasions, even if their help was not sought. But, in some cases they had been chastised by the quarrelling couple on the plea that the episode was purely an internal familial affair; whereas in some other cases the quarrel had ended up in criminal litigation and they had to be unnecessarily involved in the same as witnesses, etc. Under the circumstances, nowadays, they generally avoid these situations.

The different *lines* in the plantations are not located continuously. The average distance from one cluster to the other is around 0.3 kin , the space in-between is interspersed by tea beds, paddy field, main road and neighbouring villages, etc. To an outsider each *line* appears to be an independent and autonomous community. So, in their day-to-day lives, excepting during working hours in the plantations, there is hardly any chance for a woman to meet some other women belonging to a different *line* . The scope of interaction during working hours is also very limited. As noted earlier (cf. *Chapter Six*), if they interact beyond exchanging good wishes or so; and if the interaction is prolonged, the *sardar* generally does not take it easily and considers it a dereliction of duty if he condones their socialising.

On Sundays and holidays some of the women do visit other *lines* if they have relatives and friends. Besides, most of the Christian women on Sundays join their men and other members of the family to participate in the community prayer held in the church, located within the plantation in one of the labour *lines*. Thus, the Sunday-prayers provide the hetero-ethnic Christian women (along with the men-folk), belonging to different *lines* an opportunity to interact with one another after the prayer.

The Bi-Weekly Market and The Women-Folk

Extra-familial interaction for the tea labourers, especially for that of the womenfolk, most of the time generally remains confined within the boundaries of the plantation only. Their interaction with the outside world is at a minimal level. However, the bi-weekly floating market is an important platform that provides the people with an opportunity to interact with different people beyond the garden community. Each tea plantation has its own market that sits twice a month, on the days when the workers receive their wages. The market generally sits in an open field within the garden or adjacent to it. Flying business men belonging to different ethnic, linguistic and religious groups from the neighbouring areas generally flock together in the market and set up their stalls of ready-made garments, rice, wheat flour and other edible items, vegetables, fruits and fancy items. Almost every day-to-day necessary item is available in these markets.

With regard to Dhelakhat and Dirial, the plantations under intensive investigation, it has been observed that the bi-weekly market sits on alternate Fridays in the open field within the garden.

On the day of the market, most of the labourers, both men and women as well as children, go there to buy various items. This is not only a place of buying and selling, but also an occasion of relaxation and interaction, meeting friends, peer groups and other people having common and mutual interests. To be more specific, shoppmig is not the only attraction in these markets. These are, as a matter of fact, the centres for old acquaintances to meet, and to provide ample opportunities to the workers to have a routine outing. Alongside interacting with the people from beyond the garden community on the economic front, they also meet their co-workers, friends and relatives from other *lines*. During the present investigation, it has also been observed that a good number of women and men workers attend the market only to meet their friends and relatives living in other *lines*. They gossip about various issues. Very often they discuss other issues like marriage settlement and engagement. Besides a few stalls for light refreshment, country liquor is also openly sold in the market. Most of the people spend the whole day in the market and enjoy themselves to their heart's content. In many cases both the husband and the wife go together to enjoy a change in their monotonous daily routine. As noted earlier, besides shopping, sometimes they get the opportunity of discussing even marriage negotiations in the bi-weekly market. These discussions generally become more effective if husband and wife are both present together.

Case VII. 5.

Jayanti, aged 46 years belongs to the Parjah tribe. She is illiterate and a permanent labourer in Dhelakhat tea estate. She is married and has six children. Her husband Hikoka is also a permanent labourer in the same garden. He is 48 years old. During the time of investigation in 1998, on a payment day they received their wage amounting to Rs. 660.00. With that amount both of them went to the market to purchase the essential items for the family. While they were in the market they met Krishna aged 45 years, belonging to the Parjah tribe, working as a permanent labourer in the same garden. He is a resident of *line* no. 2, while Hikoka and his wife belong to Mottapung line. During the course of their conversation with him, they came to know about his eldest daughter who had attained marriagable age. So Hikoka and his wife talked about their son, for whom they were looking for a match. Hikoka offered him a bowl of *haria* and requested him to accept the offer. Finally they settled the marriage.

Therefore, the bi-weekly market is a place of interaction, strengthening of relationship, development of new relationships and extension of mutual invitations for further interaction. They not only meet their friends, but also make new friends. In fact, this is one of the most interesting places where any one can interact with the labourers, irrespective of their age and sex, without any inhibition.

During the present investigation it has also been found that there are some intelligent young labourers who carefully observe the business psychology of the shopkeepers before they purchase a commodity, in order to pay the minimum price.

Case VII.6.

George, aged 23 years belongs to the Munda tribe. He is a permanent labourer in Dhelakhat tea estate. On the market day as usual he went to the market. Though he was intending to buy vegetables, he had been going around meeting his friends. At the same time, he had also been asking the prices of various items, but he did not purchase anything and went back home. He presumed that the prices would fall towards the evening as the raw vegetables would lose their freshness by then. Besides, these would fetch a still lower price on the following day, so the business men would prefer to sell these vegetables at a lower price towards the closing of the day. Accordingly, George went to the market for a second time in the evening to do the marketing. As expected, he could actually purchase the desired vegetables at a much lower price.

Women-Folk and The Media

The most important function of the mass media is to communicate with the masses. Mass media transmit information to a very large audience, irrespective of age, sex, education, ethnicity and religious denomination, within a short period of time. The more a group of people is exposed to the media, the more it becomes aware of, and involved in, the affairs of the larger society of which it is a part.

The newspaper, radio and television are the three most important impersonal media of contact with the wider society. In a very few of the families under investigation, there are battery operated radio sets. But users rarely seem to be interested in listening to news broadcast. Most of the time, programmes are tuned to Hindi songs. While listening to the songs, they usually do some domestic work simultaneously and as such, the volume is always turned up very high. The people are yet to develop the habit of listening to the news. Incidentally, the newspaper is an unknown item among them. Even the club does not subscribe to any newspaper.

Television is a very effective means of communication for both the educated and the uneducated, and the literate and the illiterate. It provides a lot of information as well as education to all the viewers. In the modem society, television has reached the remotest of the rural areas and has proved to be one of the best sources of information as well as entertainment.

In both the plantations under investigation almost in every *line*, at least one or two families possess television sets. Through various programmes in the television, both men and women workers, and both the young and old ones receive a lot of relevant information about the goings-on in the larger society. Since most of the labourers are illiterate; and since their movements outside are restricted for some reasons, this is one of the best means through which they can have contact with the outside world. Moreover, for the women workers, who are otherwise overburdened with their productive and re-productive pre-occupations, television is a major source of relaxation.

On Sundays and other holidays, some visit the neighbouring families that have television to view different programmes, especially to watch films. Some of the young women are so addicted to Hindi films that they are very familiar with the names of the popular Bollywood actors and actresses.

Besides, once a month, the management also makes an arrangement to show films in the tea garden free of cost. Most of the womenfolk go to enjoy the film show, and thereby enjoy some relaxation and entertainment. This is also an occasion for them to interact with one another and to be exposed to the outside world which is not very familiar to them. All these exposures and experiences no doubt have some influence on their thoughts and life style.

Women Workers and The Trade Union

A discussion on the community life of the people under investigation remains incomplete unless some mention is made about their relations with the industrial authorities. This, in turn, calls for a brief passing reference to the trade union activities in the plantations, and the degree of participation, particularly of the women workers, which participation may be construed as a scale to measure (in terms of quality) their position in the labour community as well as with regard to the industrial authorities.

A trade union is an association of workers for the purpose of safeguarding their interests as well as of improving the working conditions of the worker through collective discussions and negotiations with the management. The Indian Trade Union Act was passed in 1926, and it gave a formal recognition to the workers' right to organise themselves and to safeguard their interests.

As noted earlier (cf. *Chapter Three*), in the initial stage, the work conditions for the plantation labourers were very unsatisfactory. But most of the people being illiterate and recruited from very backward sections of the society, they had to reconcile themselves to the situation without any sort of protest. Very often, they submitted to the rigours of the situation without much opposition on their part. Whatever opposition there was, came from the educated public in India as well as in Great Britain. In spite of all these odds, trade unions in the tea districts of North East India had a comparatively late development. The labourers were in fact quite unable till 1939 to take any organised action to promote their common interests.

An organised trade union activity on a sustained basis, however, started in Assam for the first time in 1939. Its Chairman was Shri A.K. Chanda and Vice-Chairman Shri Sanat Kumar Ahir, both then members of the Assam Legislative Assembly.

In May 1945, five individual garden unions and one Assam Tea Labourers Association were formed in Sibsagar district through the efforts of Prof. P.N. Sarwan, a member of a tea labour family from Jorhat.

After the second World War, the labour movement spread rapidly among the tea garden workers. In 1947, a branch of the Indian National Trade Union Congress was formed among the labourers. All India Trade Union Congress also had its unit functioning among the tea garden labourers.

At present, there are the following trade unions among the tea plantation labourers in Assam.

1. *Assam Chah Mazdoor Sangh*
2. *Assam Chah Mazdoor Union*
3. *Assam Tea Labourers Association*
4. *Assam Chah mazdoor Sramik Sangh*
5. *Assam Chah Mazdoor Parishad*

The *Assam Chah Mazdoor Sangh* is the only union that has been functioning for the labourers of the plantations under investigation. It is affiliated to the Indian National Trade Union Congress with its headquarters at Dibrugarh. It has around 20 branches throughout Assam.

In each tea estate, a garden unit is constituted. Its activities are confined to the particular garden, and it looks into the affairs of non-fulfillment of certain small-scale demands of the labour community by the authorities. In case an issue becomes a stalemate, the garden unit seeks the intervention of the circle or the Central Body.

It is relevant to emphasise here that although considerable attention has been paid to the study of trade union activities in general, any exercise with regard to the participation of women workers in these activities has received very little attention. The following pages, therefore, have been devoted to a brief discussion on the extent of awareness and the involvement of women tea labourers in the trade union activities.

It has been observed by a good number of researchers (e.g. Kar, 1981) that the general labourers, irrespective of their sex, age and ethnic affiliation, do not show any genuine interest in the affairs of the trade union. This is mainly because of the fact that most of them do not have faith in the office bearers and the executive members of the union. By and large, they consider them to be not only inefficient and indifferent to the general labourers' problems, but also self-seekers. The female seems to be relatively indifferent to the activities of the union which is dominated by male leaders.

In the present setting, however, the situation with regard to women's participation and involvement in the union activities seems to be a mixed one. Notwithstanding the domination of the male members, there are some women members in the executive body. A good number of women have also been found not only to attend the general meetings, but also actively to participate in the deliberations and proceedings of the meetings.

It may be noted here that the executive body and the office bearers of the garden unit of the union is formed through election/selection for a term of three years in a general meeting, attended by all the labourers with the outgoing president in the chair, and occasionally having some observer from the management/circle office.

Incidentally, during the present investigation, the election of the office-bearers and the new executive body of the Dirial unit took place on 4th July, 2001 at 4.30 p.m. It was an organised meeting about which information was communicated to all the labourers, through the *line chowkidars* of the respective *lines* as well as through the *sardars*. The Asst. Manager of Tingrai branch, (Tingrai branch consists of 38 gardens) Shri. Bansilal Sahu, presided over the meeting. The venue of the meeting was the playground.

It was, in fact, a huge gathering. Around 500 labourers attended the meeting, out of which around 200 were women workers. It was interesting to note that all of them along with their plucking baskets, etc., arrived at the venue very punctually. They came straight from their work-spots to be at the meeting on time.

While beginning the meeting, Shri Sahu introduced the purpose of the meeting, and told them to consider some criteria while proposing the name of a prospective union leader. With regard to the criteria for a person to be eligible to be proposed for the purpose, he added, the person should be (i) a permanent worker in the plantation, (ii) able to speak at a public gathering (iii) in good health so as to be able to move here and there at short notice and (iv) preferably, literate . After this short introduction, he read out the names of the labour *lines;* and specified the number of members to be elected from each *line.*

The entire exercise was a very lively one in the sense that there was much whispering and lobbying among the members of both the sexes before the names were proposed by one person and seconded by some others. It was interesting to note that a section of the members vehemently opposed the proposals for re-electing some old members. Similarly, there was opposition when some names were proposed to be elected in absentia.

As a member was declared elected, he/she was brought in front of the gathering to be congratulated by the people through collective clapping. A total of 36 members were elected in the meeting who in turn elected the office bearers, namely, the President, the Secretary, two Asst. Secretaries and a Treasurer. There were four women members in the executive committee.

The meeting, however, could not be brought to a natural conclusion. With regard to the election of some members, murmuring started among some workers, and after a time it developed into unruly shouting and counter-shouting, among the different sections of the participants. There was apprehension of group-clashes, and as such, most of the people, particularly the women-folk, started leaving the venue, and the meeting also came to an abrupt unceremonious end.

This, however, does not depict the total picture with regard to women's participation and involvement in the trade union activities. There are a good number of women workers who are not at all bothered about these meetings, proceedings and elections. They are not only indifferent in this regard, but also some of them are even allergic to discussing these activities. As a matter of fact, most of them are not only over-burdened with their indoor and outdoor pre-occupations, but also they firmly believe that the union leaders work more for the interest of the management than for the welfare of the 'destitute' labourers.

Case VII.7.

Rita Surin, aged 32 years, belongs to the Munda tribe; and subscribes to Christianity. She has been working in Dhelakhat tea estate as a permanent worker. Her husband, too, is a permanent labourer in the same garden. When asked about her awareness, participation and involvement in the trade union and its activities in the tea garden, she simply said that neither had she heard about it, nor did she know what a trade union meant. She had also never bothered to acquire any knowledge and information about the trade union activities in the tea garden. She added that she did not have any confidence in the leaders. She maintained that the leaders were, by and large self-seekers, and worked more for the interest of the management than for that of their co-workers.

Case VII.8.

Somari Tanti is 45 years old. She has been working as a permanent worker in Dirial tea estate for the last 25 years. She is married and has five children. Her husband, too, is a permanent labourer in the same garden. When asked about her knowledge of the trade union and its activities, she said that those activities were meant for the male workers only, who had no other concerns and household worries . According to her, trade union activities were mainly meant for the male workers and she gave more importance to her productive and re-productive activities than to the trade union activities. She went on to say that even otherwise she was quite indifferent towards the activities of the union as she did not have any confidence in most of the leaders who were at the helm of its affairs.

Notwithstanding these observations, it seems, the women labourers are gradually coming forward to participate in trade union activities. With time, it is expected that their awareness of the same is likely to increase.

Woman and The Wider Society

The tea labourers, since their migration to the Assam plantations have by and large led the life of islet communities. The reasons for the same were both physical as well as man-made. Besides the very poor transport and communication network, the plantation management also did not want that the labourers should come in contact with the people from beyond the garden. Visitors' movements in the labour settlements were also controlled, and prior permission of the management was needed for visits from outsiders. This was done deliberately to keep the people detached from the wider society so that they perpetually remained submissive and servile.

As a matter of fact, initially the labourers were exploited to the maximum extent, and were maltreated and abused as if they were sub-humans. As such, the management did not want the people to come in contact with the wider society that might instil awareness among the people which might herald protests and unrest among them against their inhuman living and working conditions.

After the end of the colonial rule; and with the development of the transport and communication network the situation gradually changed. The horizon of contact as well as awareness among the tea garden workers (both men and women) gradually expanded.

Dhelakhat and Dirial tea estates are connected with the outside world through the township of Tinsukia. As noted earlier, people go to Tinsukia on various occasions. Many of the people (both men and women) from the gardens visit Tinsukia which is located at distances of approximately 8 km and 13 km from Dhelakhat and Dirial respectively.

Tinsukia being a commercial centre, they go there for major and minor shopping. They purchase different items from different shops. In the process, they interact with the people of different cultural and personal backgrounds.

They learn to bargain. With some people they develop intimacy, sometimes leading to friendship. Some of the intelligent women utilise their experiences with the prices of different commodities in Tinsukia, in making good bargains in the biweekly market in the gardens. In general, in the bi-weekly market, the businessmen want to make exorbitant profits by hiking the prices of almost all the commodities. The customers having some idea about the standard price can thus bargain better in the market.

The women-folk, especially the younger ones, on Sundays and holidays, sometimes go to Tinsukia to view movies in the cinema hall. They view especially Hindi films when these are screened. The influences of film actors and actresses can be observed in their dress and hair style. In some families, even the children are named after the popular film personalities.

On the whole, all these exposures seem to have broadened their world view, and they no longer seem to live in islet communities.

Woman Workers and The Voluntary Organisation

Women's movement in India proves itself to be unique as compared to the similar movements in other countries. The movement began much before the country became independent in 1947. The social reformers and political leaders were very much aware of the low status of women, particularly in the 18th and 19th centuries. For centuries together, women in India suffered from being placed at a lower social status because of the prevailing social customs and taboos.

During the pre-independence period, the main issues of the movement were to provide social equality to women by emancipating them from evil social customs and traditions. But after independence, the issues changed and all the women's movements spoke for their economic upliftment through eradication of poverty, imparting education, creation of awareness and creating jobs for women. Thereafter, women's empowerment was emphasised through participation in the decision making process (cited in Rath and Rath, 1999: 238).

The women's movement also grew out of the grassroots participating organisations of women. It has also been held that the grassroots organisations of urban and rural poor women are vital instruments to provide them collective strength, bargaining capacity and collective articulation of their interests (Banarjee, 1995).

Since independence, national development strategies under different plans and programmes have promoted women's grassroots organisations like *Mahila Mandals*, etc., for the delivery of services to women or for creating income generating activities for them.

With this background in mind, in the following pages an attempt has been made to find out whether the tea garden women workers participate in any such grassroots, organisation/s that aim at raising their total status in the society.

During the present intensive investigation it was found that none of the woman workers belonged to any organisation excepting some of the Christian women who were found to be members of *Mahila Sangh*.

Mahila Sangh is an association for the Catholic women of Dibrugarh. It is not a registered organisation. It aims at the total development of women as well as their families. Its membership is open to all Catholic women above twenty years of age, irrespective of their marital status and ethnic identity. Its main objectives are:

(i) to arouse the latent power of women

(ii) to foster respect for human life, especially the girl child

(iii) to encourage self-confidence through education and exposure to wider society.

As a normal practice, the different local units of the *Sangh* organise a formal meeting once in a month where all the members participate. They discuss various issues of a general nature, particularly those related to women, and also take some decisions as to how to minimise/undo, the problems. The general body meeting involving all the local units is convened annually. Members from all the units participate in the meeting to take stock of the preceding year's activities, and also to prepare some agenda for the succeeding year.

A still larger meeting is organised at Diocese level once in three years. The convention is generally participated by the Catholic women-folk to share various issues and experiences pertaining to their life and activities. The convention normally continues for three to four days and a good number of eminent personalities are also invited to speak on different issues related to the improvement of the quality of women's life.

Incidentally, during the present investigation, one such convention was held in Dibmgarh on 26-29 September, 1998 at the Bishop's House, for the women-folk of Dibrugarh Diocese.* The focal theme of the convention was "Women : agents of change and transformation". There were around 2500 woman delegates from the thirty *parishes.*** A good number of women from the field,

* For the conveniece of administration and management, the entire Catholic Church is divided into a number of Dioceses, each having a territorial jurisdiction. The Bishop is the head of a Diocese.

** A Diocese is again divided into a number of *Parishes* (each having some defined territorial jurisdiction). The Parish Priest is the head of a *Parish*.

where the present investigation was conducted, took part in the convention. Most of them were the leaders of the *Mahila Sangh.*

The inaugural function of the convention commenced at 7 p.m. on 26 September, 2001. Rev. Fr. Leander Kerketta, the Vicar General, presided over the entire function and hoisted the convention flag. In his message to the delegates , he advised them to be responsible members of the family and society, so as to become agents of change and transformation. There was also lighting of the lamp and a prayer invoking God's blessings on all the participants.

On 27 September, the morning *bhajans* and prayers started at 6.00a.m.. A series of sessions were then conducted by Ms. Sugandhi Subramani who works for the development of women through NGO and had come from Delhi. During her sessions she dealt with various issues like alcoholism and illiteracy , that hinder the growth and development of women and society. She, therefore, exhorted them to form small groups in their own settlement units and to work unitedly for the common cause of progress and development. She also conducted a few group discussions where the participants could share their problems, difficulties, and concerns, as well as experiences of success and failure.

On 28 September, the first session was conducted by Ms. Monica Devi, a lawyer from Dibrugarh. She spoke on the legal rights of women and advised them what to do in case of harassment and exploitation. There was a very lively interaction from the participants in the session.

That afternoon, Fr. Albert Tirkey the Parish priest of Golaghat addressed the audience on the need of having a woman's organisation. He conveyed his message through songs and dramas and made it very interesting to the audience, consisting, by and large, of the rural women.

In the evening, the participants drew up some action plan based on their needs. The most urgent need was identified as education of children and also stopping drinking habits (alcoholism) so as to save money as well as preserve health. In the night a cultural show was arranged by the participants.

On 29 September, 2001, during the concluding function, Rt. Rev. Bishop Joseph Aind (Bishop of Dibrugarh Diocese) urged the women to carry the light that they had received during the convention, and spread peace and development in their own areas as they returned to their families.

The entire programme was interesting and enriching to all the woman participants. Most of them were illiterate, yet there was a lot of participation during the group discussions. A good number of them were lactating mothers and their babies were brought along with them. Their whole-hearted participation aroused enthusiasm and zeal among them. They involved themselves to such a great extent that they asked to have such gathering organised more frequently.

In fine, with regard to their community interaction and interpersonal relationship within and beyond the tea garden, it seems, more and more working women are gradually coming forward to build new relationships, especially by actively involving themselves; and by opening new horizons beyond their tea garden setting in almost all spheres.

8

SUMMARY AND CONCLUSION

This chapter is a recapitulation and summary of the data presented and discussed in the preceding chapters. In the process, some concluding remarks have also been incorporated. An endeavour has been made to highlight the salient features of the findings of the present study with regard to the status of women working in the tea plantations in Upper Assam.

The *term* status has to be used with a double significance. A status, in abstract, is a position in a particular pattern and the status of each individual in each facet of life varies in degree according to the level of participation in these different patterns. The status of any individual means the sum total of these positions which one may occupy. It represents one's position in relation to the total society. The individual comes to occupy a status assigned to him in relation to the status of other persons within the society.

From the anthropological point of view, status is primarily a position in a social structure which involves rights, duties and reciprocal expectations of behaviour that do not depend upon the personal characteristics of the individual. Thus, Status is simply a collection of rights and duties played out in a society at a given time.

A role is the expected behaviour associated with a social position . The people are conscious of themselves and others occupying positions which carry with them certain rights and duties, and when the individual puts the rights and duties into effect, he/she is performing a role.

Thus, *status* is a relative term and it differs in its meaning from individual to individual and from society to society. So, too, the status of women differs from time to time and from society to society.

In the present study, *Status of women working in the tea plantations: A case study in Upper Assam*, an attempt has been made to examine and understand the prevailing status of women workers in the Assam tea plantation in the context of the existing socio-economic setting to which they have been exposed since their emigration there some one hundred and fifty years ago.

Though different studies have been carried out among the tea labourers from an anthropological point of view, yet no systematic and in-depth study has till date been undertaken this regard among the people under investigation.

For a better, more intensive and holistic understanding of the problem, the microfield for the purpose of investigation has conveniently been confined to two tea plantations located in Dibrugarh and Tinsukia Districts in Upper Assam.

Further, view of the fact that women's status varies from society to society and from one religious group to another, data has been collected from members belonging to different ethnic and religious groups. As the tea labourers in Assam are distributed in around 60 tribe and 40 caste groups; and in mainly two religious groups (the Non-Christians and the Christians), data has been collected, for the sake of convenience, from two tribes and one caste group and also from both the Christians and the Non-Christians.

An intensive investigation has been carried out in the micro-field to generate as much empirical data as possible, broadly with the following objectives in mind:

1. To have a detailed idea about the various activities of the woman labourers.
2. To understand the role of women in the socio-economic development of their family and community.

3. To get to know about the problems and needs of women in relation to education, wage earning, employment, expenses, and also to identify the factors that hinder their socio-economic development.
4. To attempt an evaluation of the position of working women in their family life as well as in the place of work.
5. To understand the level of participation of the working women in politics (Trade Union Activities).
6. To study the general health of woman workers (as reflected in the indices like age at marriage, fertility, infant mortality, etc.).
7. To find out whether the provisions of the Plantation Labour Act, with regard to the social securities and other facilities supposed to be made available to both men and women labourers, have actually been miplemented properly in the tea plantations under investigation.

The study has been guided by the following hypotheses:

1. Sex variation in status exists among the tea labourers : women workers enjoy a relatively low status.
2. Women have less accessibility to educational facilities : The majority of the tea garden woman workers are reluctant to send their daughters to schools.
3. The level of education of the couple has a direct bearing on the education of women: An educated couple is more inclined to send the daughters as well as sons to schools.
4. Literacy has a direct bearing on age at marriage: Literate women are relatively less interested in being married early.
5. Hard labour with sub-standard nourishment enhances morbidity: women workers are more prone to various diseases.

6. Hard labour with less nutritious nourishment reduces life span: women labourers in the tea garden live a relatively shorter life compared to the norm for women nationwide.
7. The level of awareness in political and community activities varies with sex: women labourers have a lower level of awareness.
8. Different levels of awareness in political and community activities prevail on the basis of outside exposure : women labourers with better outside exposure have a better level of awareness.
9. Leisure and recreation facilities are inequitably distributed : woman labourers get much less leisure time and far fewer recreational facilities as compared to their male counterparts.
10. Religion influences women's status : Christian women labourers, enjoy a better status in all spheres as compared to their Non-Christian counterparts.

Standard anthropological methods and techniques have been applied throughout the study, which has have been carried out in various successive stages. These are as follows :

The first stage was to formulate the problem (topic), and to choose the population and the micro-field.

To start with, exploratory visits were made to a number of plantations in Tinsukia and Dibrugarh Districts to ascertain their ethnic composition and the numerical strength of the different ethnic groups composing the labour population of the different tea plantations. Also, due consideration was paid to the accessibility to the plantation as well as the assured co-operation of the management. Taking into consideration all these factors, as well as consultations with the supervisor of the project, two plantations, namely; Dhelakhat tea estate in Tinsukia District and Dirial tea estate in Dibrugarh District (Upper Assam) were selected for the purpose of the present intensive investigation.

The next stage involved consultation of relevant literature, formulation of the research design, including preparation of relevant schedules, and preparation for initiating the field investigation. During the initial stage, a period of about six months was devoted to the preparatory stage of the study. For this purpose, intensive and extensive library work was carried out. In the meantime, a few visits were also made (i.e., prior to the actual field work) to the plantations, to meet the management personnel as well as the people, so as to establish a better rapport; and also to arrange accommodation for camping during the course of the intensive field work.

Because of their numerical preponderance and also because of some other considerations, intensive data has been collected from the Tanti, Munda and the Parjah families. Besides, the Christian (Munda) families have also been covered in the investigation. Initially, it was proposed to cover, preferably, at least one hundred families in each group so as to cover a total sample of 400 families. But, because of some unavoidable circumstances certain changes were effected in this regard. For the Parjah and the NonChristian Munda, data has been collected from 100 families in each group. But, in the case of the Tanti and the Christian Munda, the total available number of families were 70 and 80 respectively. Therefore data has been generated from these 150 families only (and not 100 families each). Thus, the total sample size stands at 350 families (and not 400).

After the selection of the sample population, a door-to-door census survey was carried out in these two tea plantations with the help of a prepared schedule. This helped the investigator to collect the basic demographic as well as other factual information, related to the families of the woman workers of the tea plantations. Besides, the survey also provided the researcher with an opportunity to introduce herself to the people and explain clearly the purpose of the visit and the academic aims of the study; and also to seek the respondents' co-operation during the followup investigation. Above all, the exercise provided the researcher with a prolonged opportunity for establishing a very good rapport with the people in general.

The initial phase of the study was done with the help of the *Line Chowkidars*. This was followed by intensive field work for the collection of in-depth qualitative data. During this period a number of anthropological techniques were used in the field either independently or in collaboration, depending on the nature of the data in question. The important techniques used were (i) observation (both participant and non-participant) (ii) interview (both individual and group; structured and unstructured) and (iii) collection of concrete cases.

It is obvious that the research tools and techniques used for the purpose were not uniform throughout the study. There are many aspects in a group's day-to-day life, as well as in their social and community life, where one's participation and indepth understanding remain inadequate with pre-detertnined tools like interview schedule, and questionnaire etc. Many of the interview processes with the people are symbolic, the meaning of which can best be understood by close observation and careful scrutiny.

After the completion of the field work, systematisation, classification and analysis of the mass of the generated data have been done and the dissertation has been prepared. The quantitative data analysed by using the simple statistical tools and techniques. All the possible attempts have been made to co-relate the data with different variables. The qualitative data have been generated and systematised according to the reliability. To make the dissertation more holistic and communicative , photographs, maps and figures have also been incorporated where relevant.

The entire mass of data, after being systematised and organised has conveniently been presented in eight different chapters in the thesis.

In the *First Chapter* an attempt has been made to introduce the theoretical background of the problem in its proper perspective. It embodies discussion on the study, review of literature, the objectives, working hypotheses, relevance of the study, the method and the techniques followed in the study and an overall plan of data presentation.

While introducing the specific problem for the purpose of the present study, all efforts have been made to incorporate as much detail as possible with regard to the discussion on the concepts, the objectives, working hypotheses and the relevant methodology.

Chapter Two begins with a discussion on the origin of tea as a beverage, and it provides a brief history of the introduction and development of tea plantations in Assam. It may be noted here that the cultivation of tea plants and the manufacture of the finished tea leaves has long been a major industry in Assam and at present it occupies a very important place in the economy of Assam. There are around 760 full-fledged tea plantations in Assam covering an area of approximately more than 51 percent of the total area under tea in the whole of India. Besides, there are around 2,500 small scale (producing green leaf only) tea plantations in Assam.

Assam produces 410,430.000 kilograms of tea every year to bring in a revenue of not less than Rs. 500 crore per year to the country. The Assam tea plantations at present have a resident labour population of more than 20 lakhs and a work force of more than 9 lakhs.

In keeping with the contents of the problem under investigation, in the discussion, special emphasis has been laid on the various modes of recruitment of labourers in the plantation. A detailed discussion has been made on the circumstances under which the heterogenous groups of labourers had to be brought from different states. Due to the acute labour scarcity in the state, the labourers were brought mainly from Bengal, Bihar, Orissa, Madhya Pradesh, Uttar Pradesh, Andhra Pradesh and Tamilnadu with the false promises of "less work and high wages". *Contractor system* and *Sardari* system were the two ways the planters used to recruit the labourers.

While concluding the chapter, an idea has been provided of the ethnic composition of the labourers, working in the Assam tea plantations.

The land and the people where the present investigation has been carried out, have been briefly introduced in *Chapter Three.* Along with an overall idea about the heterogenous nature of the population composition, the discussion begins with a brief geographic and historical note on North-east India in general and Assam in particular. An attempt then has been made to introduce Dibrugarh and Tmsukia Districts (where the micro-field is located), from the historical, geographical and ethno-demographic points of view.

Around 30 percent of the plantations of the state are located in Dibrugarh and Tinsukia districts and it is also estimated that around 25 percent of the population of the districts is composed of tea and ex-tea labourers and their dependants.

In Tinsukia district alone at present, there are around 1')9 tea gardens belonging to various companies, covering an area of 80,000 hectares. Besides, there are a good number of recently opened small-scale tea plantations that produce green leaf only.

The micro-field for intensive investigation has been introduced with some details with regard to the two plantations' location, social boundary, area of coverage, and history of establishment . Along with this, a discussion on the physical features (e.g. climate, communication and transport, labour settlement, creche, drainage system, important public places, etc.) has also been incorporated here in brief .

The chapter also deals with the ethnic composition of the labourers in the two tea plantations. There are a total of 1035 families distributed in 36 different ethnic groups. Among the tribal groups, the Mundas, however, are the numerically dominant one and the Parjahs occupy the next position. Among the caste groups, the Tanti families have the highest numerical strength.

The chapter concludes with brief ethnographic accounts of the three communities under investigation.

Chapter Four deals with some important aspects of social life of the people in general and the womenfolk in particular.

In view of the fact that the family is the most important element in the social life; and also view of the fact that the women's role in the family as daughter, sister, wife and mother are fundamental for understanding their status in a society, an attempt has been made in the chapter to have a reasonably detailed understanding of the different aspects of the family life of the people. Marriage being very intimately related with family, a brief discussion has also been made on some aspects of the institution. All possible efforts have, however, been made to put particular focus on the role of women in different spheres.

Broadly classified as patrilocal, the family among the people, in practice is however, neolocal though patrivicinal. It is very interesting to note that the socially recognised marital union is not a pre-condition for establishing a family. An adult boy and a girl having mutual consent to live as husband and wife in order to establish a new family (of procreation), can go ahead with their plan without necessarily being married Immediately. The society however, prescribes that the couple should get married any time before they give their children in marriage.

Data on family size show that on average there are 5.64 members in a family. The model size however, is 5.21 with a modal frequency of 56.57 percent. Families with 10 and more members are very rare whereas the 'single member' family has been found to be absent among the people.

With regard to the type and composition, it has been found that the nuclear type of family is numerically dominant (72.00%). The majority (93.00%) of these families are composed of the parents and their unmarried children. The data make it apparent that in the present setting, the communities, irrespective of their group affiliation, by and large, prefer to have a relatively small size family, preferably having only the parents and the unmarried children as the inmates.

While dwelling some more on the size and structure of the family, it seems, this trend has an important implication on woman's status in the family. In an extended family, in the midst of all the elderly kin members, the newly married woman's liberties are curtailed to a great extent. In a nuclear family, on the other hand with the co-operation of the husband, many of her liberties are restored and by and large, she can participate in many of the decision making processes in the family.

A family being the initial platform for socialisation and inculteration, it was expected that an overall idea of the family life involving the members of the two sexes would be reflective of the position of a woman in the family in particular and the society in general.

As revealed by the data, it seems, the woman members, by and large, are not treated equally with their male counterparts in the family. The differential treatment appears to start right from childhood. The data show that a very small number of people (14.00%) prefer to have a girl child in their family and that too, mainly because of the prospects of a better domestic assistance as well as a sustained emotional attachment with the natal family even after the girl is given in marriage. During the pregnancy period the majority of the parents (51.50%) become worried about the sex of the prospective child; and in this regard the women are by and large more in number to be worried about the same. women's worries are however, more for their kin members than for their ownselves. All these worries and apprehensions relate to the period before the birth of a child. Afterwards, the picture, at least apparently seems to be a different one. It has been found that the majority of the people (79.50%) do not consider the female child as a burden, and the people accept the birth of a female child relatively more liberally. Nevertheless, it has also been observed that in a good number of families discriminatory treatment is meted out towards the female children right from childhood in terms of equal access to education, food, health, recreation and many other spheres.

With regard to inter-group variation in this regard, it seems, the discriminatory treatment favouring a boy-child is maximum among the Christian Mundas. This apparently contradicts the hypothesis **Religion influences women's status : Christian woman labourers enjoy a better status in all spheres as compared to their Non-Christian counterparts.**

Marriage among the people appears to be a social contract and is generally reversible. Monogamy is the general practice, and the usual mode of acquiring a mate is through negotiation. However, marriage by mutual consent and elopement is reasonably frequent among them. Now-a-days the marital union among the younger generation, by and large, has been found to be more a personal affair than an affair of the two families and the two sets of kinsmen. Interestingly, as noted earlier, marriage among the people is not considered as a pre-condition for the establishment of a family. The marriage formalities may be observed conveniently at a later period.

Child marriage is not practised among them. The hypothesis, **Literacy has a direct bearing on age at marriage,** could not be tested, since most of the people under investigation happen to be illiterate. The age difference between the spouses is around 5 years. Divorce, though socially permitted has not been reported from the population under investigation. A few cases of inter-group marriages have been reported to have been socially accepted by the respective communities and the majority of these couples belong to the Christian Munda. During the present investigation, a good number of women have been found to be leading a widow's life. Widow re-marriage is permitted in all the four groups, but many of the young widows did not go for re-marriage only to avoid the element of uncertainty in smooth bringing up of their children.

While dwelling some more on the family life, it may be noted that the husband-wife relation is of love and affection along with due respect and responsibilities towards each other. Both of them spend their earnings in the smooth running of the family. But in most of the cases, the husband's decision dominates the course of events; and it seems, the wives by and large, accept this domination as a matter of fact. Nevertheless, it seems, in certain vital issues like marriage and education of the children , both the husband and the wife by and large do discuss together; but, generally the husband's decision dominates. Notwithstanding this dominance of the husband in the decision making process, it may be noted that in the major decisions regarding day-to-day affairs of the family expenses and domestic activities, etc., the wife has a greater say.

With regard to the daily life of the inmates of a family, it seems, though there is a broad division of labour on the basis of sex, the woman members, as a matter of fact, are relatively much more pre-occupied as compared to the men. A detailed understanding of the daily life of the people makes it apparent that women generally do not get much leisure time in the midst of their domestic, motherhood and job preoccupations. From early morning till night, they remain very busy with their work at home as well as in the tea bed, in addition to child bearing and child rearing activities. The hypothesis, **Leisure and recreational facilities are inequitably distributed: woman labourers get much less share as compared to their men counterpart** has thus been found to be valid in the present study.

Chapter Five is devoted to health and education among the women workers of a tea plantation. In the first part, the factors that have a strong bearing on the general health of the woman workers have been discussed. These include, housing condition, nature of environmental sanitation; and quality and contents of food and drink, etc., that have been dealt with in detail. With regard to the housing facilities provided in the plantation, it is observed that these do not conform to any uniform plan; and often the accommodation seems to be unhygienic. By and large, the living rooms are devoid of proper light and ventilation; and the floors very often remain damp. Most of the houses have been found to be in dilapidated condition and the repairing works are usually not done regularly. So too, the common bathing enclosures and the toilets have been found to be unhygienic and ill-maintained.

The drainage system seems to be very poor and during the rainy season the entrances of the houses become very slippery causing inconvenience of accessibility to the same.

With regard to their food and drink, it has been found that the basic diet of the people consists of rice, wheat, vegetables and black tea with salt. The adults, irrespective of sex, working in the tea plantation take principal meals twice a day. It has also been found that the people, irrespective of their sex, by and large, are in the habit of taking alcoholic drinks, especially the locally made haria.

With regard to the morbidity scenario, most of the woman workers have been found to suffer from various diseases like chest pain, knee pain, back ache, gastritis, anaemia, and cough and cold, etc. According to the garden physician, many of the diseases result from malnutrition and undernutrition. Thus, the hypothesis, **Hard labour with sub-standard nourishment enhances morbidity : woman workers are relatively prone to various diseases,** seems to be valid in the present study. Further, in view of the fact that there are relatively more widows (51 as compared to 35 widowers) in the population, apparently it seems, the hypothesis, **Hard labour with less nourishment reduces life span : woman labourers in the tea garden live a relatively shorter life** is not acceptable. However, it has been observed that in most of the cases a woman worker generally looks older than the real age; and this may be due to hard work and less nourishment.

In case of a pregnant woman it has been found that the people by and large, do not provide any special nutrient food to the expectant mother, neither during pregnancy, nor after delivery. Most of them do not seem to be aware of the need of such special care. Pregnancy wastage due to abortion and still birth however, is not significantly high. But infant mortality and child mortality is quite frequent among them.

With regard to the fertility performance, it has been observed that the average number of live birth in the population is 3.75. However, it varies from group to group. The figures range from 2.89 (Tanti) to 4.48 (the Christian Munda).

In case of a child-birth, it may be relevantly noted here that, the people by and large, have been found to prefer home-delivery with the assistance of untrained but experienced *dais* (mid-wives) from the tea labour community. As a result, in many cases, there arise complications that probably could have been tackled if the venue of delivery would have been the hospital.

While dwelling on education, it may be noted that the highest level of educational attainment is seen among the members between 10- 19 years of age. This probably indicates that education has been making an in-road only among the members of the growing generation. While making a group-wise analysis of the data, it has been found that the level of education in the caste group is better than that among the tribes. When the comparison is made between the two tribes, the Mundas are found to be relatively in an advantageous position as compared to the Parjahs. Within the Munda again, there is a conspicuous difference between the Christian and the Non-Christian Mundas. The Christian Mundas are relatively more literate than their Non-Christian counterpart.

In all the four groups under investigation, it has been seen that the literacy level of the females is much below as compared to that of their male counterparts. Though there is a tendency to send their children to school, it is seen that the first preference is given to the boys. In other words, it seems, the women have lesser accessibility to educational facilities and the majority of the tea garden woman workers are reluctant to send their daughters to schools. They maintain, for the girls, from their childhood, primary importance is to be given to domestic training.

With regard to infra-structural facilities for education in the plantation, it has been observed that, the schools are relatively ill-equipped in terms of both teaching staff as well as accommodation and housing condition. Poor economic background, coupled with lack of proper incentives may contribute towards the relatively higher rate of absenteeism and drop-out among the school going children.

The hypothesis, **Level of education of the couple has a direct bearing on the education of women : The educated couple are more inclined to send their daughters (along with the sons) to schools** could not be confidently tested in the present study, because most of the couples under investigation were illiterate. Even otherwise, the very few literate ones have also not been found to be interested in sending their daughters to school. This observation with the very limited number of families, however, contradicts the working hypothesis noted above.

A broad outline of women's level of participation in the economic activities as well as the problems that they encounter in the process has been discussed in *Chapter Six.*

Tea is one of the labour intensive industries that depends mainly on woman workers. Plucking of the tea leaves is an important operation as the quality of the manufactured tea depends upon the care and attention with which the plucking is done. In India, plucking is done by hand, and women are largely employed in the operation.

Thus, the numerical strength of the women workers in the plantations under investigation has been found to be relatively more than that of their male counterparts.

The majority of the woman workers are engaged in plucking. Only four of them are engaged in other pursuits, viz, primary teacher (1), *sardarin* (1) and hospital attendant (2). They are better paid and also enjoy a better status.

It has however, been observed that more than 50 percent of the woman workers are casual labourers who do not enjoy any social security benefits and many other fringe benefits.

It seems, economic compulsion is the main driving force for this large number of women seeking employment in the tea plantation. Their income is by and large contributed to the common family fund. Though an earning member, a woman worker very often does not enjoy any liberty in spending her income, a sample survey in this regard reveals that more than 80.00% of the respondents do not have the liberty to spend their income without their husbands' approval. The Christian Munda and the Parjah husbands seem to be relatively more liberal in this regard.

With regard to their position in the work-place, the only parity seems to be in the wage rate. Prior to 1985, the daily wage for a woman labourer was Rs. 1. 52 less than that of a man labourer. Now it is equal. However, the opportunity for a woman worker, even for a simple promotion is so rare that stagnation in the work place is the characteristic feature. Obviously, depression is a common expression in most of them. Besides, in the work place, they very often encounter a host of physical as well as psychological problems. At their work place they generally lack drinking water and toilet facilities. At times they are unable to respond to nature's call due to lack of toilets nearby. Over and above, at times, the members of the supervisory staff have been found to deal with them in a very unkind way.

Alongwith their outdoor pre-occupations, a woman also has to look after the domestic front as a wife, mother and a home maker. By and large, they do not get the required help and assistance from the male members of the family. A woman labourer is thus subjected to plurality of role expectations which at times become naturally incompatible.

On the whole, the woman workers lead a very busy daily life with practically no time to have leisure and relaxation. They are generally overburdened with their productive, reproductive and other domestic activities. This is more so in the nuclear families. Sometimes these multiple responsibilities result in role-conflict for many of them.

The role and participation of women in the community life as well as in the political sphere with special reference to trade union activities have been focused in *Chapter Seven*. The chapter begins with a discussion on the nature, degree and extent of exposure of the womenfolk beyond the familial context . A detailed discussion has been attempted as to their interaction with the plantation community as a whole; and the same with the immediate and remote neighbourhood.

Within the garden it is seen that the labour lines are their immediate neighbourhood, where they experience a close-knit relationship among the members of the respective *lines*. They share their daily life of joys and sorrows with one another. Also they come in contact with the members of the *lines* during the bi-weekly market. The bi-weekly market is not considered a place of econonuic transactions only. It has a significant social dimension too. It is very often used as a platform for strengthening the existing relationship as well as of initiating the establishment of new relationships.

In the chapter, an attempt has also been made to have a brief appraisal of the trade union activities vis-a-vis the woman labourers. It has been observed that the woman labourers do take part in the affairs of the labour union, and some of them contribute quite actively as general as well as executive members. Notwithstanding the domination of the male members in the union some of the woman members do try to exert their views on some specific issues. But, at the same time, there are many more who have been found to be habitually indifferent towards trade union activities. They however, have their own arguments to defend their behaviour.

Nevertheless, as a whole, it seems, a sense of awareness is gradually making in-roads among the woman workers, a good number of whom are now-a-days taking active interest in the collective activities including those of the trade union.

The study further reveals that their exposure to nearby urban centre as well as to various mass media has observably broadened their world view. They no longer seem to live in islet communities. The outside exposure, however, has been found to be relatively more among the members of the younger generation and specially those subscribing to Christianity. With regard to their participation in the activities in some voluntary (women's) organisation, it seems, none of them is associated with any organisation barring some of the Christian women who have been found to be the members of *Mahila Sangha*, a voluntary association for Catholic women.

Within the limitations of the present study, it is thus apparent that with some minor inter group variations here and there, there exists, in varying degrees, sex variation in status among the tea labourers, and the women workers, by and large, have a relatively low status. Though in the overall economic and developmental pursuits, the participation of women is substantially impressive, though they are now economically more or less independent, women still seem to be voiceless or have a very minimal voice in most of their life situations. Their participation in the decision- making process is very marginal and they still find themselves relatively weak in taking decisions at home and outside independently.

Notwithstanding the observable gap between the male and female status, it may, however, be pointed out here that in comparison to the past, there are some positive developments in the status and role of the working women under investigation. Further, it seems, a sense of awareness in this regard is gradually developing among a section of the younger women who are taking active part in the activities of the labour union and other accessible organisations.

In view of their mass illiteracy, in fine, it may be emphasised that they can be made conscious of their identity, dignity and self-respect only through education. Education is necessary also to do away with the dependence syndrome to make the womenfolk more self-reliant, self-motivated and self-directed.

In the prevailing situation, it is expected that the plantation management, the State Government, different women's organisations and the various NGOs would contemplate appropriate steps in this regard so that there is a perceptible improvement in the overall status of woman workers in the tea plantation. To be more specific, for example, the State Government may be relatively more vigilant to see that the labour welfare measures incorporated in the Plantation Labour Act, 1951 and the Plantation Labour Rules, 1956 are implemented and sustained by the plantation management in letter and spirit. The plantation management, in addition may contemplate some schemes to do away with the child labour system in a phased manner which in all probabilities, and in the long run will contribute towards achieving a better education and health status of womenfolk in particular and the labour community in general.

Similarly, the NGOs and the women's organizations could initiate several programmes to take care of grass-root level conscientization, adult literacy and social education, etc. for the promotion of overall welfare of the women and their children. Education should be provided for the younger generation so that they may be able to live a better life in the future. The women could be taught to save part of their income so that in times of need they may not borrow from the money lenders. Similarly , the women workers should be made aware of the harm they cause due to their heavy drinking habits. Promotion of qualified personnel in different sectors are also very much needed. since lack of leadership is one of the major problems, the children who are interested in studies should be given free education not only in primary school but also in higher education.

Above all, political awareness should be created among the women workers. The mangement should provide more opportunity for them to expose themselves to the outside world so that they may be able to widen their horizon and be motivated to progress and development.

REFERENCES

A committee of the Royal Anthropological Institute of Great Britain and Ireland. 1971. Notes and queries on anthropology (Reprint, Original, 1874). London: Routledge and Kegan Paul Ltd.

ALTEKAR, A.S. 1938. The position of women in Hindu civilisation. Delhi: Motilal Banarasidas.

AWASTHI, R.C. 1975. Economics of tea industry in India with special reference to Assam. Guwahati: United Publishers.

BADER, CLARISSE. 1958. Women in ancient India. London: Martin, Mary E.R.K. Tubner and co. Ltd.

BAIG, TARA ALI (Ed.). 1958. Women in India. Delhi: Publication Division.

BANERJEE, N.K. 1995. "Grassroot empowerment(1875-1990). A discussion paper," occasional paper No. 22, Centre for Women's Development Studies, New Delhi.

BANTON, MICHAEL. 1989. "Role" in the Social science Encyclopaedia. Edited by Adam Kuper and Jessica Kuper, London: Routledge. pp.714-716.

BARUAH,- TUL TUL. 2000. Mundas in tea plantation: A study in their health behaviour. Dibrugarh: N.L. Publishers.

BEALS, L.RALPH. HOIJER, HARRY and ALAN R. BEALS. 1977. An introduction to anthropology. New York: Macmillan Publishing Co. Inc.

BEDI, YASH PAL. 1980. Social and preventive medicine. Delhi: Atma Ram and Sons.

BELFOUR, G. EDWARD. 1976. Encylopaedia Asiatica comprising Indian subcontinent Eastern and Southern Asia Maidah-Nyasa. New Delhi: Cosmo Publication. Vol. 11.

BHADRA, MITA. 1992 Woman workers of tea plantation in India. New Delhi: Heritage Publishers.

BHADRA, MITA. 1997. "Changing family, authority, role and status of the tea plantation women workers in Darjeeling District", in Plantation labourers of North East India. Edited by R.K. Bhadra and Mita Bhadra. Dibrugarh: N.L. Publishers, pp.229-46.

BHADRA, R.K. 1990. "Some features of tea plantations and surplus labourers in Assam", in Tea garden labourers of North-East India. Edited by S. Karotemprel and B. Dutta Roy. Shillong: Vendrame Missiological Institute.

BHOWMICK, S.K. 1981. Class formation in the plantation system. Delhi People's publishing house.

BHUIYAN, N.C. 1960. Cha Bagichar Banua. Jorhat Ahom Sahitya Sabha.

BHUYAN, B.C. (Ed.) 1993. The tribal women. New Delhi: Cosmos Publications.

CHAKRAVORTY, R.N. 1997. Socio-economic development of plantation workers in North-east India. Dibrugarh: N.L.Publishers.

CHALIKA, JYOTIPRASAD. 1997. The North East Times (an Assamese Daily Publishing from Guwahati), June 8.

CORMACK, MARGARET. 1953. The hindu women. New York: Bureau of Publications, Teacher college, Colombia University.

COUSINS, M.E. 1947. Indian womanhood today. Allahabad: Kitabistan.

CRAWFORD, T.C. 1924. Hand book of castes and tribes employed on the tea estates of North East India. Calcutta: Indian Tea Association.

DAS, KRISHNA. 1998. North East Sun, September 1-14 p. 18.

DAS, R.M. 1961. Women in Manu and his seven commentators. Varanasi: Tata printing works.

DAS GUPTA, PRANAB KUMAR. 1978. "Tribal women in industrial Context", in Tribal women in India. Edited by a committee on

Tribal women in India. Calcutta: Indian Anthropological Society, pp. 192-99.

DAS GUPTA, P.K. and L.A. KHAN. 1983. Impact of tea plantation industry on the life of tribal labourers. Calcutta: Anthropological Survey of India.

DAVID, JOEL and KARL SCAPHIRA. 1975. The book of coffee and tea. New York: St. Martin's Press.

DEKA USHA and PRADEEP PATOJOSHI. 1978. " Fertility and Pregnancy Wastage", in Cultural and Biological Adaptability of man with special reference to North East India. Edited by Kar R.K. Dibrugarh: Department of Anthropology, Dibrugarh University. pp. 193-199.

DESROCHERS, JOHN. 1987. Education for Social change. Bangalore: Centre for Social Action.

DIGUMARTI, BHASKRA RAO and PUSHPA LATHA DIGUMARTI. 1998. International Encyclopaedia of Women: The Status of World's women. New Delhi: Discovery Publishing House. Vol. 1. pp. 193-217.

DIGUMARTI, BHASKRA RAO and PUSHPA LATHA DIGUMARTI. 1998. International Encyclopaedia of Women: Women challenges and advancement. New Delhi: Discovery Publishing House. Vol. 3. pp. 37-38.

FIRTH, RAYMOND. 1958. Human types. London: The new American Library.

FIRTH, RAYMOND. 1961. Elements of social organization. London: Walts and Co. (First published in 1951, 3rd ed 1961).

FORTES, M. 1945. The dynamics of clanship among the Tallensi London: Oxford University Press.

FORTES, M. 1949. The Web of Kinship among the Tallensi. London Oxford University Press.

GAIT, E.A. 1926. History of Assam. Simla: Thacker, Spink and Co.

GHONGLAH, HALLEHOHIM. 1996. "The church and health care in the North East" , in Impact of christianity on North East India. Edited by J. Puthenpurakal. Shillong: Vendrame Institute Publication.

GISBERT, S.J. 1984. Fundamentals of sociology. Bombay: Orient Longman Ltd.

GOHAIN, R. 1974. Karam Puja aru jhumur geet (in Assamese) Jorhat Assam Sahitya Sabha.

GRIFFITHS, P. 1967. The history of Indian Tea Industry. London: Welden Feld and Nicolson.

GUHA, A. 1977. Planter-Raj to swaraj: Freedom struggle and electoral politics in Assam 1826-1974. Delhi: Council of Historical Research.

HALAYYA, M. 1972. An economic analysis of the Indian tea industry and public policy. Dharwar: Karnatak University.

HAMMOND, DOROTHY and JABLOW ALTA. 1976. Women in cultures of the world. California: Cummings publishing company.

HARLALKA, S. S. 1975. Tea garden labour in Assam. Dhubri (Assam): People's Publishing House.

HARLER, C.P. 1964. -The culture and marketing of tea. London: Oxford University Press.

HATE, C.A. 1969. The changing status of women. Bombay: Allied publishers.

HERSKOVITS, M.J. 1974. Cultural anthropology. Delhi: Oxford and I.B.H. publishing Co.

HURLOCK B. ELIZABETH, 1981. Developmental Psychology: A life span approach. New Delhi: Tata McGraw - Hill Publishing Company Ltd.

I.L.O, 1938. Industrial Labour in India. Series A, Industrial relation, No. 41. Geneva.

ICSSR. 1955. A synopsis of the report of the national committee on status of women in India. New Delhi: IIPA Hostel Building, Indraprastha Estate.

INDRA, M.A. 1955. The status of women in ancient India. Banaras: Motilal Banarasidas publishers.

JAIN, S. 1983. The tea gardens in Assam: Patterns of recruitment, employment and exploitation of tribal labourers. Social Action. Vol. 33 No. 4, pp. 262-284.

JHA, J. C. 1996. Aspects of indentured inland emigration to North East India 1859-1918. New Delhi: Indus Publishing Company.

JHA, MEHTA and MENON. 1998. Status of Indian women: crisis and conflict in gender issues. New Dehli: Kaniska, publishers distributers.

JOAN and JANE. 1974. Some growth points in cultural anthropology in the United States. Man in India. 54 (1): 230-244.

KAPADIA, K.M. 1956. Marriage and family in India. Madras: Oxford University Press.

KAPUR, PROMILA. 1974. Changing status of the working women in India. Delhi: Vikas Publications.

KAR, R.K. 1975. Unity in diversity: A note on the process of adaptation in the tea industry. Bull. Dept. of Anthropology. Dibrugarh University, Vol. IV. pp 11-15.

KAR, R.K. 1979. A migrant tribe in a tea plantation in India: Economic profile. Anthropos. 74 pp. 770-784.

KAR, R.K. and GEETANJALI BARUA, 1979. Tea labour: preliminary appraisals of common identity in a multi-ethnic community. A case study in Assam. Man in India. Vol. 59. No. I . pp. 33-42.

KAR., R.K. 198 1. Tea industry in Assam: A chronological account. Man and Life. 7 pp. 131-150

KAR, R.K. 1981. The Savaras of Mankotta. New Delhi: Cosmo Publications.

KAR, R.K. 1994. The tribes of North East India; an overview. in "Tribes of North East India, edited by S. Sengupta. New Delhi: Gyan Publishing House. pp. 1-20.

KAR, R.K. 1996. "Christianity and development: Some field data from among the tea garden labour in Assam", in Impact of christianity on North East India. Edited by J. Puthenpurakal. Shillong: Vendrame Institute Publication. pp. 384

KAR, R.K. 1997. Tea plantation and its labour in Assam: An overview. An unpublished paper presented in the seminar on Society and Development in the Tea Gardens of the North East with special reference to Barak Valley, organised by the Department of Sociology, Assam University, Silchar in September.

KAROTEMPREL, S. 1990. "The future of the Adivasi community in Assam and the role of Christian Churches", in Tea garden labourers of North East India. Edited by S. Karotemprel and B. Dutta Roy. Shillong: Vendrame Institute Publications pp. 394-405.

KARVE, IRAWATI. 1967. The Indian women in 1975. New Delhi: Indian Institute of public administration.

KATTAKAYAM, J.J. 1983. Social Structure and change among the tribals. Delhi: D.K. publications.

KUPER, ADAM and JESSICA KUPER (Ed.). 1989. The social science encyclopaedia. London: Routledge. pp. 714-16.

KURMI, S. 1981. Cha Bagichar Katha (in Assamese) Jorhat: Asom Sahitya Sabha.

LAL A.K. 1979. Status of women in an urban setting: An analysis of role-differentiation in the family. Man in India. 59 (4): 289-297.

LINTON, R. 1921. The study of man. New York: Tree of culture. Alfred A. Knopf.

LOWIE, R.H. 1929. Primitive society. London: George Routledge and Sons Ltd.

LOWIE, R.H. 1950. Social organisations. London: Routledge and Kegan Paul (1969 Reprint).

MAHARANI OF BARODA and S.M.MITRA. 1911. The position of women in Indian life. London: Longmans Green and Co.

MAJUMDAR, D.N. and T.N. MADAN 1956. An introduction to social anthropology. Bombay: Asia Publishing House.

MANDELBAUM, DAVID. 1972. Society in India. Berkley: University of California press.

MANOHARAN, S. 1974. Indian tea: A strategy for development. New Delhi: S. Chand and Co. (Pvt) Ltd.

MAZUMDAR, VINA. 1982. " Towards equality, status of women in India", in Women in the third world. Edited by Urmila Phadnis and Indira Malani. New Delhi: Vikash publishing house. Pvt. Ltd., pp. 17-29.

MEHTA, SUSHILA. 1982. Revolution and the status of women in India. Delhi: Metropolitan Book Co. (pvt.) Ltd.

MERTON, R. 1963. Social theory and social structure. Illinois: Free Press Glencoe.

MISRA, REKHA. 1967, Women in Mughal India. Delhi: Munshiram Manoharlal.

MISRA, SIB RANJAN. 1986. Tea industry in India. New Delhi: British Publishing House.

PARSONS, T. 1954. Essay in sociological theory. New York: Free Press.

PERRY and PERRY. 1973. An introduction to sociology (2ND ed). New York: A development of Harper and Row publishers Inc.

PHUKAN, U. 1984. The ex-tea garden labour population in Assam. Delhi: B.R. Publishing Corp.

PRITCHARD, E.E.E. 1965. "The position of women in primitive societies and our own", in The position of women in primitive societies and other essays in social anthropology. Edited by Pritchard E.E.E. London: Faber and Faber Ltd. pp. 37-58

QUINN, NAOMI. 1977. Anthropological studies on women's status. Annual Review of Anthropology. Durham: Department of Anthropology. Duke University. pp. 181-225.

RAJU, REKHA DEVI, 1988. Status of women. Poona: Dastane Ram Chandra and Co.

RATH, NAVANEETA, 1999. "Women in India. Past and Present" in Women in India: A search for identity. Edited by Sharada Rath and Navaneeta Rath. New Delhi: Anmol Publications. PVT. LTD. pp. 33.

RATH, SHARADA and NAVANEETA RATH. 1999. Women in India: A search for identity. New Delhi: Anmol publication Pvt. Ltd.

ROY BURMAN, B.K. 1968. Socio economic process in tea plantations with special reference to tribal labourers. Delhi: Census of India, 196 1. vol. 1. part VII-A.

ROY, J.K. 1975. "Dietary and some allied investigation in tribal India", in Bio-Anthropological Research India. Edited by H.K. Rakshit. Calcutta: Anthropological Survey of India.

RUSSELL, C.S. 1974. Transition to parenthood: Problems and gratifications. Journal of marriage and the family. 36: 294-301.

RUSSELL, V.K. and HIRA LAL 1975. The tribes and castes of Central Provinces of India. Vol. IV. Delhi: Rajdhani book centre.

SACHIDANANDA. 1978. Social structure, status and mobility patterns. Man in India. 58 (451- 4) 1-112.

SAIKIA, D. 1978. Cha bagichar shramik aru sanskriti. Tezpur: People's Book Stall.

SARAN, A.B. 1974. Murder and suicide among the Munda and Oraon. New Delhi: National Publishing House.

SERVICE, ELMAN.R. 1971. Primitive social organisation. New York: Random House.

SHAH, P.D. 1950. Tribal life in Gujarat. Bombay: Gujrat research society sansodhan sadan.

SHARMA, J.C. 1992. Nutrition factor in health, physical growth and development and politics. Presidential address in the section of Anthropology and Archaeology in the 79th Session of the Indian Science Congress Associations at Baroda.

SILLS, DAVID L. 1968. International encyclopaedia of social sciences. Vol. 15. U.S.A. : The Macmillan and Free press. pp. 250-350.

SINGH, AMAR KUMAR and C. RAJYALAKSHMI. 1993. "Status of tribal women in India", a discussion paper presented in the seminar on Status of tribal women in India, held in C. S.D., New Delhi in December.

SRINIVAS, M.N. 1977. The changing position of Indian women. Man. 12(2): pp. 221238.

STICHT. T and MACDONALD, B.A. 1990. Teaching the mother and reach the child. Geneva International Bureau of Education.

SULLEROT, E. 1971. Women, society and change. London: World University press.

SUMMERS,, L. 1964. Investing in all the people educating women in developing countries. Washington: Education development. Institute of the World Bank.

THOMAS, P. 1939. Women and marriage in India. London: George Allen and Unwin Ltd.

THOMAS, P. PENTON and MARY. J. HEFFRON. 1987. Women in third world. New York:ORBIS Books, Mary knoll.

THOMPSON, and A, FINALYSON.1953. Married women who work in early motherhood. British journal of Sociology; 114:150-68.

TRIPATHY, JAYASHREE. 1999. "Women and their work environment", in women in India: A search for identity. Edited by Sharada Rath and Navaneeta Rath. New Delhi: Anmol publications Pvt. Ltd. PP. 129-147.

VEERAMANI, R. and T. RAVI. 1999. "Women in Indian society: Prospects and perceptions in women," in Women in India: A search for identity. Edited by Sharda Rath and Navaneeta. Rath. New Delhi: Anmol Publications PVT. LTD.p. 58.

VIDYARTHI, L.P. and B.K. RAI. 1977. The tribal culture in India. Delhi: Concept publishing company.

WEBWER, MAX. 1978. Economy and Society. Berkely : University of California Press.

INDEX

PLATE NO.1

1. A young girl washing the utensils early in the morning.

2. Two young girls looking after the siblings while their mothers are at work.

PLATE NO. 2

3. A lactating mother feeds her baby during the short break.

4. Two women washing their clothes after their work in the garden.

PLATE NO. 3

5. A view of women cleaning the tea beds after pruning.

6. A view of women going in search of fire wood on Sunday.

PLATE NO. 4

7. Women gossiping during their annual leave.

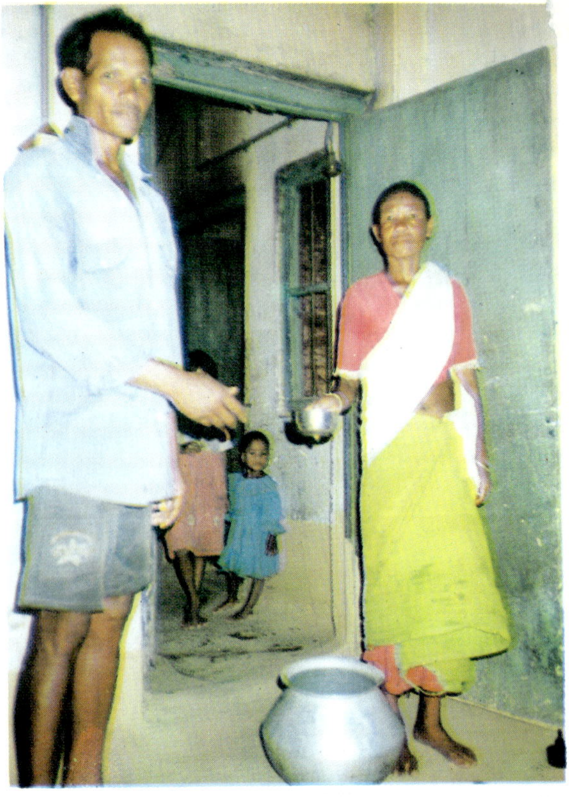

8. A Munda woman selling *haria*.

PLATE NO. 5

9. A view *dai-budi* (mid-wife).

10. A Non-Christian Munda couple during their late *Sindhur* (marriage) ceremony.

PLATE NO. 6

11. Discussing their marriage affairs in the bi-weekly market.

12. A view of women purchasing the vegetables.

PLATE NO. 7

13. A view of men and women gathered for the selection of the new executive body of the union.

14. The newly elected women in the executive body.